Also by Bobbie Ann Mason

Clear Springs

Bobbie Ann Mason

Clear Springs

A Memoir

 Random House New York

RANDOM HOUSE and colophon are registered trademarks of Random House, Inc.

Portions of this work were originally published in The New Yorker.

Library of Congress Cataloging-in-Publication Data

Mason, Bobbie Ann.
Clear Springs : a memoir / Bobbie Ann Mason.
p.   cm.
ISBN 0-679-44925-6 (acid-free paper)
1. Mason, Bobbie Ann—Childhood and youth.   2. Women novelists,
American—20th century—Family relationships.   3. Kentucky—Social
life and customs.   4. Mason, Bobbie Ann—Family.   5. Farm life—
Kentucky.   6. Family—Kentucky.   I. Title.
PS3563.A7877Z77   1999
813'.54—dc21
[B]   98-37173

Random House website address: www.atrandom.com

Printed in the United States of America on acid-free paper

24689753

First Edition

Book Design by Barbara M. Bachman

For my mother

And in memory of

my father and

grandparents

Preface

My grandmother baked cookies, but she didn't believe in eating them fresh from the oven. She stored them in her cookie jar for a day or two before she would let me have any. "Wait till they come in order," Granny would say. The crisp cookies softened in their ceramic cell—their snug humidor—acquiring more flavor, ripening both in texture and in my imagination.

"Coming in order"—an apt phrase for writing a memoir. My life is coming in order, as memories waft out of that cookie jar. But what is the recipe for those cookies? Who knows? My grandmother is dead, and her knowledge and memories are lost.

Like many Americans, I long to know the past. There's a sense of loss in America today, a feeling of disconnectedness. We're no longer quite sure who we are or how we got here. More and more of us are rummaging in the attic, trying to retrieve our history. We draw genealogical charts and hang old quilts on the wall. We seem to hope that if we can find out our family stories and trace our roots and save the old cookie jars and coal scuttles, we just might rescue ourselves and be made whole.

I grew up on a small family farm, the kind of place people like to idealize these days. They think the old-fashioned rustic life provided what they are now seeking—independence, stability, authenticity. And we did have those on the farm—along with mind-numbing, back-breaking labor and crippling social isolation. Farm life wasn't simple. I remember a way of life before I Love Lucy and credit cards and Watergate, a time when women churned butter and men plowed the fields with a team of mules and children explored the fields and creek beds. Sometimes I think I can remember the nineteenth century. When I was born in Kentucky, in 1940, farm ways had not changed much since pioneer times. No true cultural upheaval had hit Clear Springs, the rural community my family came from, since the Civil War. We seemed to live outside of time.

But World War II hurled us into the twentieth century. After my father came home from the Navy, we got a radio the size of a jukebox, and we started going to drive-in movies. I began dreaming of a rootless way of life, one that would knock me loose from that rock-solid homestead and catapult me into the fluid, musical motions of faraway cities. All three generations of our extended family were challenged simultaneously by news from a fast-moving outside world. My elders had to carry on with their inevitable labors, but seductive promises seemed to whirl in front of my eyes like a fireworks pinwheel. I was mesmerized, churned up by popular songs and Hollywood images that filled me with longing.

Suddenly it was possible for the newest generation of country people in our region to go to college, travel to Europe, and even choose a life off the farm. (I had a notion to work as a secretary for a record company.) My parents encouraged even my most ill-informed ambitions, for like most Depression-era parents, they wanted their children to have easier lives than they had had; and they wanted us to rise above the shame so many country people felt. The movies and the radio insisted that country people were inferior and backward. "Put your shoes on, Lucy, don't you know you're in the city?" There was a fatalism in my parents' hopes for their children, a fear that we would move on up to some highfalutin place where, cocktails in hand and spouting our book learning, we would look down on them.

I didn't want to spend my life canning beans and plucking chickens, so trundling my innocence before me like a shopping cart, I headed for New York—where else?—and got a job on a movie magazine. But I wasn't a glamour-puss, I hated cocktail parties, and writing celebrity gossip soon palled. I wanted to be a real writer, which I thought meant I had to become a Greenwich Village bohemian. I didn't know that the postwar portrait of the Village artist was already turning into a caricature. Bob Dylan—Nick Carraway's country cousin—had arrived in the Village some time before, not as a starry-eyed tourist like me but as a revolutionary messenger from the boondocks. But it was a long time before I understood how Dylan affirmed the very resources I had left behind.

Confused, unsure of my direction or purpose, I left the city for an upstate New York graduate school. Then the sixties exploded. In one ear I heard the Beatles singing the magic of transcendence, and in the other I heard about my grandmother's nervous breakdown, apparently caused *by her worry over me—the innocent who had "gone off up North" to the evil big city. I teeter-tottered between two worlds. As I struggled to become sophisticated, my folks and their country culture were always present in the deepest part of my being. Yet I was estranged from them, just as I was a stranger there in the North. I was an exile in both places.*

This book is the story of a family trying to come to terms with profound change. It truly centers on my mother. If she'd had the chance, she might have busted out to the big city years before I dreamed of doing so. Many of the impulses I felt burned in her breast, too. But she remained caught in a household dominated by my cautious, worried, tight-stitched grandmother. To understand what happened to my mother and subsequently to me, I recently began to sort through the scraps of the past, looking for the patterns of our quilted-together lives.

—BOBBIE ANN MASON, KENTUCKY, 1998

Contents

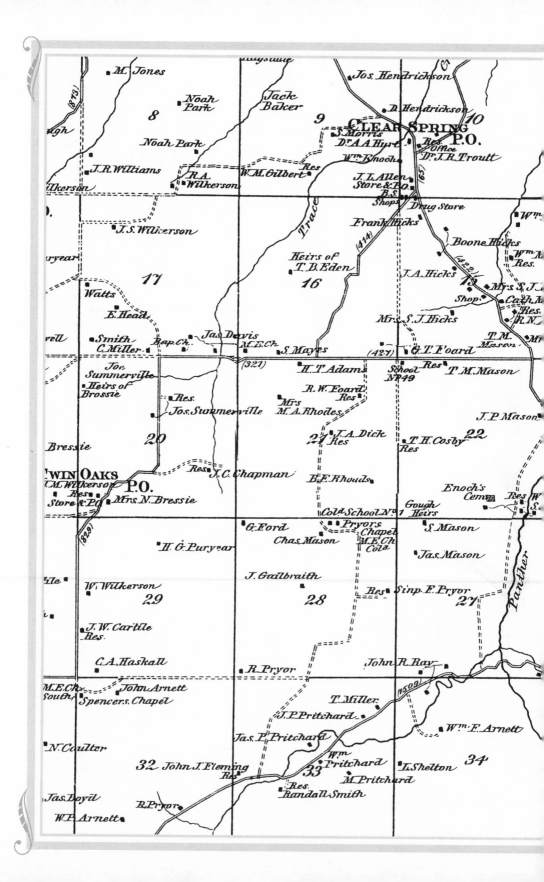

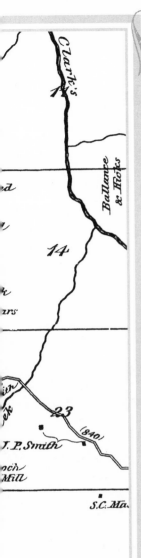

Clear Springs
1880

PANTHER CREEK PRECINCT

POP.: 1,422

MOST OF BOBBIE ANN MASON'S NINETEENTH-CENTURY
FOREBEARS SETTLED IN CLEAR SPRINGS, A FARMING COM-
MUNITY IN GRAVES COUNTY,
IN WESTERN KENTUCKY.

The Masons

THE MASON HOMEPLACE IS STILL LOCATED AT THE
SITE OF J. P. MASON'S RESIDENCE (22),* ON
PANTHER CREEK, WHERE HUNGRY PIONEER
PEYTON WASHAM ATE HIS SEED CORN.

The Arnetts

BOB MASON JOURNEYED WEEKLY FROM HIS PARENTS'
HOME (T. M. MASON, 22) TO THE ARNETTS
(W. P. ARNETT, 32). HIS HORSE-AND-BUGGY TRIPS
WENT ON FOR THIRTEEN YEARS BEFORE
ETHEL ARNETT AGREED TO MARRY HIM.

The Hickses

IN 1919, ROBERT E. LEE STOLE EUNICE'S HORSE
AND BUGGY AT THE FARM (NOT SHOWN,
CENTER OF BLOCK 22) WHERE MAMMY HICKS
LIVED WITH HER PIG, PET.

The Lees

THE LEE FAMILY ARRIVED IN THE AREA AFTER 1880, SET-
TLING NEAR DR. A. A. HURT (9–10). THE IRISES STILL
BLOOM AT THE ABANDONED LEE HOMEPLACE.

* THE NUMBERS DENOTE THE NUMBERED MAP SECTIONS.

The Mason-Lee Family Tree

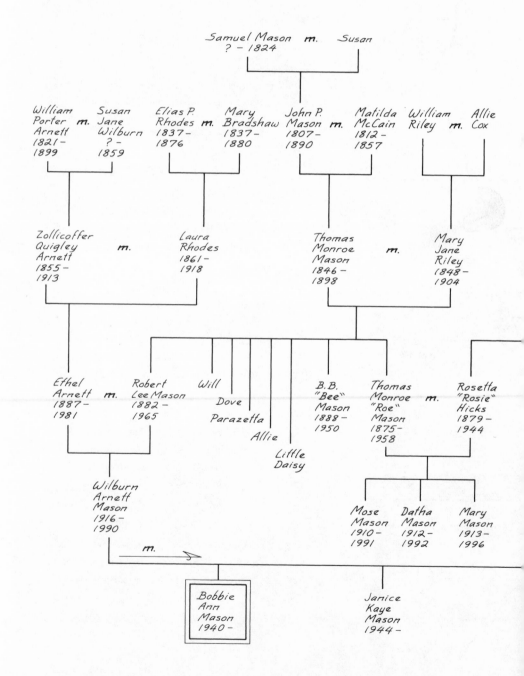

Main Characters

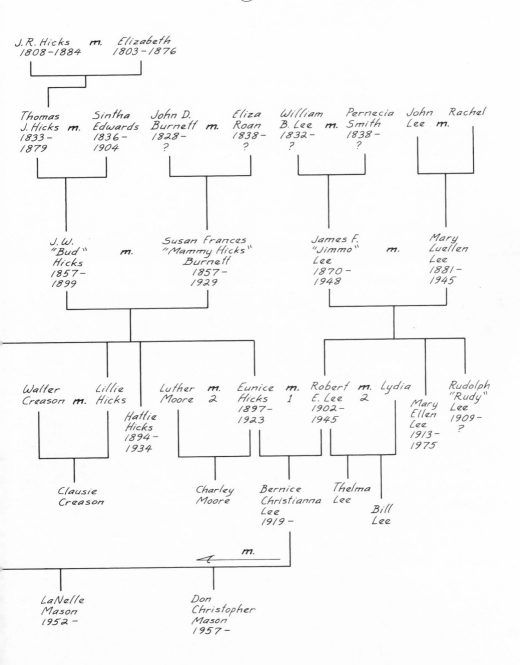

One

The
Family
Farm,
1994

It is late spring, and I am pulling pondweed. My mother likes to fish for bream and catfish, and the pondweed is her enemy. Her fishing line gets caught in it, and she says the fish feed on it, ignoring her bait. "That old pondweed will take the place," Mama says. All my life I've heard her issue this dire warning. She says it of willow trees, spiderwort, snakes, and Bermuda grass. "That old Bermudy" won't leave her flower beds alone.

The pondweed is lovely. If it were up to me, I'd just admire it and let the fish have it. But then, I'm spoiled and lazy and have betrayed my heritage as a farmer's daughter by leaving the land and going off to see the world. Mama said I always had my nose in a book. I didn't want to have to labor the way my parents did. But here I am, on a visit, wrestling with pondweed.

I'm working with a metal-toothed rake, with a yellow nylon rope tied to the handle to extend its reach. I stand on the pond bank, my Wal-Mart Wellingtons slopping and sucking mud. I fling the rake as far as I can, catch the pondweed, and then tug it loose. An island of it breaks off and comes floating toward me, snared by the rake. I haul it in and heave it onto the bank. The pondweed is a heavy mass of white, fat tendrils and a black tangle of wiry roots beneath the surface scattering of green leaves. Along with my rakeful of weed comes a treasure of snails, spiders, water striders, crawfish, worms, and insect larvae—a whole ecosystem, as in a tide pool. I haul out as much as I can lift—waterlogged, shiny leaves and masses of tendrils, some of them thick and white like skinned snakes. I rescue a crawfish. It wriggles back into its mud tunnel. As I work, the bank gets clogged with piles of weed. I am making progress. There is an unexpected satisfaction in the full range of athletic motion required for this job. I think about hard labor and wonder whether some of my fitness-minded friends with their rigid exercise routines could be talked into helping me out.

I've seen water lotus covering a lake, smothering it with plate-sized pads. Water lotus are giant lilies—double-story affairs that make gigantic seedpods resembling showerheads. Water lotus are a disaster if what you want is fish. Even without any lotus, this pond has seen disasters before—three fish kills: a fuel spill from the highway, warmwater runoff from a tobacco-warehouse fire, and a flood that washed the fish out into the creek.

In the early eighties, my father hired a backhoe to create the pond so that my mother could go fishing—her favorite pastime. He cut down a black-walnut tree so she could have a view of the pond across the field behind the house.

There used to be blackberries at the site of this quarter-acre pond—banks of berry bushes so enormous that we tunneled through them and made a maze. The blackberries were what we called tame. Back in the forties, my parents planted a dozen bushes to keep the fields from washing into the creek. The blackberries spread along all the borders. The berries were large and luscious, not like the small, seedy wild ones, but we never ate them with cream and sugar—only in pies or jam. Every July we picked berries and Mama sold gallons of them to high-toned ladies in the big fine houses in town. They made jelly. We got twenty-five cents for a quart of berries, a dollar a gallon. It took an hour to pick a gallon, and I could pick up to four gallons in a morning, before the sun got too hot, before I got chiggers implanted in the skin under my waistband. My fingers were full of thorn pricks and stayed purple all summer. The blackberries haven't disappeared, but they used to be more accessible, less weed-choked. They grew up and down all the creek banks, along the edges of all the fields, along the fencerows, along the lane. My father burned down masses of them before digging the pond.

The pond feeds into Kess Creek, which cuts across this farm—the place where I grew up, and where my mother still lives. The farm is fifty-three acres, cut into six fields, with two houses along the frontage. We are within sight of the railroad, which parallels U.S. Highway 45. We're on Sunnyside Road, a mile from downtown Mayfield, somewhere between Fancy Farm and Clear Springs, in Graves County. We are in far-western Kentucky, that toe tip of the state shaped by the curve of the great rivers—the Ohio meets the Mississippi at Cairo, Illinois, about thirty-five miles northwest of Mayfield. To the east, the Tennessee and the Cumberland Rivers (now swelled into TVA lakes) run parallel courses. Water forms this twenty-five-hundred-square-mile region into a peninsula. It's attached to the continent along the border with Tennessee. Historically and temperamentally, it looks to the South.

There aren't any big cities around, unless you count Paducah (pop. 26,853), twenty-six miles to the north. The farm is typical of this agricultural region. A lane cuts through the middle, from front to back, and two creeks divide it crosswise. The ground is rich, but it washes down the creeks. The creeks are clogged with trash, dumped there to prevent hard rains—gully-washers—from carrying the place away. At one time this was a thriving dairy farm that sustained our growing family. It was home to my paternal grandparents, my parents, my two sisters, my brother, and me. There were at least eleven buildings along the front part of the farm, near the road: two houses, a barn, a stable, a corncrib, a smokehouse, two henhouses, a wash-house, a milk house, an outhouse. I even had a playhouse.

The gravel-and-mud county road ran in front. Sometimes the school bus couldn't get through the mud. Before the road was paved and fast cars started killing our dogs and cats, we would sit on my grandparents' porch and say "Who's that?" whenever anybody passed. My grandparents' house was a large, one-story building with a high gabled roof—a typical farmhouse. The other house, a small white wood-frame structure that my parents built when I was four, stood on a hill in the woods. When the road was paved, the roadbed was built up, so the house seemed to settle down to the level of the road. We still say the house is on a hill.

The farm is one field to the east of the railroad track that used to connect New Orleans with Chicago. The track runs beside Highway 45, an old U.S. route that unites Chicago with Mobile, Alabama. Highway 45 goes past Camp Beauregard, a Civil War encampment and cemetery, and leads toward Shiloh, a Civil War battlefield, and continues to Tupelo, Mississippi, where Elvis Presley was born. On this highway when I was about ten, my dog Rags was killed, smashed flat, and nobody bothered to remove his body. For a long time, it was still there when we went to town—a hank of hair and a piece of bone. It became a rag, then a wisp, then a spot. It's hard to explain the indifference of the family in this matter, for my heart ached for Rags. It had something to do with the immutability of fate. To my parents' way of thinking, there was nothing that could be done to bring Rags back to life, and besides they were behind on the spring planting or perhaps the fall corn-gathering. There was always something.

When I was in junior high, a motel opened up on the highway. It was the first motel in Mayfield. I could see it from my house. Marlene lived at the motel. I envied her. The allure of rootlessness—strangers passing through, stopping there to sleep—is a cliché, but if you live within sight of trains and a highway, the cliché holds power. Marlene's father built her a frozen-custard stand—to my mind the definition of bliss. It was a cozy playhouse on the side of the open road: a safe thrill. But Marlene was popular at school and grew too busy for any sidelines. Her father put an ad in the paper: "FOR SALE: Marlene's Frozen-Custard Stand. Marlene's tired."

Long before this, back in 1896, across the field in front of our houses, an amazing thing happened. Mrs. Elizabeth Lyon gave birth to quintuplets. For a brief time they were world-famous, until curiosity-seekers handled the babies to death. The quintuplets' house stood right beside the railroad track, and passengers from the train stopped to ogle. They were five boys—Matthew, Mark, Luke, John, and Paul. The names had come to Mrs. Lyon in a dream. President Grover Cleveland and Queen Victoria sent congratulations on the babies.

I am a product of this ground. This region is called the Jackson Purchase. In 1818, Andrew Jackson signed a deal with Chinubby, king of the Chickasaw Nation, and soon white settlers swarmed in, snatching up sweeps of prairie. Most of them came from Middle Tennessee, where the Cumberland Settlements had led to the founding of Nashville. One of the Cumberland pioneers was my great-great-great-grandfather, Samuel Mason. Several of his ten children headed for the Jackson Purchase, and four of them settled on Panther Creek, at Clear Springs, from whence all the relatives I have ever known sprang. In 1920, a century after my ancestors settled in Clear Springs, my grandparents boldly moved away from there, from the bosom of generations. The land had been divided up so many times that sons had to leave and find their own land. For Granddaddy, it was a long journey of eight miles. In 1920, he bought the fifty-three and one-tenth acres by the highway for five thousand dollars. The house, only six years old, was sturdy and attractive. The land was cleared and fertile, and it was only a mile from town, so trading at the town square or the feed mill would be an easy journey by buggy or wagon.

At one time, much of the land of the Jackson Purchase was covered with tall grass. The Chickasaws had apparently burned it periodically to create grassland for buffalo. When my father plowed in the spring, he turned up arrowheads. The land is not delta-flat, but it's not at all hilly either. It resembles rolling English farmland, both in the natural lay of the land and in the farming habits the farmers imposed upon it. It has small fields, and the fencerows are thick with weeds, vines, oaks, wild cherries, sumac, and cedars.

The landscape is still changing. On the highway, not far from our farm, are a tobacco-rehandling outfit, a John Deere business, and a chicken hatchery. The little frozen-custard stand, fallen to other uses and then to ruin, stood there until fairly recently, but the motel disappeared long ago. In its place is a collection of grim little buildings, including the House of Prayer. With the Purchase Parkway close by, industries have located near the interchange. My birthplace is now at the hub of industrial growth in the county, and the road in front of the houses is now a busy connector to highways and factories. When the cars rush by (ignoring the speed limit of thirty-five) on their way to work, or when a shift lets out, my mother sometimes stands at the kitchen window and counts them. "That's sixty-eight that have gone by in five minutes," she announces.

The farm now lies entirely within the Mayfield city limits. To the east, the subdivisions are headed our way. Behind the farm, to the south, we can glimpse an air-compressor factory. Just across the railroad, to the west, the four-lane bypass leads around town and to the parkway and to everywhere on the continent. Across the road, in a thirty-acre cornfield, which is like an extension of our front yard, is the landmark of the town.

I call it the chicken tower. It is the feed mill that processes feed for all the chickens that fuel Seaboard Farms, whose chicken-processing plant is on the other side of town. Construction workers came in 1989 and put up the tower in continuous twelve-hour shifts, while my father watched in fascination. The thing rose faster than hybrid corn shooting up. A chain-link fence girds the field. A deer was caught on the fence almost as soon as it went up.

The tower is a tall, gray concrete structure, without windows. It's a hundred and fifty-six feet high. If you see it at dawn, it's hard not to think about a space-shuttle launch. Adjoining the chicken tower are six cylindrical towers, attached like booster rockets. The architecture is unrelievedly functional. The word "Soviet" comes to mind. The tower has a framework of pipes crawling over it, and the six cylinders have earned the nickname "the concrete six-pack." These silos are a hundred and ten feet high. The mill hums, and big trucks come and go. It's like a huge refrigerator running. The chicken feed smells a bit like the mash of a whiskey distillery. The chicken industry, proliferating throughout the South, extravagantly promises prosperity, and many local farmers have grabbed the chance to raise chickens for Seaboard. The plant hatches the eggs and makes the feed, and the farmers raise the chicks in houses built at their own expense. Then low-wage workers cut up and package "poultry products" when the birds are six weeks old and sporting their first full plumage.

Beyond the chicken tower is the site where the Lyon quintuplets were born in 1896, and beyond that there's the feed mill where my mother's soybeans go, and beyond that is town. And then there's the wide world I eventually left home to see.

It's summer now. I am back again. With Oscar, the family dog, I'm visiting the pond on a warm evening, feeding fish. I'm flinging pellets of fish food out onto the water, trying to get it beyond the pondweed, which extends out all around the banks of the pond, except for the clearings I've made. When I pick up the empty fish-chow bucket—a plastic ice-cream tub—I find three crickets caught in it. They can't jump more than two or three inches straight up. There are two small ones and one large one. The smalls have striped backs like lightning bugs. They have feathery arms and legs and feathery feet. The large one has a long antenna it loops toward itself, then extends out tentatively, searching. The other antenna is grossly shortened—cut off by some vicious fighter-bug? Or did it come like that? Suddenly I realize that looking at crickets this way is the essence of what it was like to be a child here, immersed in the strange particulars of nature.

From the pond, in the green lushness of early summer, in three directions you see only fields of soybeans and corn, with thick fencerows and washed skies. A movie could be filmed here, a historical drama set in 1825, and it would seem authentic—except for the soundtrack: the noises of the highway, the air, the feed mill; the blare and thud of music from cars whizzing past. If you turned the camera in the other direction, toward the road, you'd get all the visual cues of the present day—the wires and poles, the asphalt, the Detroit metal, the discarded junk-food wrappers and beer cans thrown from cars that have "twentieth century" written all over them. You would also see a brown farmhouse with two rickety outbuildings, a red stable, and a small white house in a lovely woods that is mowed and trimmed like a park. And you would see the chicken tower, lord of the landscape.

Late September. The soybeans aren't quite ready to harvest. Some of the leaves are still green, but the pods are fuzzy and brown. The crop this year is full of weeds from outer space because the strongest herbicides have been banned. Something short of Agent Orange has been used this year, and the path to the pond is bordered with weeds, some a good ten feet tall.

Mama and I walk down this path to the pond. She uses her fishing rod to fight the weeds and snakes. Oscar trots along, thrilled to go with us. Miraculously, he never goes near the road.

"That's Johnsongrass," Mama says, pointing her rod at a clump of what looks like a trendy ornamental grass. "You can't ever get rid of that. Your Daddy used to cut it off and dig it up and dump it in the creek."

"What's that one?"

"Hogweed? Horseweed? I can't remember. But at the joint sometimes there's a big knot and inside is a worm that's good to fish with."

"It's horseweed," she says presently. "Not hogweed. Hogweed is what you call presley—pig presley I always called it. The hogs like it real well. It's got real tender leaves."

"Pig presley?"

"When we raised hogs I'd pull it up and give it to them, and Lord, they'd go crazy."

"What does it look like?"

"It grows along on the ground on a stem and has tender leaves. It looks rubbery."

"Purslane? Parsley?"

"I always called it pig presley."

"Is that one of your weeds that will take the place?"

"No, pig presley's all right. It's good."

We reach the pond just as a small heron escapes in a slow-motion flight over the creek. The pondweed has died back a lot, and the reflections in the pond are clear and still. The main house, inside its army of old oak and maple trees, is reflected in the pond. The chicken tower rises above the trees. The tableau is upside-down and innocently beautiful and abstract.

Mama gestures to the southeast and says, "If the wind is this way, I smell horse piss, and that way I smell cow mess, and over yonder it's tobacco curing, and from the north it's chicken feed." Her rod follows her directions. She laughs: her big, loud laugh. "If that don't beat a hen a-rootin'!" she says. Her laugh supposedly comes from her grandfather, "Jimmo" Lee, who had red hair and an Irish or Scottish burr in his voice. (Nobody remembers whether he was Irish or Scottish, but about half of the settlers were Scots-Irish, Protestants who came to America long before the Great Famine.) My mother uses idioms that are dying out with her generation, right along with the small family farms of America. Her way of talking is the most familiar thing I know, except maybe for the contours and textures of this land. Mama's language comes from the borderlands of England and Scotland and from Ireland, with some other English dialects thrown in, and it is mingled with African-American speech patterns acquired along the way. It is much like Mark Twain's language in *Huckleberry Finn*. It's spoken, with variations, in a band of the upper South stretching from the mid-Atlantic states across the Appalachians to the Ozarks. In the Jackson Purchase, this old dialect rested in the farmlands and changed with the weather and the crops and the vicissitudes of history as news filtered in from other places. Today there's a good chance you won't hear many people under sixty say, "If that don't beat a hen a-rootin'." It's an expression that comes from a deep knowledge of chicken behavior. Mama has contended with many a settin' hen. On free-range chickens, she's an expert.

Mama casts out a long rubber lure, a sort of Gummi Worm, and reels it in. She's casting for bass. "I'd rather fish for bream because they bite like crazy," she says.

The beanfields are leased out to a neighbor, and Mama frets about their proper cultivation. Dense growth from the creeks is creeping out into the fields. She hates weeds, insects, snakes, and bad weather. And she rails against the haphazard and violent methods of mechanized farming. A crop-spraying machine called a highboy straddles several rows, and the driver rides on tall wheels. One year, the combine missed so many soybeans that I imagine she was ready to go gather them up in a bucket and carry them to the mill herself. Another year, she chopped out all the pokeweed that had infiltrated a soybean field. She was afraid the pokeberries would stain the feed. "Them beans would have been purple by the time they went through the mill!" she said. "I don't know if hogs would appreciate purple feed. And pokeberries is poison."

. . .

Now it's winter. A tree is down, blocking the path across the creek. It has split, rotten at the center. I remember when that little tree hollow was a good hiding place for secret messages in fantasy girl-sleuth games—forty years ago. At the creek, a jumble of memories rushes out, memories of a period in my own lifetime which links straight back to a century ago, and even further: hog killing; breaking new-ground; gathering dried corn in the fall; herding cows with a dog; churning; quilting. I have a snapshot of myself as a child, sitting on a mule. I know the textures of all of these experiences.

What happened to me and my generation? What made us leave home and abandon the old ways? Why did we lose our knowledge of nature? Why wasn't it satisfying? Why would only rock-and-roll music do? What did we want?

With my family, the break started in 1920, when Granddaddy moved away from Clear Springs to find land, and we ended up living right on the edge of town. The stores around the courthouse square were tantalizingly near. Who wouldn't rather go shopping than hoe peas? And the radio told us that we weren't quite so isolated: we were in Radioland! The highway called us, too. Our ancestors had been lured over the ocean to America by false advertising—here was the promised land, literally—but once arrived, they had to clear rocks and stumps and learn to raise hogs. We inherited their gullibility. We wanted to go places, find out what was out there. My sisters and I didn't want to marry farmers; we were more interested in the traveling salesmen. By the time my brother—the youngest of us four, born too late—came of age, a family farm seemed to require more land and machinery than it once had in order to prosper. So again it was time to move on.

We didn't want to be slaves to nature. Maintaining the Garden of Eden was too much work—endless hoeing, fences to fix, hay to bale, and cows to milk, come rain or come shine. My mother, who knows more about wind and weather and soil and raising chickens than I ever will, approves of progress, even though she finds much of it scary and empty. The old ways were just too hard, she says wearily. She and my father expected better lives for their children. They knew we'd leave.

But I keep looking back to see where I've been. I am angry that my father died before I could ask him all I wanted to know about the life of a dairy farmer, because I think he knew all about the earth and the seasons.

The winter light is heavy and stark. Dim skies, silhouettes of black trees, mud. The pondweed lies dormant; the soybeans were recently harvested, and here and there stray beans have spilled out onto the soil. The dampness deepens these brown-and-black tones of the landscape. Oscar and I cross the creek and head out through the cornfield. The corn has been harvested by a big machine that gobbled up the stalks, moiled the shucks and spit them out, then glommed the kernels off the cob and spun them into a hopper. I recall the way dried corn comes off the cob when you do it by hand. You mash two cobs together hard and loosen a few of the kernels till they pop out like teeth. Then you can rub the cobs together more lightly and pop the rest of the kernels out of their sockets. I also recall shelling corn for the chickens with a corn sheller; it had a crank handle and an iron maw with teeth. Now I can hear corn being crumbled and gnashed in the tower.

The cedar trees on the fencerow along our western border have grown thick and tall and have lost their youthful prickliness. We always had a young, scraggly cedar from one of the fencerows for our Christmas tree. Now these are full of bluish berries and conelike cocoons made by some insect that shrouds itself with a dead cedar twig.

The chicken tower has a star on top for Christmas. From up there, you would see the lay of this farm, reduced in its significance, a small piece of the earth.

It is late afternoon, and the ominous winter light accents the trees. Then the harsh electric light of the chicken tower floods the area. It is never dark at night here the way it used to be, when there were just stars and moon.

There's a loneliness about the homeplace now. But the family straggles home each Christmas to renew itself, and the place returns to life. In the way of rural families, Mama doesn't invite us to come, but she expects us all to be there. And we always are. The family is small, only fifteen of us. Mama cooks a dinner for her four children, their three spouses, her five grandchildren, and two more spouses. She has turkey with cornbread dressing and giblet gravy, a ham, potato salad, dressed eggs, Jell-O salad, cranberry relish, her special Sunset Salad, broccoli casserole with cheese sauce, yeast-raised rolls. And from her freezer she may offer creamed corn, green beans, shelly beans, and brown field peas—all grown in her garden. Then she loads the table with fruit salad, boiled custard, her special uncooked fruitcake, co-

conut cake, German chocolate cake, peanut bars, decorated refrigerator cookies. She makes all this food herself because we don't really know how to do it and it is her joy to feed us amply. She makes enough for about thirty-six people. The feast seems always to be prepared for some imagined larger family.

This dinner defines the family and replenishes us for another year. We get here, regardless of what it costs us in money or trouble, or whatever difficulty with weather and flight delays. We're far-flung. We have not scattered simply to Paducah or Nashville or Louisville, places within reasonable reach. We didn't leave the farm for Pittsburgh or Hattiesburg or Racine. My sisters and I first headed to California, Florida, and New York—the meccas. One niece worked at Disney World; one sister works in special-effects computer graphics in Hollywood. The movies, Disney World, Manhattan. Those were the fishing lures that came over the airwaves and reeled us in. I stayed in the Northeast for many years, chasing literary dreams. Even my brother, who stayed closest to home, works for the quintessential American corporation, Coca-Cola.

We've been free to roam, because we've always known where home is.

Oscar and I turn back. As we approach the pond, a heron—a great blue one this time—takes off from the water, not far ahead of us. Its flight path cuts across the face of the chicken tower, which looms beyond the house and the bare winter trees. The dying pondweed is dissolving into the muddy murk of the pond. As I look into the reflections on the surface of the pond, I think about all the death on this soil: the oaks that Mama says were "barked up and skinned" by lightning; the hogs and cows and calves and chickens we've slaughtered for food; all the cats and dogs smashed on the road after it was paved; my grandparents; my father. Before my grandparents moved here, a farmer died of epilepsy, in the garden. I think about what a farmer knows up there on his tractor or walking along behind his mules—the slow, enduring pace of regular toil and the habit of mind that goes with it, the habit of knowing what is lasting and of noting every nuance of soil and water and season. What my father and my ancestors knew has gone, and their idioms linger like fragile relics. Soon my memories will be loosened from any tangible connection to this land.

I don't know what will happen to this piece of land eventually. Urbanization has hardly begun here in the Purchase. Kentucky is an agricultural state, ranking fourth in the nation in the number of family farms. The tension between holding on to a way of life and letting in a new way—under the banners of Wal-Marts and chicken processors—is the central dynamic of this area. There are no malls, no cinema complexes, no coffee bars here. But a Wal-Mart Supercenter is looming over the horizon like a UFO. The town is poised on the edge of the future.

As a family farm, this piece of land may be doomed. The family has fragmented. I live too far away to deal with a soybean crop. I wouldn't know how to make the ground say beans, the way Thoreau wanted it to, and would probably just prefer to read his musings on the subject. My nephew fantasizes a golf course; my brother dreams of building a minimart; someone has mentioned llamas. When land is spoken of these days, it's usually in an opportunistic tone. Someone sees a buck to be made. But the big bucks are usually made by someone else, not the people who know the land. I do not know what industrial or technological analogue of pondweed will take over this land. What is tame and what is wild seem to go through cycles of varying perspectives. I'm sort of wishing for a comeback of the blackberries. It's tempting to think of just holding on to the land while industries close in around. We could call the place a nature preserve. I think of those alligators and long-necked birds you see moving lazily in the foreground of a space-shuttle launch.

Our two houses face the chicken tower like cats staring at a stranger. My mother lives in my grandparents' old place, and the other house is unoccupied. It's the higgledy-piggledy house my parents kept adding onto periodically. I grew up in that house. The picture window is empty, and the shutters sag. The overgrown forsythia bushes reach the roof, and a mock-orange tree grows right smack atop the cistern. The house seems desolate, abandoned.

I own an oil painting of that house when it was in its prime—with trim green shutters, a white picket fence (which I once had to whitewash, like Tom Sawyer), a red-white-and-blue flower bed, a blue snowball bush, a pink climbing rose, and tall leafy trees hovering above the roof. My mother painted this scene; she painted one copy for each of her children and one for herself. It has been a long journey from our little house into the wide world, and after that a long journey back home. Now I am beginning to see more clearly what I was looking for.

Two

Country People

2

In the summer of 1949, when I was nine, my mother and I traveled to Detroit to visit Mama's aunt Mary, her father's sister. Mama had made the trip several years before, and she was excited about showing me the big city.

"I want you to see them big buildings," Mama said. "They're so tall your eyes'll pop right out of your head."

"Are they as tall as the trees around the house?"

"Taller than that. Heaps taller."

"Taller than the courthouse?"

"Ten times that high."

It was a peculiar promise, like something from the world of "Jack and the Beanstalk." But what struck me more than the imagined height of the buildings was my mother's joy at the prospect of showing me Detroit. She sparkled like a Coca-Cola that had just been opened, and her laughter accentuated her beauty.

Mama washed and ironed our best clothes, made me a new dress, polished my shoes. She packed everything in a heavy-cardboard suitcase snake-striped on one end. Secretly, I thought of it as a valise. In my reading of girls' mystery series books, suitcases were called valises, which I pronounced "*vall*-is" in my mind, since I had never heard anyone say the word. The idea of packing a valise fascinated me—the notion that we could stow our necessary belongings and then just vamoose.

We were country people. We didn't ordinarily go on vacations because there were cows to milk, chickens to feed. The dairy farm held us back with invisible fences as confining as the real barbed wire bordering our pastures. Summer was for work, not for gallivanting. Earlier in the summer, I had gathered at dawn with a bunch of kids at a small grocery in Mayfield; from there, we rode in the bed of a pickup truck out to some strawberry fields. We picked strawberries in handies—flat wooden crates that held six quart-sized boxes. For our morning's labor we received a nickel per quart. The fruit went to Paducah, where berries from all over western Kentucky met to travel north on the trains so that people in the fine hotels and restaurants of northern cities could enjoy farm-fresh strawberries.

During the Depression, country people from the South had begun trekking northward to find work. Farm people were actually on the move then. Many of them, after planting crops in the spring, left their families and traveled to Detroit to sweat on the auto assembly lines until fall harvest. They came home to get the crops in, then returned to Detroit for the winter. My father's people, the Masons, were rooted on the land like gnarled old trees, but some of my mother's paternal relations, the Lees, joined the migration north. Mama's aunt Mary Lee had moved to Detroit in the thirties, and Mary's brother Rudy followed during the war, finding work at U.S. Rubber.

"Mary and Rudy make good money up there," Mama told me.

In front of the hotel in Mayfield, Mama and I boarded the flashy red-and-white Brooks bus. The Brooks Bus Line, a family operation based in Paducah, hauled people back and forth between western Kentucky and Detroit, a distance of six hundred and twenty-three miles. The company had started out as a guy with a car, an entrepreneur who realized that Kentuckians got homesick and needed to make quick trips home.

I was throbbing with excitement. As we rumbled across the bridge over the Ohio River into Illinois, I felt I was soaring into a new freedom. Mama and I were escaping, riding the bus together, leaving the farm behind, with the cows, the dog, the cats, my grandparents, my father, my little sister—the whole world known to me. Coconspirators, Mama and I were heading for a bigger and better place, one that would somehow transform us. Several black people sat in the rear of the bus, and I wondered if they were escaping too.

For the journey, I brought along *The Bobbsey Twins in a Great City*. I had read it several times, and I was under the spell of New York City, the Bobbseys' destination. The twins chased enormous clanging fire trucks, got lost on an underground train, and became involved with an Italian organ-grinder and his monkey, who did tricks. I loved it. In a big city, any adventure might happen. Nothing ever happened at home.

"You read it too," I begged Mama. I wanted to share it with her.

"It's for children," she protested. But she gave it a try. I thought she was bored with the book because she soon fell asleep. A chatty man across from us lowered the green paper shade so that the sun wouldn't glare in her eyes.

"Don't you touch that emergency cord, now," he whispered to me. "That 'ere's liable to get the *po*-lice after us."

We rode the red-and-white Brooks bus all night. The bus traveled catty-cornered across the bottom of southern Illinois and on up through Indiana. I woke up intermittently as we passed through strange towns. Late in the night, we tumbled from the bus into the smoky station at Fort Wayne, Indiana, for a rest stop.

"Fort Wayne," I said to myself over and over. I had never been anywhere farther than Paducah. In the *Weekly Reader* at school I had read about Brazil and Africa and Holland. I wouldn't have been surprised to see mountains or giraffes or people in wooden shoes there in Fort Wayne. The bus station was a stage in our journey to the unknown, where passengers demanded hot dogs and grilled-cheese sandwiches in the middle of the night. The scene was as strange as if I were dreaming it—or reading about it. A black couple from the last row of the bus, sad-eyed and shabby, walked down the sidewalk to the corner. I heard the woman say, "We never ought to have left her," and the man said, "We couldn't have brought her. We couldn't have brought her."

We continued into the night. Strains of "Cow-Cow Boogie" by Ella Mae Morse and "How Are Things in Glocca Morra" swirled alternately through my head, the sounds textured like a marble cake, until I finally fell asleep. The green paper shades shut out the shock of dawn, but as soon as I was awake I peeped out to see where we were. I saw flat fields of corn. I wondered what would happen if I touched the emergency cord. But I knew I wasn't ready to stop yet.

De-troit! Everybody said "*De*-troit." They said "Polacks" lived there. "Don't let the *Po*-lacks get you," Granddaddy had told me. He didn't explain what he meant.

Mama had visited Mary in Detroit when I was two. She stayed for two weeks, leaving me at home with Daddy and my grandparents. When she returned on the bus, the driver let her out on the highway, a quarter mile from our house. Carrying her suitcase, she headed down the road. She saw me playing in the yard, and she says that when I saw her, I ran straight to the house. My grandmother declared that Bobbie didn't know who her mother was, she had been gone so long. But Mama said Bobbie recognized her and had run into the house to tell everybody that her mama was home.

The story was repeated all my life, how I didn't recognize my mama when she finally showed up after traipsing off to Detroit. But Mama still insists that I *did* know her. And I'm sure she's right.

We got off the bus in Wayne, a suburb of Detroit, where Aunt Mary lived in a neighborhood of postwar houses. The houses were all similar, as if they had been created simultaneously, like a paper-doll chain. I was amazed that they were so close together. I marveled at Mary's house number on a post—number three-three-five. We didn't have a number at home, except for the one I had painted on my playhouse. Mary lived with her husband and daughter; and her brother Rudy, who was lame, was staying there, too, during our visit. Mama and I slept in the attic, where the knotty-pine ceiling smelled so fresh and sweet it made me giddy. The smell was the essence of promise.

I was eager to go into downtown Detroit, where there were tall buildings and museums and theaters and magnificent stores. I had seen two souvenir postcards from Mama's previous trip: pictures of the De-troit Institute of Arts. It wasn't taller than the courthouse, but it was grand—a stone building with arched doorways and a splendid row of 1940 and 1941 cars out front. The other postcard, an interior view, showed the Court, a room two stories high, with tropical foliage and a fountain and immense paintings on the walls—and what appeared to be a statue of a donkey on a pedestal.

"I'll show you that," Mama had promised.

But our hopes collapsed on our first morning in Michigan.

"Bad news," said Uncle Rudy, brandishing the newspaper at the breakfast table. "The buses are going on strike."

We couldn't go into the city because the buses weren't running. I had never heard of a strike. It sounded like something to do with clocks. Or baseball. I imagined a ball bat poised to make a loud crack. Even though Aunt Mary explained the meaning to me, I envisioned the buses disabled by violent crashes.

Mama moaned. "Just our luck," she said. "Of all times for us to pick to come up here."

"They may settle it before y'all head home," Aunt Mary said. "You never know. Or they might drag it out till Christmas."

"Don't worry, littlun," Uncle Rudy said, patting my head.

Mama gave me a little squeeze. "I got your hopes up for nothing," she said.

Every day the news was the same—the strike continued. A neighbor gave us a ride to downtown Wayne. But it wasn't a big city. I was surprised to see the familiar Woolworth's sign on a store. Woolworth's was in Mayfield—it was odd to see it here too. We went in, and I bought souvenirs—two dainty little ceramic pots with MADE IN JAPAN labels stuck on the bottom.

"Dust catchers for whatnots," Aunt Mary said.

"We beat them Japs and put 'em to work making pots and things," said Uncle Rudy. "That keeps 'em busy so they won't be a-making guns."

There was no Detroit. It was disappointing. A dim image of a promised city formed in my head, like the pearly gates and golden streets of heaven. I did not know how to readjust my desires to the ambiguities I was discovering in my early travels. It would be absurd to find Woolworth's everywhere I went.

But what I remember from that trip more than my disappointment was my mother in this new setting. She was comfortable with her kinfolks, and she let loose with them in a way she didn't always manage to do at home. She seemed happy just to be somewhere different. Although she was always spirited and full of gaiety, she seemed to burn even brighter up here in the North. I remember how pretty she looked, with her black curls piled on top of her head and the rest of her hair hanging down around her neck like a curtain. Her hairdo was like one of Joan Crawford's, but Mama was prettier, I thought. If she was so pretty, why wasn't she a movie star? I wondered.

I loved the North. There were sidewalks to skate on—if only one had skates. I played jacks and Old Maid with a neighbor girl, but she made fun of the way I said "fire." I said "far." And I said "tard" for "tired." Her family had a television set—the first I'd ever seen. We watched a blurry picture of Howdy Doody. At home we had a splendid console radio with wonderful programs—*Jack Benny* and *Fred Allen* and shows that played records. Listening to our radio, I had to imagine the faces behind the voices. Now I hoped they didn't look like Howdy Doody.

Every night the adults played cards and whooped it up. Mary drank beer and smoked cigarettes. Her raucous laugh encouraged Mama's own laughter. Mama giggled and let loose her best laugh—a trill of little ha-ha's as gladsome as a rooster crowing at sunrise.

"I can't stand the taste of beer," Mama said, making a face when she tried a sip. She smoked a few cigarettes, though.

"Wilburn got me started smoking," she explained. "I don't really smoke."

"I started before I got here," Mary said. "When the war was on, all the women commenced to smoking, but I beat 'em to it!"

Mama shuffled the deck of cards. "When Wilburn come home from the Navy, he'd be a-laying on the bed, and his cigarettes would be across the room. And he'd say, 'Light me one, hon.' So I'd go get a cigarette and light it up for him and bring it to him. Once in a while I'd tell him I was going to have one too, if it was that good."

From the living room, where I sat on the floor coloring in a coloring book, I could hear the adults at the kitchen table, slapping cards down in a boisterous game of catch-the-deuce. Mary's raspy voice cut through the smoky air like the sound of Daddy's truck cranking up. She had adopted a Northern brogue, talking sharply and to the point. She was a big-boned woman, and she wore wide-legged pants. Uncle Rudy wore a brace on his leg, which had been damaged by polio when he was a child.

"They didn't call it that then," he had told me.

"It was polio, all right," Mary said. "We just didn't know it till now."

The great polio scare was on that summer, and Mama worried that I would come down with it. But Mary said it came from public swimming pools. I longed to know what living in Michigan would be like, in a place that had swimming pools, in a lovely house like this on a street with a sidewalk, so close to the magic towers of Detroit.

Wandering around the living room, I gazed at pictures of dead people: my great-grandparents and my grandfather Robert Lee. I remembered him, but I didn't remember when I learned he was dead. He was Mary's other brother. He was Mama's daddy. His portrait was on a lamp table. He had a sly grin and a thick head of hair. He stared across the room as though he had something to say, but it would be a long time before I knew his story. I had noticed that Mama wouldn't look at his picture. I thought she didn't like him.

I remembered him, even though I was only four when I was around him. I remembered his red hair. I recalled a cold, bleak day at a cabin on a hillside out in Clear Springs. The ground was bare, and chickens roamed through the yard. He showed me a wonderful thing. He dug a hole in the side of the hill and built a fire in it. Then he placed a potato in the hole and covered the entrance. Later, we came back and found a hot potato there—steaming, its skin charred. I had never had a potato cooked in the ground before. At home we always had boiled potatoes-in-the-jacket.

I stared at his photograph. Then I opened my Bobbsey book again, and the New York skyscrapers renewed my longing to see the tall buildings of a big city. In the kitchen, the adults were ending a hand, yelping and puling in their teasing. I heard Mama cry melodramatically, "You fixed *my* little red wagon!" After a while, I heard her mock boo-hoo's when she lost a hand. I could imagine the pout on her face. And then later I heard her sing out, "Shoot the moon!" I could hear my mother's laughter rising above them all, and I could feel her triumph as she gathered the pile of winning cards to her bosom, raking them across the table in glee. Upstairs later, in our cozy pine-paneled loft, she hugged me as though she were sharing a secret with me, something she desperately thought I needed to know.

My mother was an orphan. I was her first child. She says it was hard to wean me from her breasts. And she says that when I was little and company came, I would cling to her and look to her for what to say. Today, my awareness of her missing parents makes me cling to her still, because I have never been able to bear the thought of such a hole in my own life.

Her father, Robert Lee, abandoned the family just before she was born, and Mama lost her mother in childbirth when she was only four. She was left to grow up without affection or closeness or indulgence. Yet she wasn't thrown into an orphanage or adopted or shuttled around to foster families. She lived at first with her grandmother, then in the teeming household of her aunt and uncle. Her kinfolks took her in, out of obligation. But they gave her little love. "You're lucky to have a roof over your head," they said as they put her to work. She says she felt like a lost kitten, crouching beneath the passing shadow of a hawk.

For me, the image that most illuminates her childhood is the Christmas orange. One Christmas, in the houseful of kinfolks she was raised with at Clear Springs, the older cousins got dolls, but all she got was an orange.

She remembers how, as the smallest child in the household, she was made to work in the garden, the fields, the tobacco patch. "I was just an extra mouth to feed," Mama says bitterly. "But I was always a hard worker. I guess I got that from my mama. They said she was a hard worker. I don't know what else I got from her."

I believe she also got her black hair, a tendency toward plumpness, and her sense of humor from her mother. Maybe she got her enduring spirit from her, too. Mama has a few tiny memories of her mother, Eunice Hicks Lee. And Mama remembers that everybody said Eunice was short and fat with a good disposition, and that she liked to laugh.

"I had hair when I was born," Mama tells me. "They said my mama had heartburns all the time she was carrying me, so that's why I had hair. They said I didn't have any fingernails or eyelashers. I was real little and didn't cry for two months, and when I did it liked to scared them to death."

Although my mother has told me about it many times, I still can't quite manage to grasp the facts of her losses, the darkness of her painful upbringing. My own childhood was sunny and privileged, thanks to her efforts, and so my own choices were wildly different from hers. By the time she was seventeen, my mother had quit school and eloped.

After her grandmother died, my mother, Christianna Lee, was raised by the Mason family in Clear Springs, on the original Mason homeplace. She was taken in by her aunt Rosie, who had married Roe Mason, my father's uncle. My parents weren't related, even though they shared a set of cousins, and they did not grow up together. Yet my mother was dominated by Masons all her life.

In May, 1936, she was not quite seventeen. My father, Wilburn Arnett Mason, was twenty. They had met the year before. When they decided to marry, Wilburn kept it from his parents. Christy told no one except Aunt Rosie, who was relieved that Christy would marry into a respectable family. "I was afraid you'd fall in with somebody no-'count like your mama done," Rosie said. Christy crammed her meager belongings into a suitcase Rosie let her borrow. Then Christy and Wilburn drove across the state line, to Tennessee, where they were married by a justice of the peace named Squire McDade, a popular performer of spur-of-the-moment, no-frills marriages. Wilburn brought Christy home to his parents' house that night, long after his parents were in bed. The mantel clock was ticking loudly in the living room, where Bob and Ethel slept in the summer because it was cooler there. Wilburn and Christy crept into the north bedroom and settled onto a narrow bed that folded out Murphy-style from an elaborate piece of cabinetry containing a carved headboard and drop-down legs. Wilburn was clumsy, and the racket he made rigging up the bed made Christy giggle. The night was black, and she could see only vague shapes in the room, like people crouching.

When he heard his parents stir at first light, Wilburn jabbed Christy awake and quickly they pulled on some clothes. He led her from the bedroom to the kitchen. Through the tall windows Christy could see a vast, unobstructed expanse of fresh pasture and newly plowed fields. The fields, a geometric design bordered by tree lines, receded in the distance. The dew glistened in the coming sunlight. Bob and Ethel were standing in the kitchen, already dressed. Bob was stropping his razor, and Ethel was drawing a bucket of water from the cistern. When they saw her, they seemed to freeze. Slowly, Ethel lifted the bucket onto the edge of the cistern. Christy had never seen anyone thunderstruck until this moment.

Ethel steadied the bucket, and Bob let loose his leather strop. It dangled from its hook on the kitchen wall. Ethel replaced the cistern lid. They seemed to be waiting for words to come to them.

Then they said, "Well!"

Ethel said, "I'll say!" A little smile flickered. She dipped water from the bucket into the kettle and set the kettle on the stove. The wood fire was already going.

Wilburn said, "Got enough grub? She eats like a horse."

Christy gave him a little slap on his arm. She didn't know what to say. What had she gotten herself into?

Many times I've tried to imagine this scene—the shock of the new, the embarrassment of the unspeakable, my parents as young kids daring the future with a radical act. My grandparents knew Wilburn had been courting Christy—or sparking, as they called it. They had watched her growing up over the years when they went to the gatherings at the Mason homeplace in Clear Springs. It wasn't as though Wilburn had brought some stray home. They were pleased, actually, and probably relieved that the union had been accomplished with so little fuss and discussion. I can fairly well imagine the quiet astonishment of my grandparents—the little toss of Granny's head as she tried to accommodate the surprise, the tickled exuberance beneath Granddaddy's placid grin. I try to envision my parents emerging from the bedroom. He guides her by the shoulders, like a calf he's bought at the stockyard. Her eyes are wide, as she enters her new life with a paradoxical mix of meekness and audacity. But I have trouble truly comprehending my parents' courage in conducting this surprise incursion into the Mason household, knowing it would come to such an awkward scene. If they had the daring to spring this on my grandparents, why didn't they have the nerve to announce their intentions openly?

They can't have been afraid the Masons would say no. Their boldness was really more like cowardice, their inhibition creating a scene that perversely fulfilled their fears of embarrassment. What could have been more embarrassing than straggling out of the bedroom together that fine morning?

I've gone over the scene in my mind many times. Maybe their secret act was simply a way of avoiding debate. Marriage requires a jump of faith into the unknown, but their elopement literally came down to slipping in through the back door. Of course I believe they were in love, but what that odd morning scene tells me is that people can dive into marriage for no better reason than a desire for adventure. Or perhaps, even, a sense of fate—the willing leap over the edge. An alluring, dark feeling of wonderment—what would happen if we took the plunge? Maybe it would be like flying; we wouldn't fall. But today when she tells me about the early days of her marriage, my mother always says, "I jumped from the frying pan into the fire."

After breakfast, the men went to milk, and Ethel showed Christy how she washed her dishes. Aunt Rosie worked in a variety of creative ways, but Ethel seemed very precise, Christy observed. She was particular about her meat-grease can and the leavings that went into her step-pedal slop-bucket for the hogs. She washed her dishes in hot water in a pan on the woodstove and scalded them in the "rinch water" in another pan, using water and soap very sparingly. She had made her soap from hog fat and ashes and lye in a kettle over a fire outside. Christy was surprised that the soap was perfumed. Aunt Rosie didn't perfume hers.

As soon as the men returned from milking, Christy went down to the milk house and helped them bottle the milk so they could deliver it to customers in town. She watched Bob handle the cream separator; he was careful and slow, like Ethel. Wilburn slapdashed through his work with a grin—to aggravate his parents, Christy realized.

She followed Ethel through her routines that morning, remembering herself as a little girl following her grandmother around. She helped Ethel with the hoeing, the washing, the sweeping. Her natural high spirits surged forth; she chattered about her cousins and the others at Aunt Rosie's. With minimal small talk, Ethel concentrated on hilling up her beans, pulling the dirt close to the stalks with her hoe.

"I'm a hard worker," Christy said. "I can turn out work. Lead me to it. I ain't lazy. I'm work-brittle!"

In the afternoon, after dinner, Ethel sat down on the porch to rest.

She told her new daughter-in-law, "After your grandmother died, we thought about adopting you. But now we have you anyway!" She smiled, but she offered no embrace or other gesture of affection. She said, "Rosie thought you'd be better off out there at Clear Springs with some of your own people."

Christy pondered what it would have been like growing up with Bob and Ethel and Wilburn. That was a strange idea, she once told me. She said she was glad they hadn't adopted her; Wilburn would have been sort of a brother, then, not someone to marry. I find this a chilling thought. If they had adopted her, our family—my parents and grandparents—would have been in place. But I would never arrive.

It was common for newlyweds to live with the man's parents. Since Wilburn was an only child, it was expected that he would stay with his parents. Besides, my mother knew that a son could not readily establish his own farm, especially during the Depression, so she did not expect to have a house of their own. She settled into her new life. Bob and Ethel were thrifty and purposeful, giving her the impression of a pair of secure, steady old workhorses. Their lives followed a firm cycle of work. But their routine was so quiet. Christy missed being around a crowd of people. She was normally sassy and full of fire. Instead of taunting her, the way her cousins had done, her in-laws were reserved and watchful. Wilburn teased her plenty, though. She fought him, and the more she fought the more he teased. He laughed at her and provoked her and got her to chase him. He behaved like a collie dog nipping at the cows' ankles. But he was excessively shy around groups, and he would not go to church, just as he had not gone out to Clear Springs with his parents to the Mason family get-togethers. On those occasions he stayed home and explored the fields and creeks with the neighbor boys. He cared more about the natural world than he did about human events, Christy realized. He was always pointing out a bird nest or a strange bug.

Bob read only the newspaper and the Bible, but Christy could tell that Ethel had education. She didn't say "hit" for "it" as some of the older folks did, and she owned some books. Christy dabbled in them, fearful that Ethel would catch her when she was supposed to be working. Christy wanted to learn. Wilburn often told her she was dumb, because the school at Clear Springs was inferior to the Mayfield school he had attended. But even if she had wanted to continue her education, she couldn't now. Married people were not allowed to attend school.

The days and weeks went by. Wilburn and Bob milked twice a day, bottled the milk, and peddled it to their regular customers in town. Sweet-milk was twelve cents, buttermilk a nickel. Christy washed and scalded the narrow-necked, thick-lipped bottles in the milk house. She liked working with the bottles and the bottle-capper that snapped in the paper-plug caps printed with MASON GRADE A DAIRY. As she worked, she listened to a radio soap opera called *Stella Dallas*, about a mother's love for her ungrateful daughter, who had married into society. The story was so riveting it made Christy weep. She listened to a music program with an announcer whose limpid voice she loved. She hummed along with "Pennies from Heaven" and "I've Got You Under My Skin." Bob and Ethel had bought the radio so they could hear some local programming (farm and community news, and some fiddling), but they did not care for anything that came from far away. Christy and Wilburn listened devotedly to *Fibber McGee and Molly*, *Amos 'n' Andy*, and *Charlie McCarthy*.

Wilburn got work sacking feed. After milking in the morning, he walked a mile up the railroad track to the feed mill, which was adjacent to the house where the Lyon quintuplets had been born. After Wilburn started the job, Christy helped Bob deliver the milk in town while Ethel cooked dinner. To her relief, Christy was not expected to cook. Ethel's kitchen habits were intimidatingly persnickety. She cooked certain things in certain pans and put a specific amount of meat grease in her vegetables. She often got up in the middle of the night to mix her yeast rolls to rise by morning. She cooked small amounts and was especially stingy with meat. Christy craved meat. Aunt Rosie always served chicken and ham and a large assortment of vegetables for a houseful of people, but Ethel was in the habit of cooking for only three. Supper was what was left from dinner at noon. Sometimes at night Christy and Wilburn were still hungry, so they would sneak a couple of eggs from the egg bowl in the kitchen and boil them in the fireplace in their room.

On Saturday nights, in Wilburn's rattletrap Ford, Christy and Wilburn sped to Mayfield, where they gorged on hamburgers and Coca-Colas—nothing was so scrumptious, they thought—and went to the show. Vaudeville troupes didn't come around much anymore, now that the picture shows were so popular. At the Princess or the Legion Theater they waited in line to see triumphant Westerns and side-splitting comedies. Mayfield was crowded with people from all over the county seeking some relief from their week's toil. The burger joints with curb service were jammed. One of the drugstores sent carhops all the way down the block along one side of the courthouse square. In town on a Saturday night, young people drove around the square and honked and yelled.

On one Saturday night, Wilburn and Christy went to a honky-tonk, where folks lindy-hopped to jazz and big-band records played on a Victrola. Wilburn wouldn't dance, although he loved the music. One of Christy's older cousins spotted her and Wilburn there. Later, the cousin told Bob Mason that his son and daughter-in-law were out dancing at the honky-tonk.

Bob confronted Christy, out by the wash-house.

"Did you and Wilburn go to that place that used to be Coulter's School?"

She was silent, feeling the accusation in his voice. Then she nodded.

"Well?" he said. "What were you doing out there? At such a place?"

"Oh, we just wanted to see what was there," she said. "We didn't do anything."

He said nothing. He didn't tell them not to go again. He didn't have to.

Living with her in-laws could be embarrassing and uncomfortable. Trying to get a good night's sleep on Wilburn's narrow bed was like sleeping with a mule, my mother often says. "He was long-legged and slept crossways." Eventually, they borrowed a "bedroom suit"—a bed, a chest of drawers, and a dresser—from a neighbor. The bed was larger than the one that let down from the wall, but the wooden slats kept falling out of the frame beneath the mattress. Often they clattered to the floor in the middle of the night, when Bob and Ethel were asleep. Sometimes Wilburn and Christy got up and put the slats back under the mattress. At other times Christy would just sink into the hole and Wilburn would fall asleep on top of her. "Why don't we rope the bottom so it won't spraddle out?" she said to him once. "I don't know," he said. They didn't get around to fixing the bed.

"Wilburn bought me my first pair of silk stockings," my mother tells me. "And I got a run in them first thing. He was surprised that I had brought so few belongings with me. 'Is this all you've got?' he said."

From his earnings, Wilburn had to pay his father for their keep. Everything the farm brought in went back into it, into livestock and seed. Even though these were the Depression years, the Mason farm was doing well, without any debts. The farm would be Wilburn's one day, but meanwhile Bob was in charge.

"We were just kids," my mother says. "We wanted to play." She learned to ride a neighbor girl's bicycle and scratched up her knees falling onto the gravel roads. Wilburn chased her as she rode down the driveway, distracting her and getting in her way until she landed in the potato patch. "I never was so mad in all my life!" she says with a laugh. Wilburn had always wanted a bicycle, but his parents would not buy him one. He told Christy that the two things he had always wanted were a bicycle and a goat. "I'm going to get me a bicycle and a goat if it takes me the rest of my life," he told her.

Bob and Ethel were old—Ethel was forty-eight, and Bob was fifty-four. They had married late, when both were already set in their ways. They were cautious, conservative, acutely conscious of good value. They took pride in their grooming, their clothing, their furnishings, their yard, their fields, their entire place. Although Ethel was a strong, rawboned woman, she nonetheless had delicate nerves. Bob called her "Ettie," pronouncing both *t*'s with a light touch of the tongue. The tip of his nose wiggled like a rabbit's. He was less restrained than Ethel, more given to chuckling and gentle teasing, but nevertheless his word was law. He was a tall, well-built man who pampered his wife.

"Bob carried her around on a pillow," my mother says. "She had an easier life than any woman I knew. She didn't have to do a man's work, like I did."

Ethel had a plainspoken way about her that was utterly unselfconscious. "She could cut you down with a word," Mama tells me. Ethel might deliver a judgment on scouring a skillet or gathering eggs. She wasn't polite, or sparing of feelings, and she did not know that her direct remarks hurt. Again and again, she made Christy feel worthless, out of place.

My mother entered a new phase of loneliness. Wilburn was restless. Before he married Christy, he had been in the habit of running around with his bachelor friends. Now, on a few Wednesday nights, he went to town with some of his old pals, leaving her at home with his parents. He and his friends went to the poolroom, a smoky, dark place off limits for women. "You wouldn't like it anyway," he assured her. She had heard there was drinking and poker in the back room.

The mantel clock kept pace with the night work. It pinged every fifteen minutes and struck every hour. Christy tried not to pay attention to it, to keep busy, to do as she was told. She hulled peas or pieced scraps of material, trying to imagine a quilt. She was glad when eight o'clock struck and her in-laws silently prepared for bed.

On Saturdays, Christy and Wilburn went to town as usual. On the way home from the show one Saturday night, he stopped at a restaurant near the feed mill.

"You wait in the car," he said.

It was late, and she knew there was no food being served. She suspected there was gambling and liquor in the back of the building. Alcohol was illegal in Graves County, and gambling was both illegal and sinful, she thought. She waited and waited. It was cold and her coat was thin.

When Wilburn finally returned, he was wobbly, but he insisted on driving. She had to reach across him to steer the car herself because he could not keep it in the road. When they reached home, he stumbled and fell into the coal pile beside the house. Angrily, she left him there and went inside in the dark to bed. The next morning he appeared, wearing a guilty grin. Coal dust was smudged all over his good pants and coat. He had crawled under the porch and slept there. His parents said nothing. They did not mention the coal dust on his clothes. But their silence was shattering.

The next chance Christy had for a ride back to Clear Springs, she told Aunt Rosie how Wilburn was behaving. Wilburn wasn't bad, Christy knew. She was crazy about him. But she didn't understand why he treated her so indifferently at times, why he wouldn't stand up to his parents, why he left her there with them and went to town.

"Was that how my daddy treated my mama?" she asked.

"Shit!" said Aunt Rosie, almost under her breath. That was a word men said when they thought women weren't listening. "You've made your bed," Aunt Rosie said with finality. "You have to lay in it."

"Well, why does he go polly-foxing around like that?" Christy asked her aunt. "Why doesn't he take me with him? I like to have a good time."

"That's menfolks," Aunt Rosie said. "They have to go off once in a while in a bunch. Just leave them alone. It don't concern you one bit. You just have to put up with it. It'll be all right as long as he comes home and don't run off and steal you blind, the way your daddy did your mama. Bob and Ethel will keep you. And don't forget you've got a roof over your head."

"I don't have a thing for anybody to steal," Christy said.

Christy had inherited none of her mother's things, but now Rosie gave her one of Eunice's preserve stands—a large, lidded glass thing on a pedestal.

"That'll hold enough preserves for a wheat threshing!" Aunt Rosie told her.

"Just what I need," Christy said. But she was glad to have it.

The work was regular—milking, washing and scalding the bottles, drying apples on a screen door laid out on the milk-house roof, setting chickens on their nests, dehorning cows, working mules. Christy helped gather corn and field peas. Bob commented to Wilburn, "I wouldn't let my wife work in the fields like that." Yet it seemed to Christy that Bob would think up things for her to do, just to watch how hard she worked.

"It makes me so mad I could spit," she told Wilburn. "They seem just amazed at how I can turn off work. They just stand there and watch!"

"They can't believe their good luck," he said with a grin. "They don't have to hire."

They had often boarded a hired hand, but now they did not. Christy threw herself into the work on the farm in a perverse effort to show how valuable she was. She labored spitefully, directing her youthful temper at weeds and shucks and mud. She tried to adjust to her married life, but she kept a little distance, saving herself, and gradually Wilburn saw it. He saw that flame of independence she hoarded—as if her mind were somewhere else, free. What he didn't know was how often she wondered if she should have gone to Detroit with her aunt Mary instead of marrying him.

Many women, even farm women, were entering what they called public work—a job outside the home. In 1938, after two years of marriage, Christy began working in Mayfield at the Merit Clothing Company, which manufactured men's suits. Bob and Ethel were scandalized, but Wilburn didn't object. The factory was a multistory brick building with oiled wood floors and hundreds of paned windows. Its enormous rooms were filled with whirring machines that hummed and buzzed and click-clacked. People were intently absorbed at these machines, working as if they were privately engaged in a fascinating puzzle. Christy was thrilled.

She spent her first week making set-in pockets and welts for vests. But she didn't catch on to the work at first and couldn't meet the production quota.

"I was so young," she tells me. "I didn't know how to put out the work. This floor lady was supposed to teach me, but she had the hots for a foreman and she didn't take enough time with me. Her job was to teach the new ones and keep tabs, but she was too busy flirting with the foreman. I did a bunch of work and done it wrong and had to take it out and do it over. They didn't have repair hands then, to go along behind and fix mistakes. So all I made was a dollar and a half for the whole week!"

She bought a dress with that first paycheck. It was white eyelet, with a gathered skirt and ruffles around the neck. It was the first dress she had ever owned that wasn't handmade.

"I hadn't been working there long, and I still wasn't making my average when the manager called me in and bawled me out. He talked to me like I was a dog, and I went out crying. He said, 'I guess you know I should fire you, but I'm going to give you another chance, and if you can't handle it, you'll have to go.' "

The manager sent her to a simpler job, sewing labels inside coats. She did that easily, and in time she performed a variety of other tasks: she cleaned coats; she ran tacking machines; she mastered vest welts.

"People worked hard to hold on to their jobs," she tells me. "Everybody knew how lucky they were to have them."

The world of the factory dazzled her. The place was steaming hot, the air was filled with lint. The pressers worked in a cloud of steam that flushed their faces. Gigantic overhead fans swept the air. Christy sat proudly on a high stool and guided heavy material through her machine. She loved being out in the world, going to town, earning money. She felt important. "The people I worked with was really something," she tells me. "There were all kinds of personalities, and I learned how to stand up for myself." She learned not to be afraid to be herself. She gabbed and giggled and kidded. She bloomed.

"They included the label sewers in some of the office parties and conventions," she says. "And all the employees got a corsage and a free big dinner once a year."

I have a snapshot of her with a group of her Merit pals on an outing to a Civil War battlefield on the Mississippi River. The picture shows several women posed around a car, eating smile-wide slices of watermelon. I love to imagine her at this time in her life, when her youthful optimism took charge of her and lifted her out of her limited past. I like to imagine that I was conceived in some supercharged instant that arose from the electric state of mind she enjoyed while she was a Merit employee.

The Merit offered train excursions. In 1939, Christy signed up for a factory trip. She had earned enough money to pay her way. Wilburn did not go with her. The group traveled by train to Biloxi, Mississippi, a resort town on the Gulf of Mexico. They went on boat rides, took a bus tour of New Orleans, ate seafood, and saw more exotic scenery than Christy had ever imagined.

I went along on that trip, too. I was a stowaway, although neither of us knew it at the time. So began another radical change in Christy's life, and so began my curious, wandering existence.

4

The first question I remember asking came to me when I was about four. Mama was sweeping our room. We lived with Daddy's parents—Granny and Granddaddy. I asked Mama why she was sweeping.

"The floor's dirty."

"What are you sweeping it for?"

"Because I have to."

"What for?"

"*Cat* fur to make kitten britches," she said, exasperated.

To me, it was and still is a fundamental question. Why work? Does everybody have to sweep? Could I get out of it somehow?

I played house with my dolls, Nancy and Johnny. Nancy could drink from a bottle, and she could pee—she was modern. But Johnny was a hand-me-down rubber doll who had been left out in the rain. He was bleached-out and lazy and no-account. In one of my earliest memories, Santa Claus left a domestic tableau across the foot of my bed—a little iron and ironing board, and a kitchen stove and sink and pantry. Mama had saved all year to achieve this surprise, to see the delight on my face.

I practiced for my destiny with my new toys. But jigsaw puzzles, not dolls, became my obsession. As soon as my hands could manipulate objects, I was working jigsaw puzzles. In my playpen, I forced the pieces into place and celebrated my discoveries. I had tantrums if the pieces wouldn't fit. "You'd stand on your head and show your butt," Mama always says, with a laugh. I loved coloring books and connect-the-dots—any sort of play that caused a design to emerge—a surprise, like the sun coming up.

When the Japanese bombed Pearl Harbor, my parents and I all had the mumps. President Roosevelt was on the radio. Worry suffused the air, and Mama was afraid for Daddy. Daddy had to stay in bed, while

Mama helped Granddaddy milk the cows and deliver the milk to our customers. Women could handle mumps, but mumps had a way of "falling" in a man, causing sterility, Mama explained to me years later.

Before the mumps, I had already been stricken with pneumonia my first winter. My parents and I slept in the unheated north room, the coldest room, and I was often sick. I slept in their bed with them for warmth. One night Mama awoke to find me completely uncovered. "You were cold as a frog," she says. When fever developed later, she fed me juice she squeezed from onions roasted in ashes, and she painted my chest with black-walnut juice, staining my skin brown. She crooned baby talk, her voice throbbing with worry. I can imagine how she must have clung to me fervently from the time I was born. At last she had something of her own in the world. She had me. And she had survived childbirth. At every point of her pregnancy, she must have been aware of her own mother's fate.

My earliest memories seem to have soundtracks. I try to make sense of the fragments of sounds I remember, but they are growing fainter. I try to grasp them from the foggy air:

My grandmother's muted, stern murmur, and her soft way of protesting, with a slight self-effacing laugh, all wrapped up in the word "Pshaw!" It was a smoothly rounded cat-spit of a sound.

Granddaddy's grinning "tee-hee-hee." He was mild-mannered and calm most of the time, and gentle in his humor.

My mother's series of little cat-sneezes.

The way she said "Shhh! Be quiet!" when Daddy was taking a snooze.

Her bursts of hilarity and Daddy's guffaws, his haw-haw-haw laugh at anything foolish.

The bull bellowing. The slap of cows' tails against their flanks, swishing flies.

The motor of the small truck, Daddy returning from his milk route.

The creaking chain of the pulley as Granny drew the bucket of ice-cold water from the cistern.

The voices of kinfolks gathering, the variety of pitches.

The individual voices—Mose, Herman, Uncle Roe, Uncle Bee, Mary, Datha. The older ones said "holp" for "help" and "ye" for "you," and they all said "mess" for just about any situation.

Sounds had shapes. Before I learned to read, I assigned a visual language to the sounds I heard. The image for Daddy, naturally one of my first words, stayed in my mind for many years. It was a dented aluminum cup of the kind used for drinking water from a cistern. (We used an aluminum dipper to sip from the bucket drawn up on the screaking pulley.) This crinkled cup flashed into my mind whenever I heard the word "Daddy." Even now, sounds always have shapes—abstract ones, arcs and shadings of spaces—and a typewritten word accompanies each one like a subtitle. A whooshing sound is long and drawn out, wide on the ends, rounded as the mouth would make it. Traveling along behind is the typed word "whoosh." A train's whistle is long and thin with a flared end, like a contrail of sound, and it covers the entire space it travels. A cat purrs a flow of dots.

The sounds linger in my head:

The electric milkers—suctioning the cows' tits, sucking the milk.

The motor that ran the electric milkers at the barn. It had a throbbing rubber-against-air rhythm. In bursts, the exhaust air flowed to the outside of the small milk house adjacent to the barn.

In the barn, the two-by-four sliding into place, locking a cow by the neck into a stanchion so she could be milked. The splash and whish of urine running down a trough to a hole through the south wall of the barn. The plop of powdery white lime splatting and scattering onto the whitewashed concrete floor to smother the stain of fresh manure. The scrape of manure being shoveled from the barnyard into the manure spreader. The sound of boots sucking mud. So much sucking.

My pacifier was made of wood. I sucked wood. My first word was "sook-cow"—the cry my family used to call the cows at milking time. I've learned lately that the lowland Scots used "sook, cow!" to call their cattle; it comes from an Old English word, *sūcan,* to suck. It is a clue to our history, which has been mostly lost to memory.

My very first memory is a scene fading into that oblivion. It was a pleasant summer Sunday afternoon. I was still an only child. I was three. We had company, and Granny made vanilla ice cream, churned in a freezer filled with salted ice. I was wearing a blue-print dress and white socks and sandals. Mama had made my dress from a muslin feedsack. It felt luxurious and finely textured, like Granny's damask tablecloth. The kinfolks gathered on the front porch, where they could see anybody passing along the road, and I was sitting alone for a few minutes at the top of the steps to the back porch. The concrete stairway had a tubular metal rail, smooth and round to hold. When I got a little older,

I would swing out under this rail to the ground, and the metal would make a slight squeak against my moist hands. But that day I sat on the top step in a quiet moment that has stayed with me always. I was concentrating deeply on a Coca-Cola bottle cap that Daddy had fastened onto my dress. He had separated the cork lining from the metal cap and then fitted the cap and cork together again, capturing the dress material snugly between. The texture of thin cork was like skin, pleasant to touch. The metal cap was cool, hard, and fluted, like the ones in Granny's bottle-capper for the grape juice she bottled from the grapes on her arbor. I tested out the fitting of this marvelous wonder—the cap separated and then reunited on my dress—and I remember feeling that I was making a discovery about how the world works in clever ways— disparate objects making delightful, unexpected connections for no real reason other than for our pleasure in discovering them.

I remember the ice cream that day, vanilla and heavenly, with the occasional tang of salt from a crumb of salted ice flicked into the cream tub. (Granny and Granddaddy called ice cream "cream.") Ice cream and Coca-Cola were imprinted on the appetite center of my brain that day. They became part of my mind's unfolding, like the patterns on my dress.

That same year a much more significant scene occurred, but I have no memory of it. I climbed onto the kitchen table, and—no doubt pleased with myself—I stood there surveying the room from my new vantage point. Granny and Granddaddy had forbidden me to climb on the kitchen table.

"I was outside when I heard you squalling," Mama says. "And I ran from the wash-house, up the back steps, to the kitchen. Bob was standing there with the razor strop in his hand. You were screaming like you'd been kilt, and he was fixing to thrash again. I jerked that thing out of his hand so hard it burnt the skin off of my fingers. Then I grabbed you up and run into the bedroom. I was bawling as hard as you were."

When my mother tells her memory, it is as if she is going through it again. I can see the hurt on her face. "Your little legs was purely black," she says. "I don't know how many times he hit you, but you stayed bruised a long time. Wilburn didn't say anything to his daddy that I know of. But Bob never hurt you again."

"I don't remember it at all," I say. I think about how mothers report they never remember the pain of giving birth. I wonder if forgetting applies to all kinds of pain, and if pain is the reason so much of our history has been forgotten. I cannot remember the savagery of the razor strop, its sting, my squalling, the black welts on my legs, the shudder of my mother's sobs. I loved my grandfather.

My legs seemed destined for trouble. In the summer of 1944, we had a new house and a new baby, my sister Janice. Shortly after she was born, I butchered my leg at the knee in an accident that required twenty-two organic, dissolvable stitches of catgut. I had a wreck with a breast pump. My cousin Sadie and I were playing with the pump someone had given my mother so she could save her milk for the baby. It was made of glass, with a rubber bulb on one end. We filled it with sand and took turns squeezing sand at each other. I was on the rope swing under one of the grand oak trees by the driveway. I was swinging as hard and as high as I could and Sadie was standing nearby, ready to spray sand at me as I swung toward her. But I slammed into the breast pump in Sadie's hand. The glass shattered, gashing the side of my knee.

It was a Sunday, and some kinfolks were visiting. Granny wouldn't let Mama see my leg. Mama was still in bed after coming home from the hospital with the baby. Now Daddy took *me* to the hospital. While someone prepared the ether, a nurse held me. She chirped about all the new babies that were in the hospital. "We've got the cutest little colored babies here now," she said. "Twins! And black as coal."

Our new baby was a white baby. I wondered, what if Mama had brought home a black baby? Did she get to choose which baby she wanted? Maybe they would send a black baby home with me and I could surprise her. The gas started flowing over my face, and a hundred little Humpty-Dumpties with high, squeaky voices began building an enormous Tinkertoy structure all over me. They worked busily. The scene was like a Katzenjammer Kids strip in the Sunday funnies, where the action is all over the place simultaneously. I couldn't read. I couldn't understand the Katzenjammer Kids, even after I learned to read. For years, I studied them hard, trying to work out the riddle of their fascinating speech.

That summer, my father was preparing for the inevitable. President Roosevelt was often on the radio talking about it. Daddy was waiting for the President to call him. He hadn't expected to be drafted because he was a farmer with little children. And the doctor had told him he wouldn't be accepted anyway because he had sensitive ears from having scarlet fever when he was a teenager. But the war grew worse, and now the word was that the government was taking anybody. Daddy began selling off his cows; he let some of them go dry.

In anticipation of the second child, Daddy built us a house—in the woods on a hill a couple of hundred yards away from his parents' house. Granny and Granddaddy didn't think much of it. It was not large and solid like their conventional farmhouse, with its porch and cistern. There was plenty of room for all of us in their house, they believed. Our new house, a white wood-frame structure, was very small, a little square divided into four rooms—two bedrooms, a living room, and a kitchen. It cost fifteen hundred dollars to build, with a friend's help. For my mother, it was a mansion—her own place at last. She had a stove and a sink and a living-room suit. She had two little girls. She was happy that summer and full of hope that clashed with her dread of the war.

Daddy knew that if he were drafted, he would probably end up in the infantry and have to slog through the war on foot. So, after waiting as long as he dared, he enlisted in the Navy, hoping for better treatment. Janice was crawling when Daddy left for basic training at the Great Lakes Naval Training Center near Chicago, and when he returned briefly on leave, she was walking. He was waiting for his orders.

At the end of his leave, Mama went with him on the bus to Nashville, where they went to the naval recruiting station and picked up a sealed envelope containing his orders. He was supposed to present it, unopened, to his commanding officer, but he kept worrying at the seal until he got the envelope open. The orders inside said California. That meant he would ship out into the Pacific, right smack in the middle of the war.

They stayed in a hotel. The night was hot and full of fear, and they couldn't sleep. They parted before daylight. At home, my mother kept busy, afraid she would never see her husband again. She saw her life stretching before her on the farm, with her in-laws. She did not get a letter from him for a month. During that time, President Truman announced the dropping of atom bombs. "It was the hardest time I ever lived through," she says. "I was nuts."

We spent the days in our new house, and Mama carried water from the dairy, for we did not yet have running water. She was afraid to be alone with us at night, so we all slept at my grandparents' house for as long as Daddy was away.

When he came home on a furlough, he was in his uniform, with his long white seabag. He slept and slept. He told us he had not been able to sleep on the ocean because of the blasts of the guns. His ears hurt. He had been on the U.S.S. *Shaw,* a destroyer that had been sunk at

Pearl Harbor, then raised and reoutfitted. Loud, echoing crashes re-verberated deafeningly in the old metal hull. In those tight quarters, the sailors had to try to sleep wherever they could string a hammock or curl up. Daddy made a pallet on a metal table in the mess and cushioned it with cereal boxes. He was an ammunitions passer, working belowdecks—he couldn't see out but sent along ammunition in an assembly line. The shells went up a dumbwaiter onto the deck where the heavy guns were. He said that down below, he could not know what was coming, a kamikaze or what. The noises battered his ears.

I remember him packing his clothes to go away again after that furlough. He rolled up each item and stuffed it into his seabag. It was an enormous bag, with many items of clothing in it. He wasn't patient when working with his hands, and he couldn't get the clothes rolled precisely enough to fit them all in the bag. Frustrated, he dumped them out and started again, rolling up the jumpers and bell-bottoms as tightly as he could.

Mama has often said that when he first got to California he had his choice of a battleship or a destroyer. He chose the destroyer. She says, "The battleship was the one that carried the bumb over, and on the way back it sunk. The boys he trained with died." She always says "bumb" for "bomb."

Daddy told us about the high waves, higher than those in a storm at sea we saw in a movie. He told us about a tribal chieftain he saw on a Pacific island. The chieftain wore mostly feathers. Daddy told about swabbing the decks. He told about the Panama Canal. Of the fighting itself, he would not speak.

While he was away, he sent Mama some chewing gum. He had always hated to hear her chew gum. It irritated his sensitive ears. But he wrote, "I'd give anything just to hear you crack this gum." He also sent her a Heath bar, for fun. In his letters, he addressed her as "Sugar."

One day, Mama and Granny stood across the road at the mailbox. I ran out from the new house through the woods to the road to meet them. Mama was clutching a letter, and they were both crying. She told me Daddy had been transferred from the Army to the Navy—or that is the way I remember it anyway, even though it makes no sense. Mama doesn't remember that. She remembers a different crying scene at the mailbox, when all the factory whistles were suddenly blowing.

I said, "Mama, what are you crying for?"

She said, "The war's over."

5

At the end of the war, crowds of sailors gave their Navy garb the heave-ho. In San Francisco they tossed their uniforms in the streets, then many fell drunk in the gutters. My father, picking his way through the drunks, gathered up an assortment of discarded garments and sent them home; they were good clothes with a lot of wear left in them.

This frugality was the tone of my family's life in the late forties and fifties, those energetic, prosperous postwar times when the discharged soldiers and sailors raced home to plow their wives and sow new houses on subdivided pastures. But Daddy wasn't released when the war ended; he had to live on a ship at Norfolk, Virginia, for months. While he was away, my mother got a hundred dollars a month from the government for family support. Of the eleven hundred dollars she received, she saved eight hundred. For three hundred dollars, she fed and clothed two children, operated a car, and met her incidental expenses. Mama had plans for her savings. She saw a chance to make a better living than was possible on her in-laws' modest farm. "I wanted your Daddy to run a little business of some kind," she says. "Something that would bring in some money and let him stand on his own feet instead of just doing what Bob told him to."

Before Daddy returned from the Navy, Mama said to his father, "Please, whatever you do, don't let Wilburn get involved in cows again. There's no money in it and this farm's not big enough to support us all." She pleaded with him, knowing she had no power. If they replenished the livestock, they would have to upgrade the dairy, now that pasteurization was the law. The expense would take her savings. "I could see myself being tied down with a piddling bunch of milk cows for the rest of my life," she says now.

At one point in his Navy travels, Daddy wrote Mama that he would take her out to see the world. He mentioned reenlisting. This vague promise excited her; it might be a chance of getting away from her in-laws. But she knew that with only one child to count on, my grand-parents were especially fearful of the changes brought about by the Depression and the war. Granny was well aware of the dangers of moving away. One of her cousins had gone to Detroit to work and had brought his aged parents up there with him. Then the unthinkable occurred—his father died and his mother was too feeble to go back to Kentucky with the body for burial. His body arrived at the depot the same night that Daddy caught the train for Portsmouth, Virginia, after his leave from the service. In her diary, where I learned these facts, Granny did not record her emotions, but these terrifying journeys, I'm sure, stayed fresh in her imagination.

Uncle Sam had spirited my father off the farm for a time, and while Mama waited for his return, she dared to dream of something differ-ent. She never seriously expected Daddy to reenlist, but now that she had two small children, she felt it was urgent to earn more money so that we could have a better childhood than she did, and she felt that he should resist his father's authority. When Daddy got home, she chat-tered on excitedly to him about the possibilities of going into business for himself—a filling station, an auto-repair shop, a grocery, perhaps. She was full of ideas, garnered and simmered during his long absence. But he had his own notions.

Within a week after his arrival, he went with his father to the stock-yard, just as he had always done. Granddaddy was trading mules. They went again. Once or twice a week, they attended sales at the stockyard. They crossed the Mississippi River to Missouri to look at cows. Within a month, they had bought a brindle cow together. Mama was crestfallen.

Daddy seemed restless and undecided. The G.I. Bill entitled him to an education, so he enrolled in automotive mechanics, a night class at the high school. But he quickly learned that he hated working on cars.

"*Why* didn't he go to college?" I asked my mother recently. It was less a question than a sputter of fury over this lost opportunity. How different our lives might have been, I thought.

Mama scoffed at the idea. "Why, he couldn't go to college. He had a family to support!"

The nearest college was twenty miles away, and he didn't have a high school diploma because he had failed the final algebra exam. He had always made good grades, but he was too humiliated—and proud, I imagine—to try to make up that one course later.

Daddy dawdled on the farm that summer. It seemed to my mother that the more she tried to encourage him to launch out in a new direction, the more noncommittal he was about his plans.

"Why don't you see about getting Wilburn a job at the Merit?" Mama asked Granddaddy. "It would pay regular."

Bob shook his head doubtfully. "Answer to a boss? I never seed the good to come of such." He added, "Besides, Wilburn wouldn't be able to do that kind of work."

My mother is angry when she tells me about this now. "Bob didn't seem to think Wilburn could do anything except milk cows and work on the farm," she says. "He never praised him or encouraged him. They both worried about him because he'd had scarlet fever, and they held him down. But he was smart, and he could have done something different."

As the days following his return from the Navy went by, it grew clearer that he was thinking about cows and mules and crops. He and his father planted corn. He set out a small patch of tobacco, which he had never done before. I can imagine his state of mind then. There was nothing as comfortable and secure as the fields he knew. I can see how he sank back into the soil. It must have been easy. The awkward challenge of training with strangers at the Great Lakes base and the dark journeys on the blank ocean were all history. Back home, he knew everybody; nobody spoke with a brogue. The two weeks he was in New York, based at the Brooklyn Navy Yard, had startled his soul. "He said he was amazed by how lonesome a big city could be," my mother says. "It was more than he could take in." I imagine that he had gone out to see the world and after a year realized he didn't need to go anywhere again. He had everything he wanted here at home. He told Mama it wasn't worth the trouble of going out there. He saw so many terrible things she didn't need to see. The roaring of the guns still reverberated in his ears and woke him out of deep sleep.

Mama was exasperated. By the end of the summer, she realized he wouldn't give up dairy farming. She knew she couldn't talk him out of it, but she thought if he was determined to farm, he should buy some more land. When a piece of land directly across the road came up for sale, she jumped. She knew they could buy it with her savings. It was a fine piece of land. It had an easy roll to it, no troublesome creeks, easy access to the highway. It wouldn't even need a barn or a house, since it was adjacent to the present farm. It seemed an ideal solution, she thought. They wouldn't have to abandon his parents, but they could have more land to work.

Mr. Coleman owned the property. One day, my parents were walking down the road past his house, and they saw him sitting in his porch swing. They called out howdies.

"I want to sell you that piece of land across from you," he said, his swing creaking slowly. "Come on up here and sign the deed," he said.

Daddy grinned and shook his head no. Mama was saying, "Yes, yes." But Daddy wouldn't say anything.

He didn't take her seriously. He found objections. He found other things to do. He didn't want to go into debt, which he might have to do if he had to outfit his own farm and hire some hands. "I'd need boys to work it," he told her. "All I've got is two little girls." Then, his father, who had taught him what everything was worth, recoiled at the price. In the end, Mr. Coleman sold the land to another neighbor, who grew corn on it.

This was the thirty acres that the chicken tower was built on eventually. In the 1940s, after the war, when America was on the threshold of prosperity, my family could have bought that land for what would now seem mere chicken feed. And where would the chicken tower be now? What if? It is frustrating, even now, to think of my father's unwillingness to take the smallest risk after the war, except for the adventure of setting out some tobacco plants. If our family had bought that land, bringing our holdings to a total of eighty-three acres, maybe we would not have ultimately dispersed. Maybe the larger farm would have been enough to hold us there. But maybe it did depend on a speedy production of sons. I was supposed to be that first son, meant to carry on the farm; the name was ready and waiting to be slapped onto the firstborn, surely a boy. Were they so hopeful of a son they hadn't even thought of a girl's name?

When another farm in the neighborhood came up for sale, Mama again urged Daddy to take a chance. From her view, this place was even better than Mr. Coleman's acreage. It was a working farm, with a house and barn. And it was over half a mile away from her in-laws. She spoke of the place to Granny. "Wilburn needs to settle down to something and get a start," she said. "He's not doing anything."

Granny was patching some work pants, and her face froze in shock. She said, "But what if he was to get sick? Who would take care of him way off yonder?"

Mama says this comment pierced her heart. Granny gave her no credit—not even for being able to nurse her husband if he caught cold. Looking back, I imagine that my grandparents were so desperate in clinging to their only son that they could not envision the second and third generation moving even a few furlongs off. Perhaps their own move from Clear Springs had been such a jolt that they could not abide this scattering. Who knew where it would end, once encouraged? After all, the Bradshaws, Granny's maternal kin, had gone out to Texas in the 1880s and had never come back. Billy Bradshaw had been shot and killed out there, leaving three little children fatherless.

Daddy dismissed Mama's newest notion. He wouldn't even discuss it. He simply proceeded—in stubborn silence—with what he had always done. Ingrained parsimony guided him like a divining rod. I suppose that close to the forefront of his mind was the awareness that his parents were often sickly. He may have imagined that he would inherit the farm in the not-too-distant future, so he probably thought it made no sense to gamble. He could get by where he was. It was what he knew. And he knew he wasn't really tying himself down, because he could still get out of the fields and take little runs to town and the stockyards. Like his father, he had a flair for trading, which was integral to a thrifty farm. Granddaddy was often sick in bed with his chronic bronchitis, but he always got better by Third Monday, the monthly gathering of farmers and stock dealers. Daddy and Granddaddy would go to sales at the stockyard and bid on a cow and come within five dollars of buying it, but then not buy it. They did not bid foolishly. They would buy a pair of mules in the morning and sell them for a profit in the afternoon, before the mules had even had a chance to eat.

At the end of the summer, Daddy enrolled in an agriculture course from the farm extension service. The textbook was *Animal Sanitation and Disease Control*. By October, he and Granddaddy were buying more and more cows, replenishing the stock from its wartime low. They bought a black cow, a heifer, a Jersey, a Holstein. They traded for some more mules. And Daddy bought the goat he had always wanted.

Mama was still determined to improve our lives. When Daddy's tobacco crop did poorly, bringing only fifty-two dollars and fifty cents, she immediately ordered a hundred baby chicks. She sold eggs to the local hatchery, and she took orders for fryers. She butchered and plucked and dressed her chickens and delivered them to people in town. In the spring of the following year, when it was clear that Wilburn had permanently settled into farming, she started work once again at the Merit Clothing Company.

"Why do you want to go back to work there?" Granny said reprovingly. "Why don't you stay home and take care of these little girls?"

"But I can give them more if I make a little money," Mama argued. "I want to be able to *do* for them."

To spare Granny from having to take care of us, Mama left my sister and me at the Clubhouse, a day-care center for Merit children. The factory was considered progressive and enlightened for having such a facility. I hated the Clubhouse. Janice loved it because there were other children to play with. I hated it because I didn't want to be around other children.

I was seven, too old for afternoon naps. I lay crumpled on a straw mat in agonized wakefulness while a sausagelike woman with squinty eyes supervised our slumber. The only thing at the Clubhouse I liked were the ten-o'clock and three-o'clock Popsicles. The days were long, and there wasn't much to do, except swing or slide in the hard-dirt playground. I tried sitting under a tree. I read a book but got teased. I wanted to stay home with Granny and help her make albums of poems and pictures. We liked to cut out cartoons from magazines. The watchbird cartoons were my favorites. The watchbird was a crazed, gangly, glum bird squatting on a branch and spouting homilies beneath the tag "This is a watchbird watching you."

After a few weeks, Mama took pity on me and rescued me from the Clubhouse. Janice had to leave too. She bawled, but I celebrated, although I missed the Popsicles. We stayed with Granny and Granddaddy during the day while Mama worked. In the early mornings, Daddy was away on his milk route. Granddaddy hadn't wanted to spend the money to upgrade the dairy for pasteurization, so Daddy now sold our milk in bulk to a company in town and then bought it back, pasteurized and bottled. He delivered it to his old customers on his prewar route.

When Daddy came home from his milk route at mid-morning, he always brought us a treat from the grocery, where he delivered milk and cream. He brought two carefully selected packages of candy for Janice and me. They might be banana kisses, cherry kisses, peanut butter kisses, cinnamon hots, or a rattling little box of Boston baked beans. They were always clever little packages with numerous individual pieces, like my puzzles, except the pieces were all just alike, pleasures guaranteed to be repeated.

Granny was piecing a star quilt. It was for me someday when I married. I helped her, learning to piece diamonds together to make stars. Granny created a pattern from a diamond she had traced onto newspaper. She cut the diamonds from flour-sack dresses my sister and I had outgrown. From her stacks of diamonds, she selected complementary colors for each star.

In her breezy hallway on a hot day, we lolled on her wicker furniture. She read the paper after dinner, after she had washed the dishes and put away her apron. Janice played on the cool linoleum floor, and all afternoon (or "evening," as we always said) I sewed quilt pieces with Granny until the factory whistle blew. The clock ticktocked loudly, and the hands jumped merrily along. I was very aware of time passing, and the whistle always blew before we were ready to quit. I tried to follow Granny's patience and guidance, her sureness as she sewed her minuscule and perfectly even stitches, tiny like kitten teeth. I was entirely absorbed. But then the five-o'clock whistle blew, and Mama, who labored in a sweltering upper floor of the Merit, came rushing home to us, whizzing into the garden and then supper. I shifted mindsets and followed my mother into a different measurement of time.

Against the Masons' ticktock backdrop of slow regularity and patient repetition, Mama roared along like a train. At night Daddy sat in his easy chair—Mama had bought him a large red leatherette cushioned rocker with her earnings from the Merit—and read paperbacks. Mama worked until midnight—canning vegetables, or sewing, hunched over her machine. She never seemed to sleep. In the morning she slapped together two pimiento-cheese sandwiches, wrapped lettuce separately in waxed paper, and flew off to work by the time the whistle blew at eight.

Daddy's white seabag stayed in our junkhouse for years. In the kitchen, we used two sets of forks—silver and stainless steel—he had filched from the mess hall. The handles were engraved with U.S.N. Daddy wore his summer whites out in the fields, plowing and harvesting. And he wore the uniforms he had rescued from the streets of San Francisco when the war ended. In my teen years, I wore one of the sailor hats, the circular brim turned down, for a beach hat. The pea jacket I inherited has the name "William Miller" in it.

6

In May, 1950, I reached my tenth birthday, the milestone of a child's survival. Granny made me a ten-year cake, the traditional way of celebrating victory over childhood dangers and sicknesses. It was a small round three-layer cake about six inches in diameter—a white cake, with boiled white icing and a maraschino cherry on the top. It was all mine. Granddaddy would admonish Janice or me when we were selfish about something. "You ought to divide," he would tell us. But I didn't have to share this cake with anybody.

I had been in the hospital with pneumonia that winter. I was alive because of penicillin. In my parents' and grandparents' time, children died of bloody flux and typhoid. They were swept away overnight by fevers. They had worms and boils and scrofula. They turned yellow and puked bile. Early, ugly death was so commonplace that parents often gave children the same names as the previous ones who had died.

I was tiny and thin. When I lay flat, my hipbones rose like the knees of cypress trees. I didn't imagine that I could die, though. None of my classmates had died—we got typhoid shots at school each autumn. I didn't feel very sick during my stay in the hospital, and in fact I soon recovered.

But I was afraid my grandmother would die. Although Granny was sturdy and tall, she had an almost dainty way about her. And she seemed so old. Mama never used delicate little handkerchiefs, the kind Granny carried to church. Out in the garden, Mama blew her nose with her fingers. Mama swore she would never dress like the older women. Granny dressed like the archetypal granny—in a bonnet, apron, and long dress over several items of cotton underwear. She wore heavy dark shoes and cotton stockings rolled on garters. This working costume was generations old. Women donned stiff-brimmed, long-tailed bonnets at a certain age of maturity, when they ran their own households and stopped letting their hair hang loose. They pulled it to the top of their heads with long hairpins. Yet within those old-fashioned conventions, Granny had her own style. She wouldn't wear a brown dress. She liked delicate "figured-y" prints and costume jewelry and hats. She always dressed elegantly when she went to town on Saturdays and church on Sundays. She wore gloves, and she draped netting or veiling on her hats. It was gracefully swirled over the brim and drooped above her eyes. It might be fastened by a gay troop of red cherries or papier-mâché peach blossoms.

Granny knew quality. She had a lovely set of blue pottery: a sugar bowl, salt and pepper shakers, a cream pitcher, and a grease jar. Her dishes—Depression-era premiums included in detergent boxes—were white, with gold filigree patterns. She had various chipped everyday dishes with faded scenes painted on them, but she saved her good things for special occasions. She brought out her fine tablecloths at Christmas and birthdays. She never used gifts, because they were too nice.

I loved her Chinese wind chimes, hand-painted glass panels that tinkled in the slightest breeze. On certain winter mornings, Jack Frost decorated her kitchen windowpanes with fancy designs like those on the wind chimes. She called windowpanes "window lights." She had an orange-juice jug with a set of little glasses, painted with oranges and green leaves. Sometimes she made lemonade, and she made juice from the grapes gathered from her arbor next to the little pool Daddy had constructed for her goldfish.

A grape arbor, a fish pool, Chinese wind chimes: Mama didn't care a thing for such frippery. She didn't own many superfluous objects, except the millefiori paperweight we all marveled over, wondering if the little flowers inside the clear glass were made of candy. Eventually, frustrated with not knowing, Daddy tried to bust it with a hammer to find out for us. But he only dented it—it wouldn't shatter.

Granny had an Oriental three-monkeys statue: Hear No Evil, Speak No Evil, See No Evil. It truly reflected her character. She didn't reveal or explain. Plain facts sufficed. She reserved her imagination and her sense of the world's complexity for her creations—her embroidery, her delicate cooking, her quilts. She sewed a fine seam, working with great care on her modest undertakings. She made a yo-yo quilt out of satin ribbons she collected from the floral arrangements left at the cemetery on her homeplace. She tatted lace trim for aprons, collars, dresser scarves. Mama didn't tat. But she could produce winter coats (made of gabardine and worsted remnants she got at the Merit), school costumes, entire school wardrobes, Sunday frocks, Easter outfits, choir robes. She whipped out circle skirts, dresses with dropped yokes, ruffled pinafores.

Mama's view of Granny as a domineering fussbudget was so different from mine. I didn't realize how my mother suffered at the hands of her in-laws, because she had learned how to hold her tongue around them. Eventually she learned an almost superhuman forbearance under the Mason regime. Granny tried to make Mama do everything the way she did it; she enforced her particular and peculiar methods for every task, from shelling beans to making cakes to killing chickens. Granny even bossed Granddaddy, manipulating him into doing her wishes. He always consulted her on matters about the farm, except on bulls and vehicles.

From Granny, I got the notion that I could have things just the way I wanted them, according to my own rules. From Mama, I got the notion that I could do everything. Granny was patient and forceful and certain. Mama was hurried, harried, rushed along by the stream of time and necessity. She slung out meals, gardens, crops, babies. She could cook supper and work all the buttonholes on a coat in the time it took Granny to boil out her stove burners.

One hot night in July of my tenth year, some men came to go frog-gigging with Daddy. Beneath a large oak by the road, I sat gazing across the field in front of the barn at swallows wheeling and dipping in the twilight. The train went by, the lights already shining in the passenger cars. Now and then a vehicle passed on the road, a neighbor on the way home from town. As the darkness grew, I had one of those feelings of eerie dislocation, when things are out of the ordinary, a routine broken. Everything was thrown into a new perspective. The men out frog-gigging struck me as deeply strange, mysterious. I could see their silhouettes moving around the pond, their flashlights briefly beaming, and hear the occasional mumbling rush of their voices. Mama was in the kitchen. She had turned the light on. She was working up green beans—breaking them and canning them in jars in her pressure canner. Tomorrow night she would fry a mess of frog legs for supper. Tonight Janice and I were going to sleep outdoors under a tent Daddy rigged up by roping his Navy blanket to three trees. It wasn't much of a shelter, but he said it would keep owl mess from slapping us in the face as we slept.

Everything was irregular. Staying up late. Sleeping outdoors in the front yard under the trees. Listening to owls and frogs and the choir of cicadas. I was seeing from a new angle, a sidling glance that charged everything with new meaning. I sought and cherished such moments.

Actually, I was afraid of the dark. The grown-ups had always told us ghost stories, to humble us and make us mind. The stories left me helpless in the night, fearful of something unseen that might get close to me and smother me, suck my breath the way a cat was supposed to suck a baby's breath. Banshees were messengers of doom. They turned all the air into sound. They shrieked—*eeeeeeeeee!*—a sound like their name. The sound would draw your breath from the roots of your lungs.

The summer light lasted until nearly eight o'clock, but in winter it was dark when I washed the milking equipment (the "milk things") for Daddy, one of my regular chores. I was afraid to walk to the milk house and back in the dark. We rarely kept a workable flashlight. I followed a path through the woods, climbed a stile (two stumps) over a fence, then made a straight run up the creek-gravel driveway to Granny and Granddaddy's. Returning home, I outran the booger-man.

The men came in now, carrying their frog gigs—poles with sharp metal points they used to stab frogs in the back—and I saw them from our makeshift tent. When Daddy peered under the blanket to check on us, Janice had already gone to sleep. He showed me the bucket of frogs, pulsating and bloody. He carried them to the house for Mama to dress. While Daddy and the men stood under the trees and smoked, I saw her in the back-porch light dressing the frogs—chopping off their long fat white legs and skinning them and dropping them into a bowl. I imagined the partial frogs twitching in the bucket. She took the frog legs inside, and later she reappeared and poured a pan of wash-water out the back door onto the rose bush.

The men left, and after a while Mama turned out the kitchen light. It was completely dark. Janice and I slept on old feather bolsters, with only a little sheet over us. I could hear frogs at the pond starting to croak again, triumphant yet diminished. I lay there feeling fear and celebration at the same time. I was so thrilled to be alive that I couldn't go to sleep. The night was full of howls and hoots and wails. Mosquito sirens pierced my ears.

One night not long after that, I was in my room getting ready for bed when I thought I heard a screech out in the woods. It was a banshee screaming its head off. I told myself it was only imagination, but I waited fearfully, not daring to tell what I had heard. Mama was in the kitchen working up tomatoes. Daddy was reading a Zane Grey Western. The radio was playing, a dance-band program.

I heard the banshee rush down the path through the dark. Then Granddaddy burst through the back door. He had to go through the two bedrooms to get to the main room. We had no hallway.

"Ettie's fell," he cried.

Daddy rushed out, and Mama followed, wiping her hands on the tail of her blouse. They called for me to stay behind with Janice. We stood in the kitchen. Two years before, our parents had added a few rooms, including a bathroom and a large kitchen. Now the house seemed large and empty, the radio playing disembodied voices. We waited uneasily.

Granny wasn't physically hurt when she fell, but she cried piteously and rolled up into a ball, as if she had to contain some internal anguish. Mama and Granddaddy took her to the hospital then, leaving Daddy to see after Janice and me. He made us go to bed, but I didn't sleep. Two hours later, Mama and Granddaddy came home, but Granny remained at the hospital. Nothing was explained to me, but later I realized that it was not clear to anyone what was wrong with her. For some time she had been nervous. She had retreated into silence, and her hands entwined each other and picked at her apron hem. I hadn't really noticed. Now I understood only that she was dreadfully sick. The suddenness of her collapse weighed on me. Everything I counted on now seemed tenuous, as loose as a feather floating to earth.

"She's worried about something and she won't say what it is," I overheard Mama say.

Granny was so sick she had to be transferred to a hospital in Memphis. There, she got shock treatments. An electric current shot through her head, skewering her mind. I was terrified that she would die in that far-off hospital. Mama and Daddy had ridden with her in the ambulance and then left her there among strangers while they rushed home to their work. It was July, and the garden was coming in. Janice and I went to the Merit Clubhouse again for a few weeks that summer, while Mama filled in for employees on vacation. This time, I discovered the Clubhouse library, a little white house thick with the enchanting smell of dusty old books that had been donated for the factory children. I could see this dust in the sunbeams that crossed the room. I discovered a row of old-fashioned books by Louisa May Alcott. I began reading

Little Women, and I longed to share it with Granny. But Granny had vanished.

Granddaddy read aloud to me a letter he wrote her. I sat in their bedroom by the oak wardrobe where he kept his cache of candy and the horehound sticks for his throat. He doled out his treasure—a peppermint stick or a few candy corns—for special treats.

His letter told about the weather and the local news and the cows and the crops and her garden and what Janice and I were doing. He had dug the potatoes, and Christy had canned more green beans and picked five gallons of berries. There was a big rain. He went to the stock sale and looked at shoats. He and Wilburn were "laying by" the corn. Wilburn helped cut hay over at Mrs. Shelton's. Roe and Mary and her girls came to pick berries. They had a little picnic with Bobbie and Janice.

Granddaddy wrote, "Now, Mama, don't you fret, times are hard, but they will get better by and by. You are ever in our prayers, and the Lord will heal thy suffering." His letter was soothing and lovely. His language was musical. It was biblical—phrases like "standing on the verge of a brighter day," "when our cares are gone," "the woes on earth vanished." It was the language of the songs in church, not actual talking. For the first time I heard strong emotions expressed in writing—not just in a story, but here at home. Granddaddy's voice was strong and eloquent. I didn't understand how he had found the words, because he could not read some of the books I was reading. It was as if by reading less he left his mind clearer for expression. I loved his letter, but it chilled me too, for I could hear the undertone. Granny was going to die.

Death was on my mind a lot, partly because I had had pneumonia, but mainly because of Beth's death in *Little Women.* Maybe Granny's mind was diseased, I thought, from reading. I had heard her niece say Granny had read too much when she was younger. "Aunt Ethel's mind was always too active," the niece said. People tended to think that you could disease the mind by what you allowed into it. They were afraid of studying. Any smart, bookish person who died young of a brain tumor or apoplexy was suspected of studying too much. Granny herself may have thought that her reading was dangerous. She had read *Gone with the Wind.* Earlier in the summer, I had been fooling around with that large red-covered book myself. Granny may have been worried that it would corrupt me. But I didn't understand the story at all. The proximity of possum hounds and crinoline-understoried ball gowns was surreal. In my imagination I transposed Tara to our farm, my frame of reference, and the opening scene with the possum hounds took place in the driveway of my grandparents' house. It didn't make any sense. I turned to Nancy Drew, who could be relied on to make sense of everything, and to Jo March, the heroine of Louisa May Alcott's novel. I would be Jo, the writer. Not Beth, the shy little sister who died.

Granny was so homesick she begged the doctors to let her out of the hospital. She could not bear to be so far away from everything she knew. I imagine she may have dwelled on her Aunt Ella, stranded at her son's in Detroit a few years before while her husband's body was sent home to Kentucky for burial. Refusing to have any more shock treatments, Granny returned to us, and she stayed in bed until fall. Mama spent many hours up there, seeing after her and keeping house for Granddaddy. Twice a day Mama gave her shots with a large steel needle that she boiled in a stewer. I glimpsed Granny's exposed buttocks, large and white.

Granny had changed. She was quiet, and she cried easily. She couldn't remember the stories we had read together in my schoolbooks. She didn't want to play with our albums. She went to the hospital again for a short period, but not in Memphis. She refused to have any more of those lightning bolts in her head. The lightning would clear out her brain's passageways, they said, so she could think more clearly, so her brain wouldn't swirl—but today I think that maybe she secretly wanted her brain to swirl, while she lay there with her eyes closed, watching a turning kaleidoscope that followed the cycle of the seasons. Her nerves were tangled up like a pile of baling twine. Her fingers would work busily in her lap, rubbing and twisting the edge of her apron.

What happened that night when the scream came hurtling through the dark? Was it merely that she fell out of bed? No one explained. She had to have some treatments. She needed rest. But that was all. Hear No Evil, Speak No Evil, See No Evil. It was a mystery, something she kept from my parents and something they kept from Janice and me. Apparently there was much that wasn't meant to be said.

The Mason household was, I realize now, filled with silences and euphemisms. My sister and I weren't allowed near when the cow had her calf. Sometimes Mama told me, a thrill in her voice, "Guess what? The sow found her little pigs last night! She'd been looking and looking for them, and she found ten little pigs." The bull's dalliances with the cows were not general news at our place. His courtships were hidden. The he-cow, as the bull was called, was so Victorian in his practices that Janice and I never knew he was up to anything. I saw Mama Cat having her kittens once, chasing her tail as the kittens popped out. She growled and pounced, as if the birth were an unexpected attack from the rear. She chased her tail like the tigers in the Little Black Sambo tale I had read in the first grade. The tigers turned to butter; the colors in Mama Cat's calico dress blended together as she spun after her tail.

Mama says now that Granny would never explain what was bothering her. Depression wasn't acknowledged then, especially in a community where strong survival instincts made depression seem like a deliberate, luxurious choice. What unspeakable horrors tormented her? Was she still upset because we had moved out of her house? Had Daddy's long absence during the war gradually worn her nerves raw? Was her own mind a horror for her? Had any of her people—parents, cousins—ever lost their minds? Was there a secret locked in her mind, chained there like an idiot child hidden in the attic?

Granddaddy and my parents talked about sending her to Hopkinsville. This perfectly respectable little western Kentucky city was identified in everyone's mind with its insane asylum. If you said you had been to Hopkinsville, people would say "How long were you in for?" or "How did you get out?" The asylum was a vast brick fortress of a place, confused in my mind with the state penitentiary, which had an electric chair.

That fall, when Granny was still recovering from her sojourn in Memphis—surely the dislocation to Memphis was more disturbing than anything else that had happened to her—Granddaddy's younger brother, genial Uncle Bee, died. Whenever he had come to visit, he always gave me a nickel, on condition that I could work it out of the knotted end of his handkerchief. At his funeral, the rows of the church pews were like furrows in the ground. I sat in the second row, very near the open casket, where he lay browned like a peach by the embalming. He was gruesome and still, motionless like the gray cat that Daddy had backed over with the truck. Everyone was crying. The preacher talked, and the more he talked the more they cried. I steeled myself, refusing to cry. I was bursting with emotion—fear and remorse and sorrow and grief. But I would not cry. It would be embarrassing. I did not want anybody to know my feelings. Like Granny, I wouldn't tell what I was feeling. I did not want to admit my vulnerability. I would defy death. I had already lived to be ten. I had received my ten-year cake. I was too special to die, I thought.

My other grandparents, Mama's parents, were long dead. I never knew my grandmother Eunice, and my grandfather Robert Lee died when I was about five. He was a drunkard, everyone said. Whiskey was evil and illegal, used only in secret. In the Mason household, Granddaddy hid his pint of "medicinal" whiskey, and occasionally he made black-berry brandy in the basement. Granny would surreptitiously take a toddy if she was sick, but she wouldn't venture near a bunch of men gathered out behind the corncrib. They might be nipping.

Nearby towns like Paducah and Cairo, on the river, sold alcohol openly. Cairo, Illinois, had a reputation as a rough river town, and boys went there for lessons taught by whores. But our county, Graves, upheld a facade of temperance. During the last decade of the nine-teenth century, alcohol had been voted in and out several times. Back then, blind tigers—houses where alcohol was sold clandestinely—kept a barrel out front as a signal. On Saturday night, a man might go to the poolroom in Mayfield, encounter some whiskey in the back room, and have to be dragged home. Or it could be worse.

> Will Sutherland and John Burnett had a difficulty at Clear Springs last Sat. night. The former was severely cut on the hand and neck. The latter was slightly wounded. Mr. Sutherland [is] on the way to recovery.
>
> —*Mayfield Monitor,* June 26, 1885

The John Burnett in this difficulty was Mama's great-grandfather. Such an incident could easily have occurred in the same place fifty years later. Mama was not allowed to go to the community dances sponsored by her Uncle Zeb—even though he could fiddle like any-thing—because there might be a knife fight. There was once a murder at one of Zeb's dances. People didn't go out on Saturday night in Clear Springs merely to shake and stomp. They wanted to get drunk.

Sometimes Daddy got drunk. He drank only beer, but he couldn't hold it. A few beers would knock him loopy. When my sister Janice was born, he arrived at the hospital staggering and laughing. Mama made him hide under the bed when she heard the nurse coming. He passed out and slept there all night. He didn't drink regularly or openly, just on occasion when he would get in a mood and go off in the car suddenly. Sometimes he didn't come home to milk the cows, so then Mama knew he was on a binge. She would start worrying, pacing the floor and looking out the window. After an hour or two, she and Granddaddy would go milk, for the cows would get mastitis if they weren't milked on time. Nothing was said about why Daddy was absent. Mama spoke only of how he might have had a wreck.

The church tried to rescue tipplers before they toppled. We attended Calvary Methodist, a small church in town affiliated with the two Methodist churches in Clear Springs. But Daddy wouldn't go; it was up to Mama to make sure her children's souls were safe. She was secretly afraid Daddy would go to hell. At church, the Women's Christian Temperance Union struggled to erase thoughts of alcohol from the minds of young people. When we reached adolescence, the W.C.T.U. made us sign a pledge never to touch a drink of alcohol in our lives. I was an obedient girl, and I signed the pledge. Anyway, I figured it wouldn't be binding after high school. But one boy refused to sign. He had already been to Cairo, and he knew something.

When I was seven—before Granny got sick and while Mama was still at the Merit—Mama sent Janice and me to the Daily Vacation Bible School at a Baptist church for a week, so Granny wouldn't have to tend us. Everyone called Daily Vacation Bible School by its full name, emphasizing the "Daily Vacation," as if to stress the dreaded dailiness as well as the oxymoronic notion of school as a vacation.

The Baptists were not our religion, so I didn't know what to expect, but the week that followed was one of delightful mornings of coloring books, stories, songs, and cutouts. I enjoyed coloring Joseph's crazy-quilt coat and filling in angel wings with the essence of cake-icing white against the off-white of the coloring booklet's pages. I liked Daniel in the lions' den. The lions didn't seem especially ferocious. Goliath was more frightening than any lion, and clean-cut David seemed no match for the shaggy giant. We sang "This Little Light of Mine." ("Hide it under a bushel—no!") Daily Vacation Bible School was like regular school, except for all the praying. I didn't know how to pray out loud and was afraid of being called on. Grown-ups prayed effortlessly, snatching prayerful phrasings out of thin air when the preacher called on them. Silently, I prayed for a bicycle to replace my velocipede.

When Daily Vacation Bible School was over for the day, Granny fed us and then rested, reading the paper in her wicker chair. She gave us scraps of material to sew together and pictures to cut out. On those hot summer afternoons, with the breeze wafting through the hallway, I felt charged up and special. And safe.

On Friday, Mama fixed us a picnic of pimiento-cheese and tuna-fish sandwiches. Cookies and drinks awaited us at the celebratory picnic at the end of Daily Vacation Bible School. (In the South, soft drinks are still usually just called drinks, as if hard liquor did not exist.) All morning we yearned for the picnic. But before they would let us have it, the adults assembled us in the hot auditorium in the church basement and talked to us. They preached for an hour or more, describing hell and urging us toward the brink of salvation. We hungered for heaven, where there would be music and manna, which was like bread and dessert rolled into one. The teachers stood watchfully against the wall. Here and there a child raised a hand. A teacher rushed over then and spoke quietly and compellingly to the child until tears streamed and grief poured out. The teacher spoke in grave and urgent tones. I could hear the teacher saying "Jesus loves you" and "He's in your heart" and "Let Him in." I was frightened. This was scarier than banshees flying into your soul in the dark, I thought. This was public, where everyone would know your sin. The teachers led several children, one by one, to the altar and made them kneel; then the preacher bent over and whispered to them. All over the auditorium boys and girls were altar-bound. I heard them confessing their crimes. They had committed every sin; they were little wretches; they had hurled rocks through windows; they had put chewing gum in little sister's hair. But if they had the courage to walk to the altar, they would be saved. Being saved meant you were reborn, and you would walk in a new way. You would walk with Jesus by your side. Nobody could see Him, but you would know He was there.

I feared that sooner or later they would get to me. I squirmed and fidgeted. Daddy had said the Baptists would get ahold of me and try to wash my feet. He said they didn't think anybody's feet were clean enough. I knew they baptized people by holding them underwater. Baptists were called dunkers. I was afraid of getting dunked. I longed for a pimiento sandwich. The sandwiches were in a paper sack at my feet. The room was sweltering. Janice was sobbing. She was only three, and fretful. "Be quiet," I whispered. "Or they'll come and carry you up there in front of everybody." She kept trying to get into the picnic sack.

I waited them out. I didn't cry. I didn't repent. I didn't raise my hand. I knew that the other children who were raising their hands were older than me. Also, I went to a different church—nobody could expect me to get baptized here. I sat silent and rigid. I wouldn't raise my hand. I wouldn't cry.

Afterwards, children with tear-streaked cheeks wolfed sandwiches as if they were manna and jelly. I didn't see any of them walking in a new way, but a couple of freckle-faced boys who had just been saved got into a little fight over a chocolate-marshmallow cookie.

Methodists didn't dunk. They sprinkled. And they tended not to pressure children with the promise of a picnic. Other than that, it was never quite clear to me then what Methodists stood for, in contrast to Baptists or Catholics or Church of Christ devotees, whom Daddy called Campbellites in a mocking tone that was supposed to convey an obscure meaning. I thought he said "camelites," so I had a mental image of people on camels riding through the desert, perhaps to Bethlehem.

The words, the stories, in church mystified me. Although the preacher took pains to draw a moral and to connect the long-ago tales of a distant land to our everyday life, it was the unfamiliarity—the strangeness—of the stories that affected me. The magic of the loaves and fishes; Lot's wife turning into a pillar of salt; Abraham about to bring down the ax on Isaac's neck, as if his son were a rooster destined for the dinner pot. The prodigal son was a favorite of mine.

In a trance, I sat through the responsive readings, the mysterious doxology, the wide-ranging prayers. In our small church, there was little to look at: the tally board of attendance and offerings, the funeral-parlor fans, the mimeographed programs. The wooden pews were hard; the slick wood sucked at our bare legs in hot weather. We couldn't see out. The windows were cloudy bathroom glass, not stained glass.

But I loved the singing. All the young people sang in the choir, whether we wanted to or not and whether we could sing or not. I had a weak voice, but I could blend in with the others and freely warble and croak without fear of being heard. Earnest Mrs. Roberts in her Easter hat pumped the pedals of the piano along with "Up from the Grave He Arose" until we thought we would rise up on Easter, too. At Easter we wore corsages and the new spring outfits Mama sewed for us. And on Mother's Day you wore a red carnation if your mother was alive and a white one if not; Mama's white flower always seemed sad to me. We had a baby-sprinkling now and then (a wet rose shaken on a baby's head). We had communion once a month, but we children did not go to the altar until we had officially joined the church, and when we did, we were disappointed to learn the holy snack was just grape juice and bits of a papery substance that tasted like the fish food Granny gave her goldfish. As we sipped, we imagined wine and blood. I loved the round silver tray of minuscule tinkling glasses nesting in their little holes like the marbles in Chinese checkers.

During the offering, the collection plate swam up and down the rows, the quarters thunking the felt lining and the paper tithing envelopes rustling discreetly. Granny and Granddaddy tithed, but we did not. We offered.

Daddy simply stayed home. He would have none of it. Mama claimed that he believed in Jesus and the whole works but preferred to avoid the social side of church. Stretching the truth, she said he worshipped privately. But her heart grieved because he wasn't a good churchgoing model for his children and because she feared for his soul. Sometimes before a prayer, the preacher asked us to raise a hand if we were praying for someone's soul. And I saw her raise her hand, her head bowed. I knew she was thinking about those times Daddy didn't come home to milk the cows. I remembered her walking the floor, aching with worry, fearing he'd had a wreck. I sensed that Mama thought he might shape up if he started going to church. But I knew he would be out of place there. He told me once that his parents were always taking him to funerals when he was little. "That soured me on churchgoing," he said. "Funerals give me the heebie-jeebies."

When I was in the first grade, a washtub of hot sandwiches wrapped in waxed paper arrived at the classroom each day at noon. We had hamburgers, hot dogs, and barbecued mutton. On Fridays, invariably, we had liver—ground into a paste and stewed in gravy and stuffed into a bun. These juicy, smelly sandwiches never appear on the buffet tables of my recurring food dreams. The following year the school built a new lunchroom, and Mrs. Hayes and Mrs. Edwards and Mrs. Rhodes cooked plate-lunches of meat and vegetables and deep-dish pie. I belonged to the Clean Plate Club—we earned gold stars for eating everything on our plates.

Before I started to school, Mama read fairy tales to me and taught me the alphabet. I attended kindergarten—for a day. While Daddy was away in the Navy, Mama enrolled me at a place in Mayfield. She dressed me up in a smart little plaid outfit and deposited me amidst a bunch of city children who had played together all their lives. Mama might as well have dropped me among the bulls at the stockyard. I didn't know which way to run. I had not been around other children, except for a few cousins on occasion. I had played a couple of times with a neighbor girl a few houses down our road. The class formed a circle for "Go In and Out the Window," and I was too terrified to follow directions. Every move I made was wrong.

When Mama returned for me, the teacher asked her if I could talk. "The cat's got her tongue," Mama explained. Crying, I followed her to the car.

Mama hugged me close. "You'll like school better," she promised me. "Kindergarten's just playing."

When I started to school, a year later, she went with me the first day. "Bobbie already knows her ABC's!" she said proudly to the teacher. I felt I was on the verge of something important. I had just had my first permanent. I wore a new dress and new shoes. I weighed forty pounds. It was August 20, 1946. School started early because it was lay-by time for the crops, a lull before the harvest began in the fall. The playground was dusty, and the air was still. Beyond the school, there was nothing to see except fields and a church and a graveyard.

Sunnyside School, the neighborhood school my father had attended, had burned the year before, so I went to Cuba School, down near the Tennessee border. The hamlet of Cuba (two general stores and a doctor) was established in 1858, when the slave states demanded that the United States annex the slaveholding island of Cuba. Old-timers called the community "Cubie." A whole different set of country people lived down there, people we didn't know. Cuba was forty-five minutes away on the school bus, piloted by amiable, apple-cheeked Mr. Bob Jones. Mr. Bob drove us deep into the country, through woodlands and past miles of corn and tobacco fields. Honey-suckle vines hugged fencerows and smothered the ramshackle sheds of aging farms. At a curve, the bus stopped before a magnificent two-story house with columns supporting a balcony. No children boarded there; the bus used the grand driveway to turn around in. This ante-bellum mansion was an anomaly, like something from a storybook plunked down in someone's potato patch.

Farther on, the Tucker children—a dozen of them, scattered throughout the grades—rumbled onto the bus like a herd of cows. You had to watch out for them because they might step on your foot or knock you down without even noticing. If any Tuckers caught you staring, they would say, "Hope you get your eyes full." They were full of mischief and wild tales about dead men they found in the woods. They sang country songs—whining, nasal laments I had heard on the radio. Another boy on the bus played the fiddle on a local radio show broadcast Saturday afternoons from the courthouse. But I didn't like country songs. Country singers sounded too much like regular people I knew. Hank Williams sounded like Uncle Roe would sound if he decided to sing for a living—a ludicrous thought. Daddy didn't like country songs either. He liked "Hey! Ba-Ba-Re-Bop."

Miss Christella, my first-grade teacher, wore a rounded rat in her hair and a smooth, puffed pompadour. Her eyes twinkled behind wire-rimmed spectacles. Her belief in children was absolute. She knew we needed to sing. We sang rounds—"Row, Row, Row Your Boat" and "She'll Be Coming 'Round the Mountain." She turned us into a marching band for the high school basketball team, the Cuba Cubs. I played tissue-and-comb, savoring the pleasant bee-buzz sound numbing my lips. For our performance at a game, Mama made me a majorette outfit—a satin skirt with a gold-trimmed weskit, and a tall hat with tassels. She fashioned the hat from a Quaker oats box.

Miss Christella assigned me to be a daffodil in a pageant. Mama bought the yellow crepe paper to make the daffodil dress.

"This won't do," she said doubtfully when she spread the length of crinkly crepe paper next to me. "Yellow's not your color."

Mama drove to school and informed Miss Christella that yellow was not my color. Blue was my color, because of my eyes. Yellow made me look sickly. "She has to be a bluebell," Mama said firmly. "Bobbie's not a March flower."

Mama exchanged the yellow crepe paper for blue and I became a bluebell.

I could be anything Mama wanted me to be. But only Miss Christella could be an artist. She drew an enormous full-feathered tom turkey on the blackboard for Thanksgiving, with resplendent bands of color on his fanned tail feathers. Miss Christella eventually slaughtered the smudged and fading turkey with the blackboard eraser, but in its place a confident and corpulent Santa Claus appeared, in a loud red suit, with a pack of colorful presents. For a while, his face was black, but she worked on him diligently with red and white chalks until she turned his face pink and she gave him a milk-white beard. Miss Christella's artistry was magic. I had never known anyone who could draw. Everyone said drawing was a talent that you either had or didn't have, a quality like dimples.

Miss Christella played "Little Black Sambo" on a phonograph and handed out purple line-drawings of a tiger for us to color. The purple ink of the ditto sheets smelled nice, like alcohol on a shot. We read the adventures of Alice and Jerry, Dick and Jane's country cousins. Their dog was Jip. They ate sandwiches and cookies after school and taught Jip to roll over. The printed word "sandwich" perplexed me. A sand witch? What fairy tale had a sand witch? Of course we didn't *say* "sandwich." We said "samwidge."

At the end of the school year, Miss Christella told my parents that I had done well enough to skip a grade. Now and then a child was allowed to jump ahead. When school ended the first of May, Mama checked out the second-grade books from the courthouse, which supplied textbooks for the county schools. I sat in Granny's front porch swing and plunged into my new books. Her gardenias smelled so sweet it gave me a headache to sit there long. The motion of the swing, with the odor of the gardenias, made me giddy. Still, I read the two readers immediately—*Down the River Road* and another Alice and Jerry. Over the summer, I completed the workbooks and read the books several times. Granny helped me some with the numbers and spelling, when she wasn't busy with corn and beans and damson plums.

"I never heard of a body getting their lessons in the summertime," Granddaddy said.

"She's smart," Daddy said.

"Don't let anybody hear you say that," Granny admonished him. "They'll think you're bragging."

In August, I entered the third grade. The girls were big, the boys rough. Two of the girls—Betty Lou and Susie Ann—befriended me. They had such big arms, I noticed. They had red hair and buck teeth and wore faded hand-me-downs. All of Betty Lou's clothes were trimmed with rickrack. These girls chaperoned me like a little sister and shielded me from the boys on the playground. They told me where babies came from and said their bus driver was a shit-ass. "Shit-ass," I said to myself over and over.

Two of the Tucker girls were in my class, Shirley and Patsy. Shirley had failed the third grade twice and was the tallest girl in the room. Under an oak tree at recess, Patsy asked me, "Do you wear underwear?"

"No!" I said quickly. It sounded dirty.

Shirley and Patsy laughed. Patsy pointed at me, sawing one forefinger with the other.

"Shamey, shamey, shamey," she said.

"You don't wear no underwear, you don't wear no panties," said Shirley.

I didn't know that underwear was what you wore under. Daddy wore "longhandles" under his bluejeans when he milked the cows in the winter. I wore panties and a slip, and in the winter I wore a T-shirt and bluejeans under my dress, but they weren't called underwear.

I thought the Tucker kids were stupid. They were fond of saying "Kiss my old rusty!" in response to almost anything anybody said.

"Have you got a nickel?"

"Kiss my old rusty!"

"The sun's out."

"Kiss my old rusty!"

I loved the third grade, the strangeness of it, with its array of bright new books issued by the county. I was looking forward to multiplication. The first and second grades had tables and little chairs, but in the third grade I had my own desk with a lid that lifted, where I could keep my colors and tablet and pencils. There was a hole for an ink bottle, but nobody used ink. JOHNNY + BONNIE SUE was carved inside a heart on the desk. The letters L-O-V-E fit neatly into the corners of the plus sign, and the letter S snaked through the plus, making a sort of dollar sign. I traced my finger over the lines. *Johnny plus-loves Bonnie Sue.* At the desk across from me, a boy called Billy slobbered and mumbled. "He can't talk plain," Betty Lou had told me. I saw Billy open his pants and play with something he was hiding inside. Spit ran down his chin. He couldn't follow the reading lesson.

One morning, about a week after school began, I was sitting at my desk working arithmetic problems, not daring to look at the boy across the aisle. In the middle of the arithmetic lesson, the principal, Mr. Jones, walked in. He stopped at my desk and towered over me. He was so tall he had to bend double to speak to me. He said quietly, "I know a little girl who's in the wrong grade. She's supposed to be in the second grade."

There was a new rule that year—no grade skipping. The teacher did not protest as Mr. Jones led me away. I retrieved my tablet, colors, and pencils out of my desk and went with him, all the eyes of the room following me like marbles rolling across a floor. He led me to the second-grade room, where Mrs. Virginia made a place for me at one of the tables, between Peggy and Jerry. I felt I had somehow visited the future, although in the week I was in the third grade we didn't get to multiplication. The second-grade class was reading *Down the River Road,* which I knew by heart.

The buildings were larger, but school hadn't changed much since my parents' and grandparents' day. Each grade occupied a room with a pot-bellied coal stove. The unfinished wood floors were oiled with heavy black oil twice a year. Above the blackboard, the alphabet was writ large on a series of placards, each letter in print and in cursive. Along the wainscoting in the back of the room, near the door, a row of black, double-pronged hooks claimed our coats, and we set our galoshes below. We had no lockers, no science projects, no aquariums, no library, no show-and-tell, no field trips, no school nurse, no foreign languages, no black students. Few students had moved in from somewhere else. No one was gifted or disadvantaged. There was no plumbing except for the water fountain. The outhouse was one building—girls on one side, boys on the other. We did not wash our hands.

Still, school was filled with pleasures. A traveling troupe, a vestige of vaudeville, might happen along and offer us a show—magic or music or acrobatics—for a dime apiece. The teachers often had to lend us the money, and some of the poor children had to sweep the classroom or fetch a scuttle of coal from the coal pile to earn their way. We saw a movie once. In the fourth grade, the school assembled to watch *Penny Serenade* starring Cary Grant—not for any educational value, but simply because it was available. If a man with a herd of goats had come along and claimed that his goats could play follow-the-leader, we would surely all have been ushered into the gym to see the show. For holidays the teachers cranked out more purple drawings on the ditto machine—simple outlines of pumpkins, turkeys, Santas. We colored them appropriately, and the teachers pinned them in a row on the wall.

I delighted in the new books each fall, the intricate puzzles of words and numbers in the workbooks, the surprises from the larger world that appeared in the *Weekly Reader*. But reading lessons were frustrating. One by one, down the row, we took turns reading aloud, and some of the feeble struggles to read were excruciating to sit through. I raced ahead in the book. In the English workbook I learned that "ain't" was wrong. We were supposed to feel shame if we said "ain't." All my family said "ain't." Everybody said it, even the teachers. But the workbook said it was wrong.

As the school years went by, I began to realize that school was not devoted primarily to learning. It seemed to be devoted mostly to basketball. In the third grade, I was a flower girl in the basketball queen's court. Carrying an Easter basket filled with flower petals, I marched down the center of the gym, scattering petals in front of the queen so she could step on them as she minced slowly toward her throne. Every year, to raise money for the basketball team, we sold seeds to the neighbors. I treasured the cardboard box with its neat row of seed packets—cucumbers, corn, radishes, pole beans, and one or two packets of flowers. And our mothers sent us to school with cookies and Rice Krispies squares and divinity fudge—all sorts of homemade confections wrapped individually in waxed paper. We sold them to each other for a nickel apiece so the team could buy uniforms.

We were herded onto the bleachers for pep rallies. The high school cheerleaders—bold in their Crayola-green corduroy circle skirts, saddle oxfords, and turned-down socks—led the cheers, stirring the student body up into a revival-night fervor. They clapped their hands in rhythm and orchestrated their elbows in a little dance.

> *Chick-a-lacka, chick-a-lacka chow, chow, chow,*
> *Boom-a-lacka, boom-a-lacka bow, wow, wow.*
> *Chick-a-lacka, boom-a-lacka, who are we?*
> *Cuba High School, can't you see?*

I didn't care for yelling and whooping. The shrieks and hollers assaulted my ears like a melody being ripped from a song. I sat like a stone. I barely comprehended the issue. Howie Crittenden, the razzle-dazzle dribbler, and Doodle Floyd, with his fancy windmill hook shot, were leading the Cuba Cubs to the state tournament. Who could have imagined this little country team would get all the way to the tournament and challenge the powerhouse teams from Louisville and Lexington?

> *Locomotive, locomotive, steam, steam, steam.*
> *Strawberry shortcake, huckleberry pie.*
> *Go, Cubs, go! Fight, Cubs, fight!*

The cheerleaders pirouetted and zoomed skyward in unison, their leaps straight and clean like jump shots. They whirled in their circle skirts, showing off their green tights underneath.

The Cuba Cubs traveled to Lexington for the tournament. In the final game they were behind at the half, but they grabbed the lead late in the game, and then Howie ran out the clock with ball handling like nobody had ever seen. And then the Cubs—the Cinderella Cubs—won the championship. The whole school—and the region—erupted in mad, unrestrained, we-can't-believe-we-did-it joy. To this day, the Cubs' 1952 victory is legendary throughout Kentucky.

As I walked past the army of trophies gleaming in their glass display case next to the high school gym, I wondered why basketball worked people up so much. Eventually, I came to a disturbing realization: each high school class dwindled from year to year as kids dropped out to marry or to help their parents farm. They gave up learning, apparently abandoning any hopes they might have had of high achievement. Basketball would do until they slipped into their fate.

Somehow, my family allowed dreams—even those dreams they'd given up for themselves. They prized learning. Mama had quit school in the tenth grade, but she always regretted it, and she wanted me to get an education so I could have the chances she missed. Daddy was always reading paperbacks. Mama subscribed to *Parents Magazine*. Granny liked to read along with me in my schoolbooks. "You might make a schoolteacher one day," she told me. She had wanted to be a teacher. When she graduated from high school, in 1905, she wanted to go to the academy in Mayfield, which took advanced pupils, but her family could not pay the tuition; besides, she lived six miles from town. Instead, her teacher let her continue attending Coulter's School, the two-room school within walking distance of her parents' home.

"He tutored me and let me borrow books," she told me. "He had me write a history composition and he made me read *eleven* books!"

Granny kept going to Coulter's School until she was twenty-two, and she postponed marriage until she was twenty-eight, but she did not get the chance to teach because she had to care for her ailing parents. She married soon after her father died. Married women didn't teach then, and once married, a farm woman wouldn't go to the library (even if one existed nearby). She had other duties. But I saw how Granny tried to keep her mind active. She read the newspaper and Reader's Digest Condensed Books and the *Saturday Evening Post*. Granddaddy read the Bible every night, following the words with his finger and calling them aloud. He sat in his rocking chair by the fireplace in winter, or in the summer he read on the porch till nightfall.

9

My grade-school teachers didn't all have college degrees, but they attended Murray State Teachers College in the summers. Mrs. Virginia, my second-grade teacher, whose Raggedy Ann–red hair waved in wings above her ears, was loud and funny. When she confronted a child with a misdeed, she would say in a singsong voice, "A little *bird* told me you've been bad." Mrs. Gisela was pregnant when I was in the fourth grade. When she mysteriously ordered us to lay our heads down on our desks for ten minutes, some of the girls decided she had had her baby then and hidden it in the desk drawer. At recess they peeked in and found chalk and erasers.

In the afternoons, the teachers read to us. Mrs. Alene, round and black-headed, read us *The Adventures of Tom Sawyer* in the fifth grade, and in the sixth grade Mrs. Isabella read us *Adventures of Huckleberry Finn* and *The Littlest Rebel*. That year an old silent film of *Uncle Tom's Cabin* arrived at the Princess Theater in Mayfield. The teachers wanted us to see it. It seemed urgent. One teacher rounded up children in her car to go. She honked her horn on the road in front of our house. "Hurry!" Mama said. "She'll run off and leave you." I rushed out the door, racing toward the promise of *Uncle Tom's Cabin*. I remember Eliza hopping the ice-floe stepping-stones, escaping from a slave trader while frantic music played.

I did not know why, in the sixth grade, we were suddenly being instructed about slave times. The messages were contradictory: slavery was bad (Simon Legree), but the loss of those old days (jovial, loyal darkies) was regrettable. We wanted it both ways. My head was full of the littlest rebel, the sorrows of her family, the persecution they experienced. The cruel Yankees burned their house down. Now and then, out in the country, I saw the black ruins of wood-frame houses with coal stoves. One morning a cluster of sad-faced children met my school bus in front of the remains of a house that had burned to the ground, all but the chimney. After that, I was consumed with fear on the bus trip home from school each day, afraid I would find our house burned to the ground. It was as if the Yankees were still in the land, spreading their havoc.

But secretly I was attracted to them. They were mysterious and foreign. They spoke a different language, rough and superior. And they were the winners. I went snooping for Yankees in books and movies, in order to spy on them and listen to their talk. But when I tried to read *Gone with the Wind*, a tale of Yankee mayhem, Mama said, "Don't read that. It might have bad language in it."

I knew that pig Latin was one way to disguise bad language. *Ell-hay, amn-day!* And then I stumbled on real Latin. Daddy's old ninth-grade Latin book was a remarkable discovery. I was astonished that there could be another language, from another time and a vanished place, in which people used strange-sounding words. *Puella* and *puer* and *agricola*. The girl and the boy and their farmer dad. I was especially intrigued by words that resembled our own. *Agricola*—agriculture. *Nauticus*—nautical. In a fit of confidence, I showed Mrs. Isabella the Latin book, and she asked me to read a page to the sixth-grade class. Standing in front of the room, I was trembling. Instead of reading the Latin words, which would make no sense and which I would probably pronounce wrong, I read my translation. It was a simple story about the farmer and the boy and the girl. I could have been reciting from the Alice and Jerry reader. The class had to take it on faith that I was extracting this spine-tingler from a page akin to hieroglyphics, secret codes, and pig Latin.

Rome was just above the knee on the Italian boot in my geography book, like the scab on my knee from one of my bicycle mishaps in the gravel of the driveway. I loved geography. In class, we copied the full-page maps from the book and colored them with crayons (which we always called "colors," as if color didn't exist otherwise). I tried to copy the maps exactly, with the shapes and proportions accurate. I wanted to go to Africa, to Indonesia, to the coast of Brazil. I colored oceans and forests and mountain ranges and printed the names in tiny neat letters. Most of my classmates did not seem interested in such faraway places. Mayfield was distant enough, with enough barriers to discourage country people. Other continents, foreign countries, were mere abstractions. But I believed in them. I knew I would go to France and Australia and Lapland one day.

The Bobbsey Twins ruined me. They went on vacations in every book and never did chores. They were Yankees. They sledded and skated and made snowmen. I languished through hot Kentucky summers, longing to go to Snow Lodge or Clover Bank or Eskimo Land. By age nine I was in a tizzy over *The Bobbsey Twins in Mexico*. Mexico was hot but exotic. I wanted to go to Mexico so badly I tried to learn Spanish.

One summer morning Mama woke me up excitedly. "Get up, get up, guess what! Surprise!"

"Are we going to Mexico?" I cried, leaping out of bed. The song "In My Adobe Hacienda" ran through my head.

No, it was Daily Vacation Bible School. I was crazy to think we could leave the cows and chickens and Granny and Granddaddy and drive thousands of miles in our eccentric gray Chrysler all the way to Mexico.

Daddy and I were walking down the lane after a cow that hadn't come up for milking. Boots, the latest dog, was with us. He was sort of a collie with golden-red hair. I said to Daddy, "When you read a book the second time, do you imagine a scene the same way you did the first time?"

"I don't read a book over. I go on to another one," he said.

"I like to read 'em again," I said. I had just reread *The Bobbsey Twins on Blueberry Island*. I was particularly fond of the scene where the Gypsies came and picked all the blueberries, but a kind boy named Tom led the Bobbseys to a secret bush that the Gypsy tribe hadn't found. When the Bobbseys picked blueberries, they were on vacation and the blueberries were there for their pleasure; when Gypsies picked blueberries, it was called stealing. We didn't have blueberries. They sounded so much nicer than blackberries.

When I reread a scene, it unerringly sprang to life the same way it had before, as if my imagination worked primarily in space and time—as though I were traveling along a familiar road. An image in my mind always had a direction and a size. And I could remember where it appeared in the book—top, bottom, left, or right on the page. But the more I read, the greater my frustration grew with my real life. When I pictured a scene in a book, it was always some variation of a familiar place—with an added element of strangeness, so that the scene appeared slightly bent from reality. Like a circus marching down our lane. Or Gypsies in the barn. Gypsies were a frequent menace to the Bobbseys, but I wanted to find some Gypsies.

I asked Granny, "How does a writer think up a whole book? Does she just make it up as she goes along?" Granny allowed as how Laura Lee Hope, the Bobbsey author, got the plot all worked out in her mind beforehand. She made plans. She didn't just write the first thing that came into her head. I studied on this idea for some time.

I went on to read mysteries, in which girl detectives solved crimes and quaint puzzles about heirlooms with the aid of a magnifying glass. These sleuths drove cars, had boyfriends, nice clothes, indulgent parents. They had time and money. They did not have to pick blackberries. I began writing my own mystery stories. I sat in a corner on the porch or under a maple tree and wrote with a fountain pen in a blue Double Q notebook, which had two interlaced Q's on the cover. I started at the beginning and followed each story, wondering what would happen next. I didn't follow Granny's advice. I couldn't think ahead. The pleasure of writing was discovering what might pop out of my mind unbidden. There seemed to be a storehouse of words that I didn't know I knew, yet they appeared at the right moment, like a girl joining a game of jump-rope.

My detectives were twins, Sue and Jean Carson, whose father was a famous detective. Jean was grimly mature, with a boyfriend. She wanted to be a nurse. Sue, the more ambitious twin, was more like me; she wanted to be an airline hostess. I had derived all the names and set-ups from the mystery series books I had read—nurse Cherry Ames, airline stewardess Vicki Barr, the Dana sisters. I stole the name Carson from Nancy Drew's father, Carson Drew. I still have a fragment of *The Carson Girls Go Abroad,* a story about a stolen stamp collection, particularly a Romanian stamp with an odd portrait of a bespectacled man whose hairline was askew. The Carson girls pursued a ring of stamp counterfeiters. In one chapter, the pursuit took Sue and Jean to the county fair, where they rode the Ferris wheel and ate candy apples and cotton candy. Then, alone, Sue entered a sideshow, "The Thing."

> In the center of the pen a woman—she looked like the wild man of Borneo—sat. Her long hair made a circle around her head, hanging down into her eyes. All around her were many poisonous snakes. Their forked tongues were darting in and out, in and out.
>
> Intrigued by the sight of the poisonous reptiles, Sue still watched. Suddenly to her horror the wild woman began playing with the

snakes, picking them up and putting them in her mouth. To Sue this was horrible. She managed to stay there longer, just for the sake of being brave. Who was going to be afraid of a woman and snakes? Especially if they had had their fangs removed, which Sue hoped with all her might they did.

Suddenly, the snake woman picked up something from the bare earth, and with a mighty lunge she flung it in Sue's direction!

The chapter ended there. I had to keep Sue hanging until I could turn the page and imagine what happened next.

CHAPTER IV

The Surprise Party

When Sue Carson spotted the woman throwing The Thing in her direction she dodged sharply. The Thing, whatever it was; Sue supposed it was a snake, hit her on the shoulder.

Sue tried to stifle a scream but a tiny one escaped her, anyway. She looked down at the ground at her feet. She just knew a snake would be there! But where was it? Sue looked and looked. Nothing was on the ground except a short piece of rope. Suddenly Sue sighed a sigh of relief. The snake woman had thrown the rope instead of a snake! What a joke on her! Sue looked down at the rope again. It appeared to be moving! Sue stepped back. The rope was still. She discovered that she had been using her foot to move it! Another joke on her. What else was going to happen?

Sue glanced at her wrist watch. It was eleven thirty, time to be eating lunch.

Answering an ad in the back of a magazine, I sent off for information about the Famous Writers' School, thinking I'd get some rules and instructions on how to write a story. The school sent me an aptitude test, which I quickly filled out and returned. Then the Famous Writers' School answered with the news that I qualified for correspondence lessons, which cost a great amount of money. After that, the Famous Writers' School kept sending me letters, asking me if I had made up my mind about the course. The aptitude test said I had talent, the letters pointed out. I thought the school was writing to me personally, and there appeared to be some urgency, so after receiving several of these letters I wrote to the Famous Writers' School, saying

I didn't have the money to become a famous writer—I was only eleven years old.

The Carson girls went to France with their father and their French maid, Mlle. Bleax (my notion of a French name). Jean's boyfriend piloted them in his own private plane while Sue played air hostess. One chapter was titled "How to Fly an Airplane." In France, they saw the famous Percheron horses Sue had read about in geography. As it turned out, the counterfeiting ring was operating right there in Provençe, France!

I didn't tell anyone at school about my writing. I was afraid they'd make fun of me. I was an earnest kid with a frown on my face. My diligence in school was absurd. I was always going overboard. Mrs. Isabella gave us word games on holidays. How many hidden words can you find in *Halloween* or *Merry Christmas*? My pencil would fly. I would find a hundred and fifty in the Christmas greeting: Cherry mist charms hammy chasm stammer retch stair mast star rat hat is it sit sir earth . . . *Merry Christmas* was nearly half the alphabet! I was free to whirl the kaleidoscope of letters almost endlessly, listening to the sounds in my mind. Mrs. Alene ordered a special school project through the mail from a school-supply house. It was a kit to be assembled—an entire Dutch village, made of hundreds of pieces of pasteboard, with little tabs to fit them all together. The village had shops and pretty row houses with mansard roofs. People wearing balloon pants and wooden shoes were sweeping the cobblestone streets. Skaters glided on the surface of the canal, their wee silver skates stuck in the ice with vertical tabs. The village was large, covering a table. To construct it, we worked in teams, by turns, but I commandeered the table, desperate to work on the Dutch village full time. It was the most splendid thing ever to appear at Cuba School.

Fortunately for my classmates and teachers, I was absent for long stretches of school, due to illness. In the winter, to keep from getting sick, Janice and I wore long pants beneath our cotton dresses, which had gathered skirts and long sleeves. We wore our dreadful brown leather high-topped plow shoes. We did not play out in the cold or snow because we were sure to catch cold. I always got sick anyway. I coughed and wheezed and spit and blazed with fever. I came down with pneumonia almost every winter.

In the first grade, I stayed out of school for two weeks, enclosed in a breathing tent—blankets draped over the bedposts to hold in the sweet fumes of boiled benzoin—while I happily colored and read and played. Mama called it an oxygen tent. I was out of school so long that Miss Christella took up a collection among her students to buy me presents. Unfortunately, I returned to school the day she planned to bring me the presents. So she returned them to the stores and I never got them. I can see her still, sitting on the bus with the shopping bag full of presents—I heard they included books and house shoes—she planned to drop off at my house. But there I was, hopping onto the bus that morning. The lost presents grew in my imagination. They made me acquisitive and desirous. Even though I always got plenty of gifts for Christmas and my birthday, there was always something else I wanted. Today it seems to me that Miss Christella's gift of art and imagination was worth much more than the gaudy lost packages.

In the winter of my tenth year, I lay in the hospital, thin and bony, my lungs tight with congestion. But I paid no attention to Mama's fretting over me. I wasn't concerned. I loved being sick. I was allowed to have ice cream and milk shakes every day. During the fever, I felt a loose plank flapping in my head; it was my mind speeding up, getting ready to fly apart. I enjoyed the sensation; it seemed to be coming from the very heart of my being.

The following year, I had two more delightful hospital stays. The first one was caused by a middle-ear infection, near Christmas. For enduring a spectacular earache, I was entitled to special presents and candy in addition to my Christmas presents. Granddaddy brought a LifeSavers book to the hospital for me. It was a carton shaped like a book that opened out to form a bookcase with a dozen rolls of Life-Savers on the shelves inside. I savored all the flavors, one by one—Pep-o-mint, Wint-o-green, Spear-o-mint, Cryst-o-mint, the colorful fruits. For Christmas I received *The Clue of the Black Keys* (Nancy Drew) and *The Spirit of Fog Island* (Judy Bolton), a cowboy shirt, and a paint-by-numbers set. I was saturated with happiness.

Later that winter, I got sick again, and one afternoon I coughed so hard I suddenly gushed up blood. Mama threw Janice and me into the car and rushed us to the hospital. She didn't even stop at the barn to tell Daddy, who was milking. I brought along a Quaker oats box to spit in. I kept coughing up blood. As we reached the waterworks on the approach to town, it occurred to me that I could die. Blood was an inch deep in the box. Even though I had passed the ten-year survival mark, maybe something had gone wrong. Mama's face was white, as if she were the one losing blood. She told me recently that she was worried that I had tuberculosis. She had seen people die from this wasting illness, and she had seen their bloody spitboxes. "I thought you were having a T.B. hemorrhage," she said.

The doctor wasn't alarmed. I merely had pneumonia again—bronchial pneumonia this time—and I had burst a bronchial blood vessel from coughing. The nurses gave me an enamel boomerang-shaped spittoon and placed me in an enclosed sunporch on the third floor of the hospital. The porch was private, enclosed by windows. With the nurses' reassurances, I relaxed, telling myself it was impossible for me to die. But I could see my mother's anxious face, hear her nervous voice. I could see her belly bulging out. I heard her say, "I'm afraid all this worry will make me lose this baby I'm carrying."

She saw me staring at her stomach. "I swallered a punkin seed," she said to me. From the way she grinned, I decided she would be all right. I was afraid another child meant more work for Mama, but I didn't dwell on how my illness was affecting her or how much it was costing Daddy.

The sunporch was drafty, so after a few days I was moved into the ward, where it was warmer. A woman in the bed next to mine chattered. She had had a D-and-C, and she apologized for passing gas continually.

"They scraped my womb," she said. "But I'll still have my baby. They didn't hurt it." She emitted explosive noises.

Mama patted her own belly. "If I have this one, it will be a miracle, with all I've been through," she said.

I preferred the sunporch, which was like having my own playhouse. But I stayed busy, even on the ward. Mama brought me books from the library, and she bought me Nancy Drews and Judy Boltons from the paint-and-wallpaper store, which had a small book section. The foot of the bed was piled with all my activities—the books, my stamp collection, a new paint-by-numbers set.

Each day I inhaled penicillin from some kind of breathing machine in the hospital basement. The acrid penicillin vapors loosened fascinating streaks of yellow and dark red in my chest. As the days went by, I coughed up large clots, hunks of brown blood like chicken livers. I studied them for clues to my being—like reading entrails or tea leaves. Twice a day, a nurse appeared at my bedside with penicillin shots, plunging the metal missiles with full force into my taut buttocks.

The kinfolks from Clear Springs showed up, although they kept the children away, in case of contagion. Mose, Herman, Mary, Datha—my parents' cousins—were in and out, dressed up for town and joking and teasing me, while I held court. They brought ice cream and candy. They all said to Mama, "Well, Bobbie Ann's got enough books to run a school."

"All those books will break you, Chris," they said.

"I paid a dollar apiece for them things," Mama said. "She says she's going to write her own books so we won't have to buy any." Mama laughed so loud she had to grab her big stomach to hold it still.

The doctors and nurses humored me along. Dr. Ellison praised my mystery novel and encouraged me to learn science. I was writing a new Carson Twins book called *The Mystery at Pine Lodge*. I had never seen mountains or a pine lodge, but I could visualize the small mountain village, the pine-scented lodge, the bushy-headed criminal, the pair of girl detectives who snooped in his room at the lodge. I had created a place I had never been, and it was tantalizingly real.

"I'm on pins and needles to find out what's going to happen next in that book you're writing," Dr. Ellison said.

"Me too," I said.

"You should study journalism when you get to college," he said. "But don't forget science." He gave me a list of words to study: *molecule, cell, atom*. He said he was going to cure me of my annual pneumonia.

Molecule. I said it over and over to myself. It was a lovely word. *Mole* plus *cule*.

King George died while I was in the hospital. And Daddy accidentally killed our collie dog, Boots. He didn't mince his words. "I backed the truck over Boots," he began. I had been reading all of Albert Payson Terhune's books—about Buff and Lad and Wolf and Bruce and Lochinvar, the whole Sunnybank cast of noble, heroic collies. I was sad about Boots; and my old dog Rags, dead on the highway, was still a vibrant memory; but the immediate reality of the hospital made events at home seem distant. And the sentimentality of the Terhune books surpassed any emotion about real, flesh-and-fur dogs.

I was getting well, and I no longer imagined that my own life was in danger. But I overheard Daddy say to Mama, "If she keeps this up, she won't live to be fifteen." But fifteen seemed so far away, years and years. I didn't even wonder if there was a special cake for a fifteenth birthday. In retrospect, I see how oblivious to suffering I was, there in my little pleasure-dome. I was enacting a typical Mason trait— retreating into my playhouse, the way Granny retreated into her mind, and the way Daddy retreated to the farm after the war.

. . .

Either Dr. Ellison or puberty cured me, and I've hardly been sick since. He gave me vitamin pills to build my strength. I liked to lick off the sugar coating and taste the mysterious flavor beneath. It was much like Fletcher's Castoria, a staple patent medicine of my childhood.

That summer, when I was well and running barefooted over the farm, Mama invited Dr. Ellison to supper. Janice and I had a new little sister, named LaNelle, and Mama was healthy and busy, operating at her usual speed. She cooked ham and field peas and scalloped potatoes and double-chocolate dump cake for our guest.

Dr. Ellison wanted to go out and walk in the fields, which I thought was unusual. He was from Detroit and he said he was enchanted by the country, an attitude that mystified me. The country was so ordinary, I thought. We climbed a stile over a fence into a pasture. He threw out his arms to embrace the landscape. "This is a wonderful place," he said. "It is beautiful, a treasure. You should always appreciate it."

"This place?" I said. I couldn't imagine he meant grass, blackberry briars, cow manure. I wanted to go to Detroit, where there were concrete sidewalks and tall buildings and traffic. Everything was so green here, and nothing important ever happened. Mama's aunt Mary and uncle Rudy came to visit from Detroit each summer. Mama fried chicken for them, and they loved the chicken so much they picked the bones clean and then sucked on them. They couldn't get good, tender chicken like that in Detroit, they said. They missed beans and corn-bread and onions. But I thought they were ridiculous to come back. Detroit was an intriguing place, with Yankees, who spoke another language and ate different food—Detroit food. That's what I wanted.

10

....

Food was the center of our lives. Everything we did and thought revolved around it. We planted it, grew it, harvested it, peeled it, cooked it, served it, consumed it—endlessly, day after day, season after season. This was life on a farm—as it had been time out of mind.

The area around Clear Springs, on Panther Creek, was one of the first white settlements in the Jackson Purchase. In the spring of 1820, Peyton Washam, his fifteen-year-old son Peter, and a third man whose name has been forgotten came to Panther Creek from Virginia with a plan to build a cabin and plant some corn. Mrs. Washam and the seven other children, whom they had left in a settlement about a hundred miles away, would come along later. Before the men could begin building, they had to slash a clearing from the wilderness. It was tougher than they expected. They had plenty of water, for the place abounded with springs, but they soon ran out of food and supplies. They sent for more, but before these arrived they were reduced to boiling and eating their small treasure (half a bushel) of seed corn—the dried corn that would have let them get out a crop. Then Peyton Washam came down with a fever. He sent for his wife to come quickly. She arrived late at night and got lost in the canebrake—a thicket of canes growing up to thirty feet high. Frightened in the noisy darkness, she waited, upright and sleepless, beneath an old tree till daylight, according to the accounts. She hurried on then, propelled by worry, but when she reached her husband's camp, she was too late. He had died during the night. Afterwards, she lived out his dream, settling in the vicinity with her children. The area her husband had chosen eventually grew into the community where a dozen branches of my family took root.

This story vexes me. What a bold but pathetic beginning! What careless, untrained pioneers. How could Peyton Washam and his cohorts have run out of food so soon? If they arrived in the spring, they should have planted that seed corn before long (between mid-April and mid-May). Why, in a mild Kentucky spring, did they not get a garden out right away? How could they have run out of supplies before they got their corn in the ground? Of course they had to clear some canebrake, which wasn't easy. But it wasn't as hard as clearing trees. You can even eat cane like a vegetable. In May, there would have been a carpet of wild strawberries. If Peyton Washam was too sick to forage, why didn't the kid and the other guy go pick something? What kind of pioneer eats his seed corn? Why didn't they shoot a squirrel?

Mrs. Washam is the hero of the tale. She survived and her children joined her. She probably could handle a gun. I'm sure she knew how to get out a garden. I picture her coming alone with a basket of cornbread and fried pies, looking for her sick, hungry husband, trying to follow directions scribbled on a piece of paper. Turn left *before* the canebrake. Follow the creek to the large old tree. Or maybe Peyton Washam's handwriting was bad—maybe he meant an *oak* tree.

This was the rough and foolhardy beginning of Clear Springs. The expedition was a man's notion, with a woman coming to the rescue. The men were starving without her. It makes perfect sense to me, in light of everything I know about the rural life that came down to me from that community. When I think of Clear Springs, I think first of the women cooking. Every Christmas we went out to the Mason homeplace for a grand celebration dinner that included at least a dozen cakes. And in the summer we went to big homecoming feasts—called dinner-on-the-ground—at nearby McKendree Methodist Church, which was on Mason land.

One day Mama and Granny were shelling beans and talking about the proper method of drying apples. I was nearly eleven and still entirely absorbed with the March girls in *Little Women*. Drying apples was not in my dreams. Beth's death was weighing darkly on me at that moment, and I threw a little tantrum—what Mama called a hissy fit.

"Can't y'all talk about anything but food?" I screamed.

There was a shocked silence. "Well, what else is there?" Granny asked.

Granny didn't question a woman's duties, but I did. I didn't want to be hulling beans in a hot kitchen when I was fifty years old. I wanted to *be* somebody, maybe an airline stewardess. Also, I had been listening to the radio. I had notions.

Our lives were haunted by the fear of crop failure. We ate as if we didn't know where our next meal might come from. All my life I have had a recurrent food dream: I face a buffet or cafeteria line, laden with beautiful foods. I spend the entire dream choosing the foods I want. My anticipation is deliciously agonizing. I always wake up just as I've made my selections but before I get to eat.

Working with food was fraught with anxiety and desperation. In truth, no one in memory had missed a meal—except Peyton Washam on the banks of Panther Creek wistfully regarding his seed corn. But the rumble of poor Peyton's belly must have survived to trouble our dreams. We were at the mercy of nature, and it wasn't to be trusted. My mother watched the skies at evening for a portent of the morrow. A cloud that went over and then turned around and came back was an especially bad sign. Our livelihood—even our lives—depended on forces outside our control.

I think this dependence on nature was at the core of my rebellion. I hated the constant sense of helplessness before vast forces, the continuous threat of failure. Farmers didn't take initiative, I began to see; they reacted to whatever presented itself. I especially hated women's part in the dependence.

My mother allowed me to get spoiled. She never even tried to teach me to cook. "You didn't want to learn," she says now. "You were a lady of leisure, and you didn't want to help. You had your nose in a book."

I believed progress meant freedom from the field and the range. That meant moving to town, I thought.

Because we lived on the edge of Mayfield, I was acutely conscious of being country. I felt inferior to people in town because we grew our food and made our clothes, while they bought whatever they needed. Although we were self-sufficient and resourceful and held clear title to our land, we lived in a state of psychological poverty. As I grew older, this acute sense of separation from town affected me more deeply. I began to sense that the fine life in town—celebrated in magazines, on radio, in movies—was denied us. Of course we weren't poor at all. Poor people had too many kids, and they weren't landowners; they rented decrepit little houses with plank floors and trash in the yard. "Poor people are wormy and eat wild onions," Mama said. We weren't poor, but we were country.

We had three wardrobes—everyday clothes, school clothes, and Sunday clothes. We didn't wear our school clothes at home, but we could wear them to town. When we got home from church, we had to change back into everyday clothes before we ate Mama's big Sunday dinner.

"Don't eat in your good clothes!" Mama always cried. "You'll spill something on them."

Mama always preferred outdoor life, but she was a natural cook. At harvest time, after she'd come in from the garden and put out a wash, she would whip out a noontime dinner for the men in the field—my father and grandfather and maybe some neighbors and a couple of hired hands: fried chicken with milk gravy, ham, mashed potatoes, lima beans, field peas, corn, slaw, sliced tomatoes, fried apples, biscuits, and peach pie. This was not considered a banquet, only plain hearty food, fuel for work. All the ingredients except the flour, sugar, and salt came from our farm—the chickens, the hogs, the milk and butter, the Irish potatoes, the beans, peas, corn, cabbage, apples, peaches. Nothing was processed, except by Mama. She was always butchering and plucking and planting and hoeing and shredding and slicing and creaming (scraping cobs for the creamed corn) and pressure-cooking and canning and freezing and thawing and mixing and shaping and baking and frying.

We would eat our pie right on the same plate as our turnip greens so as not to mess up another dish. The peach cobbler oozed all over the turnip-green juice and the pork grease. "It all goes to the same place," Mama said. It was boarding-house reach, no "Pass the peas, please." Conversation detracted from the sensuous pleasure of filling yourself. A meal required meat and vegetables and dessert. The beverages were milk and iced tea ("ice-tea"). We never used napkins or ate tossed salad. Our salads were Jell-O and slaw. We ate "poke salet" and wilted lettuce. Mama picked tender, young pokeweed in the woods in the spring, before it turned poison, and cooked it a good long time to get the bitterness out. We liked it with vinegar and minced boiled eggs. Wilted lettuce was tender new lettuce, shredded, with sliced radishes and green onions, and blasted with hot bacon grease to blanch the rawness. "Too many fresh vegetables in summer gives people the scours," Daddy said.

Food was better in town, we thought. It wasn't plain and everyday. The centers of pleasure were there—the hamburger and barbecue places, the movie shows, all the places to buy things. Woolworth's, with the pneumatic tubes overhead rushing money along a metallic mole tunnel up to a balcony; Lochridge & Ridgway, with an engraved sign on the third-story cornice: STOVES, APPLIANCES, PLOWS. On the mezzanine at that store, I bought my first phonograph records, brittle 78s of big-band music—Woody Herman and Glenn Miller, and Glen Gray and his Casa Loma Orchestra playing "No Name Jive." A circuit of the courthouse square took you past the grand furniture stores, the two dime stores, the shoe stores, the men's stores, the ladies' stores, the banks, the drugstores. You'd walk past the poolroom and an exhaust fan would blow the intoxicating smell of hamburgers in your face. Before she bought a freezer, Mama stored meat in a rented food locker in town, near the ice company. She stored the butchered calf there, and she fetched hunks of him each week to fry. But hamburgers in town were better. They were greasier, and they came in waxed-paper packages.

At the corner drugstore, on the square, Mama and Janice and I sat at filigreed wrought-iron tables on a black-and-white mosaic tile floor, eating peppermint ice cream. It was very cold in there, under the ceiling fans. The ice cream was served elegantly, in paper cones sunk into black plastic holders. We were uptown.

The A&P grocery, a block away, reeked of the rich aroma of ground coffee. Daddy couldn't stand the smell of coffee, but Mama loved it. Daddy retched and scoffed in his exaggerated fashion. "I can't stand that smell!" Granny perked coffee, and Granddaddy told me it would turn a child black. I hated coffee. I wouldn't touch it till I was thirty. We savored store-bought food—coconuts, pineapples, and Vienna sausages and potted meat in little cans that opened with keys. We rarely went to the uptown A&P. We usually traded at a small mom-and-pop grocery, where the proprietors slapped the hands of black children who touched the candy case. I wondered if they were black from coffee.

In the summer of 1954, when I was about to enter high school, my mother got a chance to run a nearby restaurant on the highway across the train track. My parents knew the owner, and one day he stopped by and asked Mama if she'd like to manage the place. She wasn't working at the Merit at that time, and she jumped at the opportunity.

"Why, anybody could cook hamburgers and French fries for the public," Mama said confidently. "That would be easy."

I went with her to inspect the restaurant—a square cinder-block building with a picture-window view of the highway. There were no trees around, just a graveled parking area. It was an informal sort of place, with a simple kitchen, a deep fryer, a grill, some pots and pans. There were five or six tables and a counter with stools. Mama saw potential.

"Catfish platters," she said. "Fish. Hush puppies. Slaw. French fries."

I was so excited I couldn't sleep. Running our own little restaurant could mean we wouldn't have to work in the garden. I wanted nothing more to do with okra and beans. Besides, the restaurant had an apartment above it. I wanted to live there, on the highway. Marlene was still running her frozen-custard stand nearby, and now I too would get to meet strangers traveling through. Mama and I inspected the apartment: a living room, a kitchen, and two bedrooms. It was all new and fresh. I loved it.

"Oh, please, let's move here," I begged, wishing desperately for novelty, deliverance, and an endless supply of Co'-Colas.

Mama's eyes lit up. "We'll see," she said.

A restaurant would be ideal for her. "It's a chance to make big money," she told me. She told the owner she would try it for a while, to see how she liked it. If she became the manager, then she would rent it for a hundred dollars a month.

"If it works out, maybe I could make a hundred dollars a *week*," she said.

I tagged along with her when she worked at the restaurant. I felt important waiting on customers—strangers driving along the highway and stopping for a bite to eat right where I was. I wanted to meet somebody from New York. When I drew glasses of foamy Coca-Cola from the fountain, the Coke fizzed over crushed ice. I made grilled-cheese sandwiches in the grilled-cheese machine. I experimented with milk shakes. I was flying.

Most of all, I loved the jukebox. The jukebox man came by to change records and insert new red-rimmed paper strips of titles: Doris Day and Johnnie Ray duets, "Teardrops from My Eyes" by Ruth Brown, and "P.S. I Love You" by a Kentucky vocal group called the Hilltoppers. I listened avidly to everything. I was fourteen and deeply concerned about my suntan, and I was saving pocket money to buy records.

The restaurant had a television set, which sat in a corner with something called a television light on top—a prism of soft colors which supposedly kept people from ruining their eyes on TV rays. I had hardly ever watched television, and I was captivated by Sid Caesar's variety show and *I Love Lucy*. When the evening crowd came in, Mama trotted back and forth from the kitchen with her hamburger platters and catfish platters. She would stop and laugh at something Lucy and Ethel were doing on the screen.

Mama had to give up the restaurant even before the trial period ended. She didn't do it voluntarily. Granddaddy stepped in and told her she had to.

"We need you here at home," he said. "Running a eating place out on the highway ain't fitten work."

Daddy didn't stand up for her. "How would you make anything?" he asked her. "By the time you pay out that hundred dollars a month and all the expenses, you won't have nothing left. First thing you know, you'll get behind and then you'll be owing *him*."

Granny said, "And who's going to do your cooking here?"

That was that. Afterwards, Mama cooked her hamburger platters at home, but they weren't the same without the fountain Cokes and the jukebox and the television. I thought I saw a little fire go out of her then. Much later, her fire would almost die. But my own flame was burning brighter. I had had a glimpse of life outside the farm, and I wanted it.

I can still see Mama emerging from that restaurant kitchen, carrying two hamburger platters and gabbing with her customers as if they were old friends who had dropped in to visit and sit a spell. In the glass of the picture window, reflections from the TV set flicker like candles at the church Christmas service.

And then the blackberries were ripe. We spent every July and August in the berry patch. The tame berries had spread along the fencerows and creek banks. When they ripened, Mama would exclaim in wonder, "There are *worlds* of berries down there!" She always "engaged" the berries to customers. By June, she would say, "I've already got forty gallons of berries engaged."

We strode out at dawn, in the dew, and picked until the mid-morning sun bore down on our heads. To protect her hands from the briars, Mama made gloves from old bluejeans. Following the berries down the creek bank, we perched on ledges and tiptoed on unsure footing through thickets. We tunneled. When Mama saw an especially large berry just out of reach, she would manage to get it somehow, even if she had to lean her body against the bush and let it support her while she plucked the prize. We picked in quart baskets, then poured the berries into red-and-white Krey lard buckets. The berries settled quickly, and Mama picked an extra quart to top off the full buckets. By nine o'clock the sun was high, and I struggled to the house with my four gallons, eager to wash the chiggers off and eat some cereal.

From picking blackberries, I learned about money. I wouldn't eat the berries, even on my cereal: I wanted the money. One summer I picked eighty gallons and earned eighty dollars—much more than Mama made in a week when she worked at the Merit. Granny said food was everything, but I was hungry for something else—a kind of food that didn't grow in the ground. Yet I couldn't deny that we were always feasting. We ate sumptuous meals, never missing dessert. Once in a while, Daddy brought home exotic treats—fried oysters in little goldfish cartons or hot tamales wrapped in corn shucks. At Christmas, the dairy he drove for produced jugs of boiled custard, and we slurped gallons of it even though it was not really as good as Granny's, which was naturally yellow from fresh country eggs. Granny complained that store-bought eggs were pale. When the cows needed feed, Daddy took a load of corn from the corncrib to the feed mill and had it ground and mixed with molasses and wheat and oats. He brought it home and filled the feed bin, a big box with a hinged lid, like a giant coffin. I would chew a mouthful now and then for the sweetening.

One spring I rode the corn planter behind Daddy on the tractor. He had plowed and disked and harrowed the ground. Sitting in a concave metal seat with holes in it, I rode the planter, which drilled furrows to receive the seed. At the end of each row I closed the hoppers so they wouldn't release seed while he turned the tractor in a wide loop. When he nosed down the next row, I opened the hoppers at his signal, so that the seed would trickle out again, evenly spaced, behind the drill. The planter covered the seed behind us. We didn't talk much in our awkward caravan. As we rode the long hot rows, rich floods of remembered music accompanied me as vividly as if I had been wearing a Walkman. Top Ten numbers like "Ruby," "The Song from Moulin Rouge," and "Rags to Riches" rolled through my head with the promise that I would not have to plant corn when I grew up.

As I look back, the men recede into the furrows, into the waves of the ocean, and the women stand erect, churning and frying.

....

11

Before this adolescent fretting began, my childhood was a fireworks display of idyllic moments. I look back at bursts of joy over daisy chains and bird feathers and butterflies and cats. These were the textures of bliss. And now I see how my eager heart must have demanded that such innocent raptures of childhood be repeated for the rest of my life, like playing a phonograph record over and over.

On summer Sundays, we often skipped church and went to the lake. Kentucky Lake was a man-made lake—one of the world's largest. It had a hydroelectric dam that was a marvel. The Tennessee River had been dammed to create the lake, a federal project intended to bring cheaper electricity to an isolated region and to control flooding. You could go down inside the dam, into a spooky tiled tunnel where there were gargantuan turbines. Most people in the region had never seen a subway tunnel or a skyscraper or even an escalator, so this engineering feat was celebrated.

Mama and Daddy and Janice and I drove for an hour to a strip of rocky beach that we had almost to ourselves. Country kids didn't learn to swim in any formal way—lessons or school teams. There were no swimming pools, the creeks were usually too shallow, and no one would swim in the filth of a pond where cows waded. Mama could perform a limited little dog paddle, and Daddy had learned to swim in the Navy. At the lake, Janice and I clung to inner tubes and pushed ourselves along with little bobs and swooshes, our toes feeling along the big rocks on the bottom. We dared ourselves to paddle outward until our toes couldn't touch bottom. Then Daddy would begin swimming. He would swim and swim until he appeared to be a floating bird in the distance. Mama had waited for him as he made his way back across the Pacific in a destroyer; now from the beach she nervously watched the lake until he swam back safely. He was confident of his ability in the water, and the lake probably seemed like a pond to him after gazing out upon the ocean.

To Mama's dismay, Daddy sometimes brought along a can or two of beer in the car. He rolled them in newspaper to keep them cold—and to hide them. He rolled the newspapers the same way he rolled his sailor jumpers, as if he were packing to go away again. Mama fussed at him when he brought beer, but it put him in a good mood. We had our picnic, or we ate catfish at a lake restaurant, and then we went exploring on the back roads. Sometimes we visited the souvenir shop at the dam. And then we played in the water some more. In the late afternoon we headed home in the hot car, our heads swirling with images of the inner tubes flubbing against the little waves. At home, we read the funnies in the Chicago newspaper, still savoring the cozy, waterlogged feeling. It was always a perfect day. To top it off, we often went to the show that night.

The first picture show I ever saw was a black-and-white Western at the Princess Theater in Mayfield. Mama and Daddy and I were ushered in late, into a hushed darkness, where people sat in silent rows, illuminated eerily by the foxfire glow of the usher's torch. As my eyes grew accustomed to the dark, I glimpsed the ornate carvings overhead, the sconces with jukebox lights on the walls, and the footlights that gleamed like lightning bugs. Buffalo thundered across the screen. I wasn't afraid.

For a couple of summers, when my little sister LaNelle was a baby, our family saw as many as a dozen movies a week. We went to two drive-in theaters, each of which changed its double bill three times a week. We went every time the feature changed. The 45 Drive-in was several miles down U.S. Highway 45; the Cardinal Drive-in was on the highway within sight of our house. Children under twelve got in free. I managed to be under twelve until I was fourteen. Many nights Mama carried a dishpan filled with homegrown popcorn she had popped. It was oily, with some burnt kernels. Of course, we preferred concession-stand popcorn.

On Tuesdays, Thursdays, and Saturdays, we drove to the 45 Drive-in, which was almost to the Tennessee border. We set out at that mellow time of day, not yet dark, when the glaring heat dimmed down. That was the era before daylight saving time, and night fell about eight. We rushed past the rendering plant, which emitted a gaseous blend of carrion and slop and bone ash and offal, and past the clay pit, a mysterious high-walled crater where trucks transported tan mud to the brickyards. We drove through Water Valley, where our water hauler lived. (He trucked water to our cistern.) After Water Valley, we passed Camp Beauregard, a sad spot where five thousand Confederate soldiers perished from the measles one frigid winter long ago. We whizzed past their graves.

As we approached the drive-in, we passed a little building perched at the edge of a bridge. We always wondered what it was—some electric transformer station or something—and we would try to guess. We came up with various notions: where trolls live; where they store highway stripes. And about then, Daddy would always say, "I hope they've got Bugs Bunny tonight." Bugs Bunny was our favorite cartoon character. We'd always know it was Bugs when the cartoon began and the Looney Tunes circle was empty, for there would be a pause, and then Bugs would burst through the circle, chomping his carrot. He'd say, "Eh, what's up, Doc?"

We loved whatever was playing—gangster shows, musicals, comedies, dramas. Gangster shows never made any sense, though. I liked the hurricane in *Key Largo* but didn't know what the people were doing out in it. Daddy favored the shoot-'em-ups. He couldn't keep still during the heavy action; he'd always root for the Indians and cheer when an arrow felled a cowboy. Both Mama and Daddy loved silly comedies. They laughed themselves sick, elbowing each other. They went into hysterics over the Three Stooges and Abbott and Costello. Daddy slapped Mama's leg so hard she yelled. The Bowery Boys were favorites of ours. I adored their New York accent and tried to learn it. I was crazy about Huntz Hall, a klunky goof, and Daddy claimed to have been in the Navy with Leo Gorcey, the "chief." This impressed me deeply.

My grandparents went to the drive-in with us only once. They dressed up as if they were going to town on Saturday. We took them to a Lum and Abner movie because we thought the country characters would be familiar. They identified mildly with the hayseed humor, but Granddaddy said later, "I never cared for stories." I wondered what he thought about the stories in the Bible, and I decided maybe he was just looking for the moral in them. Now I realize he didn't think of the Bible stories as stories, because there was nothing fictitious about them. They were the true history of the world.

We were addicted to our six nights a week. We just couldn't stop repeating this summer pleasure—the charged feeling of scurrying into the car, the landmarks along the way, the dishpan of popcorn, the jaunts to the concession stand, and the play of spotlights across the screen at intermission. Some people installed spotlights on their cars just so they could shine them on the vacant screen. Mama wasn't working at the Merit then, and we had a healthy new baby in the family. I was cured of pneumonia. Life seemed grand. Sometimes Janice and I sat outside on Daddy's old Navy blanket, leaning against the front bumper of the car. The blanket was handy the time we couldn't scrape together enough cash for admission. We rolled Daddy in the blanket and hid him on the floor behind the front seats.

We saw all the stars—Marjorie Main and Percy Kilbride as Ma and Pa Kettle, Andy Devine, John Wayne, Spring Byington, Bette Davis, Fred Astaire, Vera-Ellen, Ronald Reagan, James Stewart. There were no ratings. We saw a naughty New Orleans burlesque show. And we saw *The Prince of Peace,* which was touted for weeks in advance. It was the life story of the Lord. At intermission salesmen hawked a book about Jesus. Another time there was a sex-education movie, so roundabout it could have been about installing storm windows. Again, books were peddled at intermission—guidebooks for parents, what to tell the kids. A voice on the car speaker instructed drivers to put on their headlights for a boys' book and their parking lights for the girls' book. Mama got the girls' book but wouldn't let us see it. Later, I sneaked a look, having located it in the bottom of a drawer. The booklet advised cleanliness and caution. There was a photo of a girl on her porch waving good-bye to friends who were going swimming. She was incapacitated by a monthly affliction, like something Granny might have gone through.

Most of the movies we saw ran along an easy avenue into our emotions. But *Little Women* affected me profoundly. I had probably read Louisa May Alcott's novel five times, and then suddenly—seemingly for my personal pleasure—it came to life on screen, with June Allyson and Margaret O'Brien as Jo and Beth. The Technicolor images stunned me. The gold and ocher and red autumn leaves that blaze across the screen after Beth dies seemed to burn into my heart. To a child reading the novel, it is not altogether clear that Beth dies. Alcott tiptoed around the subject the way the sex-education film did with its taboo topic. Beth spoke of heaven and seemed to vanish like a Cheshire cat. There was so little concrete detail about her death that I cherished the absurd hope that maybe she didn't die. The movie made her demise somewhat starker. And when Jo publishes her book, *My*

Beth, the cover fills the screen and seems to scream out the loss of Beth. The book is crimson, with ornate old-fashioned gold lettering. I was flooded with the rich images of this moment at the drive-in for months, years. The movie was about the creation of a book, I thought. I had been writing my little stories in blue Double Q notebooks. In *Little Women,* Jo was always scribbling. I was determined to be like Jo, who went to New York to seek her fortune as a writer.

When I was in high school, we got a television. By then, I was busy with my studies and an afternoon job at the drugstore soda fountain, so television didn't have the impact on me that the movies did. Mama and Daddy loved it. They had whooping fits over *I Love Lucy.* We stopped going to the drive-ins. Daddy didn't see the point in shelling out money for shows when he could sit at home in his red leatherette easy chair and be entertained for free. He didn't have to buy those paperback mysteries and Westerns anymore either. To him, stories and shows were, after all, just entertainment. But I had taken them seriously. In the movies, a new world beckoned to me—those neat shady streets of cozy neighborhoods, and the golden splendor of cities. Today I rent those old movies, the Technicolor comedies and the dark dramas filled with jailhouse stripes cast by Venetian blinds. I don't remember most of them, but I keep looking for something familiar in them. I seem to recall seeing Beth's picture on the piano in some version of *Little Women.* It was vivid and close, a substitute for her presence in the group of sisters. I wonder if Beth's photograph on the piano would somehow look like me.

With the movies, my focus began to shift away from the facts of the henhouse and the oak trees and the Virginia creeper vines. Country kids knew all about mosquitoes and butterflies and frogs. We had held larvae and worms of all kinds in our hands. As a small child I saw everything up close. I saw how a flower bloomed; I distinguished pistils and stamens and pollen. I watched doodlebugs working in a cowpile, burrowing and pushing their balled burdens like tiny Sisyphean bulldozers. I identified bugs galore, though not by name. At school we didn't have science projects—frogs, bugs. We didn't seem to need them; the natural world was all around. Once, while climbing over a stile, I stepped barefoot on a gigantic stag-horned beetle. It was a surprising magenta color, and hard as melamine. I didn't make a dent in its carapace. I knew crows and blackbirds and the kingfisher who visited

Granny's fish pool. I saw a giant snake doctor—a dragonfly—with translucent biplane wings and a long red tail. I knew lightning bugs. I knew the progress of acorns. I dissected maple wings in springtime, and I knew how to slip out fresh eggs from beneath a truculent hen.

I remember a hen pecking off the smallpox-shot scab from my arm when I squatted in the yard to pee. Another time, in the outhouse, I accidentally closed the door on a rooster's neck—his head was in the wide crack above the hinge—but I noticed his glazed eyes and gaping beak in time. With our eager dog, I rounded up the cows, enjoying the easy rhythm of their plodding and frisking. Somehow, their turn toward home reminded me of Granny hanging up her apron to begin a new phase of the day.

There were always snakes—black snakes, milk snakes, copperheads, spreading adders. "Run for the hoe!" Granny cried. She could kill a snake with one whack—off with its head! She tackled snakes with the fervor of a preacher battling evil. Snakes were evil. "They'll take the place," Mama said. Whack, whack. No matter if they weren't poisonous. They were the devil in disguise, literally and absolutely.

I knew cats. Mama Cat had several loads of kittens. We installed Mama Cat and her kittens in the playhouse, but one morning I found Mama Cat eating one of them. A jealous, marauding tomcat had broken into the playhouse and killed her kittens, so she ate them.

Smoky slept with me, and Granny disapproved. "Her lungs will be coated with cat hair!" she told Mama. I persisted in sleeping with Smoky anyway, and for years I believed my lungs were lined with cat hair. He was a Maltese-gray barn cat. One time Smoky swallowed a milk strainer, a cotton disc the size of a saucer. It fit inside the metal funnel Daddy used when pouring milk into his milk cans. Smoky yowled and complained for many days without explanation, and then we saw the tip of the milk strainer appear under his tail. Milk of magnesia finished the job.

All our cats were strays. They died of untreated illnesses or unnatural disasters—car wheels. Daddy had a way of jumping into a car or truck and simultaneously taking off backwards without a glance. He always kept a cat in the barn until it got killed on the road. And then another one showed up. He was partial to white cats. We had ponies, donkeys, horses, mules, goats. We rode them all and worked them all. We barbecued the goat and hung clover-chains on the jenny donkey and teased the mule. We kept hogs, who rooted for acorns in the woods behind the house and rubbed on the trees. Their rubbing and rooting killed many of the trees and thinned out the woods. The hogs ate kitchen slop, seasoned with the dishwashing water that had lye soap in it. Hogs found lye soap larruping good. On hog-killing day Mama ground up the leavings from the butchering, packing them with several hot peppers into sausage casings—little bolster slips she sewed on her machine. "I cooked the heads and finished up the hog killing," Granny wrote one year in her diary.

I loved tiny things: bird eggshells—tiny freckled ovals and blue robin eggs, like eyeballs dropped out of the sky; the velvet-and-dust texture of a lightning bug's torch; the sweet dots of ladybugs; snail trails; book mites; bird feathers alighting on a leaf—a blue jay feather, or the bright yellow of a goldfinch; locust shells—the transparent shrouds of the seventeen-year locust of 1953. They were cicadas, actually, not the biblical plague locusts; I collected hundreds of them.

Transfixed, I watched black widows prance. They wore the black shine of patent leather, the red hourglass blazing with time's urgency. Giant gray spiders crouched at the deep ends of tunnels, their legs folded up, ready to spring. At the center of an intricate, geometric web, orb weavers posed spread-eagled, like Christ on the cross. The spiders could be cherry-red, soup-green, banana-yellow, spotted like tiger lilies. The large woods spiders carried clusters of babies on their backs. Spiders often startled me, with their grim stealth. The word spider sounded like "surprise."

Spider bites. Snakes. Mad dogs. Rising creeks that washed away the land. Bee stings. Illnesses that afflicted the livestock. Frightful electric storms. Our little house was nestled among tall oaks and hickories, and we lived in fear that lightning would strike a tree and it would crash on the house and burn us up. While Daddy was in the Navy and Mama was alone with Janice and me, a heavy storm came up one afternoon. Thunder rolled and crashed—the lightning blared hot light through the hard rain. Mama prayed. We huddled under her wings while she pleaded for a miracle to guide us through the storm. We absorbed her fear. We clenched our eyes tight, and our shudders rippled out of the house, battling the elements. Mama's grandmother had taught Mama to fear electric storms. Mama passed along her fear to us.

My goal in life was the assurance that the delights of childhood would never end. But in the very delights themselves sprouted the seeds of dissatisfaction. We were in steady conflict with nature. When Daddy rounded up neighbors and kinfolks to help him get his hay in, the timing had to be right. The hay had to be cut, dried in the sun, raked, baled, and brought to the barn before any rain might fall and spoil it. Sometimes, when a storm was approaching, the men worked frantically, far into the night.

Amid such struggles, I tried to make sense of our place on earth. If nature was our enemy, how could it be the source of some of my most intimate pleasures? What was truly important? What was liberating? Would my sisters and I have lives no different from Granny's? How could we carry forth the values of thrift and family duty and apply them to the strange new situations we would face if we left? I was sure we would go. But did we have enough moral direction to know where to leap when we got to that enticing edge? Would we wind up being sent to the hospital in Memphis for shock treatments?

One morning when I was about eight—before such questions entered my mind—I was waiting for the school bus on the gravel road in front of my house. There had been an ice storm. Ice had built up on every leaf, every twig, every blade of grass—the world was a crystal dreamscape. I wasn't enthralled by the beauty of the scene, though. For me, the landscape was to be tested, not ogled. While waiting for the bus in the freezing cold, I carelessly grabbed an ice-covered twig on a bush and broke it. But then I stopped halfway through, when I saw what I was doing. The twig dangled there like a broken bone, a twisted foreleg hanging from the joint.

After that, I noticed the twig every day as I waited for the bus. The twig did not fall off, nor did it heal. The ice melted. Spring came. The twig was still there, hanging dry and dead from a fresh green branch. Each day, I saw the twig, and it reminded me that I had attacked something for no reason. The idle act of breaking the iced twig, the satisfying snap it made, the way the twig hung from that bush for weeks, well into the summer—it came to trouble me, making me consider my pointless destructiveness. Most disturbing was the way the twig claimed my attention each day. What was it trying to tell me?

We were always destroying things, like bugs and weeds—anything that interfered with growing food or making clothing and shelter. Heedless, we children would kill bugs just to "see how they killed," as we said. I gathered jars of lightning bugs and let them burn themselves out. I collected fishing worms and let them rot, writhing together, dirtless in the hothouse of a jar. But breaking the twig brought the dawning of moral consciousness. I knew I was neither performing a useful task nor exhibiting thrift. I was mutilating a bush simply for the joy of the tactile. I didn't even need to be bored or mean or purposeful. I just did it. For the first time, the possibility of depravity occurred to me.

In a way, I wasn't surprised. As the months went by, this notion seeped into my consciousness. It seemed to confirm my secret view of myself. Usually I was on top of the world. I was the smart little girl at school. My parents spoiled me; they gave me a dollar for every A on my report card. Overconfident, I charged forth, thinking I could do anything I wanted to. I thought the world was manageable—a habit of mind absorbed from my grandmother. With her own peculiar style, Granny managed her small realm according to its necessities, abolishing whatever didn't apply. After Daddy came home from the Navy, Granny's diary reads as though the Pacific war never existed. She had patching to do, grapes to seed for jelly, and peaches to work up. Chickens to kill.

But more than anything else, it was my mother's energetic reach I emulated. Avidly I read about Amelia Earhart, Iceland, Australian aborigines, Abraham Lincoln. School—and more vividly, movies— told me about other human beings, worlds of them, in distant towns and cities and on alien continents. The postage stamps I collected were clues, the books and movies proof. I could do anything, go everywhere, have anything I wanted.

Secretly, I knew it might not be so. As I advanced through the grades, I realized that I might not deserve the privileges I desired. Down deep, I might be worthless; my heart sometimes felt like a vacuum. Sometimes when I went back to school after one of my long illnesses, I felt I hadn't been missed. I wanted desperately to live near the stores and the library, yet I was so unsure of myself when I went to town that I didn't know how to act. I wouldn't talk to anyone or look anyone in the eye. One version of me was a little queen on a throne. But another was a clodhopper. At heart was the inferiority country people felt because they worked the soil. Making my small forays out from the farm, I began to feel the centuries of shame, the legacy from Adam and Eve, who had listened to the snake and lost their paradise— their capacity for childlike wonder.

In the 4-H Club at Cuba we made projects for the county fair. Granny helped me decorate one of Granddaddy's cigar boxes to hold toiletries. We papered it inside and out with scraps of wallpaper. Decorating a cigar box for a practical purpose was a traditional thing to do, something Granny had done when she was a child. A good cigar box was a precious possession—good for collections of bird eggs and feathers and butterfly wings and Indian arrowheads.

But the 4-H Club marked us as country kids, I thought. I longed to be a Girl Scout because the Girl Scouts were in town, which automatically made them an elite group. I acquired the Girl Scout handbook and studied all the rules for earning badges, which I was eager to collect. Most of them had to do with knowledge of nature—hiking, collecting, observing birds and bugs and tree bark. I was passionate about the way you could systematize and classify and learn definitions. Best of all, you could write your findings in notebooks.

Mama took me to see a den mother in town, Mrs. Williams. "My little girl wants to be in the Girl Scouts," Mama said.

I frowned. "I'm your *daughter*," I corrected. "I'm not a little girl." Girl Scouts were sophisticated, I thought.

Mrs. Williams smiled indulgently. "All the girls want to be grown up," she said. "They can't wait, but they'll be going off and getting married before you know it. I like to see them be little girls for a while."

Mama agreed. "Bobbie likes to study," she said. "I hope she won't jump into getting married too soon, like I did."

"Girl Scouts doesn't have anything to do with getting married," I protested.

"When can she join?" Mama asked Mrs. Williams.

"The girls are having a pajama party this Friday night. First they have their little meeting, and then they're going to stay at the Joneses, where they have a big basement, and they'll pop popcorn and play games—you know, act like kids."

This was not what I wanted. I wanted to earn badges, not plunge into a group of giggling girls, all strangers. I knew then that I would hate the Girl Scouts, so I didn't join.

"Your feathers just fell," Mama said later. "You were so disappointed."

At school I was ostracized for reading books. Most of the kids didn't want to read anything they didn't have to. And now it seemed that the girls in town didn't take scouting seriously. I wished I could just have that uniform to wear to school with all my badges displayed on my carefully positioned sash.

"Now don't be different," Granddaddy always warned.

12

Music was my greatest passion. I couldn't carry on a conversation without faltering, and I never spoke up in class, but music talked directly to me and repeated exactly what was on my mind. It reflected all my longings. Listening to music was like plugging my heart into a fifty-thousand-watt radio tower and tuning into the infinite.

But I hated country music. I didn't want to be country. Daddy mocked the whiny fiddle strains and nasal voices of country music. He believed it wasn't inspired genius, like the music of Fats Waller; it didn't have the sophisticated polish of the Glenn Miller Orchestra, or the technical wizardry of Benny Goodman. My sister Janice Kaye was named for bandleader Sammy Kaye. Daddy loved quirky songs and eccentric bandleaders like Cab Calloway and Woody Herman. He'd spontaneously burst out with "Oh, Caldonia! What makes your big head so hard?" He liked Louis Prima and Gus Bivona, but he was exceptionally fond of Fats Waller. Daddy liked to sing "Your Feet's Too Big."

He and I loved Tommy Dorsey's "Opus One." One morning we played a joke on Janice, who was fast asleep. Daddy crept up to the phonograph beside the bed and placed the record on the turntable, right next to her ear. He set the needle in the groove and turned the volume up full blast. "Opus One" began with a tremendous clatter of percussion. Pleased, we watched Janice burst from her dream. This was Daddy in high form, an old Scots-Irish prankster streak erupting gleefully from his brain. "Get out of that bed and rattle them pots and pans!" he'd yell at Mama. Or he would warble "Flat Foot Floogie (with the Floy Doy)."

It was always the sounds of the songs, not the meaning, that had magic. Daddy and I enjoyed the nonsense sounds of songs like "Three

Little Fishes" and "Rag Mop." We'd turn up the radio and sing along. "M, I say m-o, m-o-p, m-o-p-p!" Words in songs, like colors and sounds, were abstractions, pure form. "Jambalaya and a crawfish pie and fillet gumbo!" was delicious gibberish.

Our grand radio resembled a jukebox, with a mile-long dial, giant control buttons, and textured brown upholstery stretched over the sound box. The radio's rigid, upright arms seemed to hold me as I sat on the floor, pressed up against the sound. I ordered a radio log, a list of all the stations in the United States, and I checked off the ones I could get—an astonishing number. At night they crowded the dial. WOWO–Fort Wayne and KLRA–Little Rock and KDKA–Pittsburgh barked out their call letters like ships in distress. Our wonder-radio could get New York and Wheeling, West Virginia, and New Orleans—all those clear-channel, fifty-thousand-watt stations. And mysterious Texas stations with call letters that began with an X would broadcast late-night evangelism with exotic mail offers for prayer shower caps or miracle elixirs.

Mama wanted me to take piano lessons because she never got to. After I began the lessons, a traveling salesman rattling off a syncopated patter conveniently arrived at our doorstep with a set of Scribner's Radio Music Library books—nine large red gold-embossed volumes containing "the world's treasures," ranging from Bach and Beethoven to Stephen Foster. They were expensive—eighty dollars—but Mama wanted to hear me play the world's treasures. It took her two weeks of work at the Merit to pay for those books. I wanted to play popular tunes like those I heard on the radio—Blue Barron's "Cruising Down the River," Del Wood's "Down Yonder," and Kay Starr's "Wheel of Fortune." The classics bored me. My piano lessons were wasted—money thrown down a hole. I wanted to play like Johnny Maddox, a recording artist whose piano had thumbtacks on its hammers to give it a special ringing sound. I didn't know at the time that it was only thumbtacks.

"I want a piano like Johnny Maddox's," I said plaintively.

Daddy mocked my tone. "A piano like Johnny Maddox's!"

What hurt was that Daddy *liked* Johnny Maddox records. It was as if he knew the limits of his aspirations while my eyes were bigger than my stomach; I had bitten off more than I could chew. Food clichés applied to almost anything. And I hadn't even heard Jerry Lee Lewis yet.

When I quit my lessons, Daddy got rid of the piano. I was sure he did it because I had been so spiteful. He sold the piano to a Mr. Smith for a hundred dollars. Mr. Smith hauled the piano away, but he never paid for it. That has not been forgotten in my family. Nor has it been forgotten what those music books cost.

My parents wanted to send us to high school in Mayfield, where the teachers and facilities were superior to those at the county schools. Daddy paid county taxes, not city taxes, so he had to pay tuition to send us to the city school—about ninety dollars a semester. Dairy farms typically brought in little cash, so my father took an extra part-time job at a filling station; Mama worked for seasonal stretches at the Merit, leaving LaNelle with Granny. After school I often saw my little sister playing by herself, with mud on her face. Twice she wandered away, and I remember running frantically through the fields and creeks, calling her name. We found her meandering down the railroad track.

Looking back at my teen years, I see that this was a difficult period for my family. My grandfather was often ill and in the hospital. My parents sank into a routine that seemed to consume all their energy and keep them unreflective. Daddy grew more reserved. Having three girls and no son to carry on the farm must have overwhelmed and distanced him. I thought he treated Mama badly, mocking her and telling her she was dumb; he rarely made kind remarks or offered praise. By the time I was a junior, Mama was pregnant again. This time, at last, the baby was a boy—my little brother, Don. But after Don arrived, Daddy went into a yearlong depression. The son he had wanted to carry on the farm had come too late. He could see that the family farm in America was dying out as a way of life. But I paid little attention to my parents' troubles at the time; I was busy being a teenager. The house was full of silences, except for music. It saved us all.

Late on Saturday nights the radio blared out strange music: "John R here, way down South in Dixie, 1510 on the dial, fifty thousand watts of joy! WLAC, Nashville, Tennessee."

John R played raunchy, stomping-and-shouting blues numbers by black singers like Big Bill Broonzy and Memphis Slim and Little Junior Parker. John R was white, but he sounded black. From the time I was a child, Daddy and I had been in the habit of staying up late and turning the radio up loud, staring in amazement at our huge console.

John R played what he called "droopy-drawers songs" (the slow stuff) and "mean, low-down songs." The mean ones sounded dangerous. I could feel the power of big men stomping into their houses and dragging out their women when they'd been untrue. In the droopy-drawers songs, they cried their hearts out. John R talked through the songs: "Have mercy, baby! . . . Come on, honey. . . . Man, don't that tear you up?" Ruth Brown's "Mama, He Treats Your Daughter Mean" tore me up bad.

Gene Nobles, another white disk jockey, played the same music on an earlier show, and he also played some bland white imitations of these risqué rhythm-and-blues songs—especially cover versions from Dot Records. Dot's artists included Pat Boone and the Fontane Sisters, but their star group was the Hilltoppers.

The Hilltoppers, I decided by the time I was fourteen, represented everything I had ever felt and dreamed about my life. As I picked blackberries or hoed vegetables in the scorching morning sun, Hilltopper music playing in my head made me feel there was a way out—some release from the cycle of the seasons. The Hilltoppers' style wasn't exactly Big Bill Broonzy and it wasn't rock-and-roll yet either—it was sort of like what would happen if Perry Como got hold of some Big Bill Broonzy material—but it grabbed me and shook me up like a religious vision, a calling. My passion for music transmuted to simon-pure hero worship. This was mainly because the group was from Kentucky. The Hilltoppers were students at Western Kentucky State College, in Bowling Green, where the sports teams were called the Hilltoppers. A Kentucky singing quartet had achieved national fame! The only famous person from Kentucky I had ever heard of besides Abraham Lincoln was Arthur Lake, who played Dagwood in the Blondie and Dagwood movies.

The Hilltoppers' first hit was "Trying," a ballad written by one of the original members of the group, Billy Vaughn. Later on they were awarded a gold record for an old Johnny Mercer song, "P.S. I Love You." Jimmy Sacca, the lead singer, had a strong, distinctive baritone that strained to be a tenor—a cross between matinée-idol crooning and big-band swing. He was a dreamboat.

I started a Hilltoppers fan club, and the day that the package of membership cards, autographed glossy eight-by-ten photographs, and buttons (I AM A HILLTOPPERS FAN) arrived seemed like the turning point of my life. Now, linked to the greater world, I felt special and important. I advertised for members in Betty Burr's fan-club column in a

New York fan magazine, and for a time my whole life revolved around the mailbox and the radio.

Over the next year, I worked diligently on the fan club and carried on a correspondence with the Hilltoppers' secretary at Dot Records. I was dying to meet the pre–Fab Four. This seemed to be so much more significant than making an impression at school, where I sat quietly, immersed in Latin or science. At last the secretary—persuaded by my fanaticism—appointed me National President of all the Hilltoppers fan clubs, and my joy was boundless. At Mayfield High I was a nobody—an outsider, a country girl. But in my new high post I had important duties. I wrote and mailed a newsletter to three hundred fan-club chapters on an addressographed list—mostly addresses in the exotic environs of New York City. I wrote to d.j.s in all the big cities. I prayed for the Hilltoppers' records to be hits. After reading Norman Vincent Peale, I applied the power of positive thinking to a tune called "Searching" so that the Hilltoppers might earn another gold record. The Hilltoppers were stars, brilliant presences, and my function was to promote their fame, so that their glow would rub off on me, like the luminescent stuff from lightning bugs.

In time, Mama and I traveled to see the Hilltoppers perform. I was growing adept at manipulating my parents. I pestered Mama until she couldn't say no; I persuaded her of the specialness of my fan-club role. Daddy seemed to acquiesce to our travels out of some kind of inertia, as if he knew I was already pursuing my own authorities and he was powerless to stop me.

The ride to Cincinnati took sixteen hours, overnight, on a bus that jolted around the curves along the Ohio River. I remember waking up at each stop and checking the town on the map, so I could say I had been there. I was so excited I couldn't eat, even though the group performing was not entirely the original Hilltoppers. While two members of the group were in the Army (they'd been drafted; this was just after the Korean War), Jimmy Sacca hired a series of replacements. This version of the Hilltoppers was appearing with Barney Rapp's orchestra at the Castle Farms Ballroom.

Castle Farms was a huge suburban dance hall that was packed with glamorous couples who drank liquor. Women smuggled in whiskey bottles under their wraps: I saw them do it. The Hilltoppers bounded onstage, wearing their red sweaters and beanies with "W" on them— the football sweaters and freshman beanies from their college. (I had ordered a beanie for myself from Western and had considered wearing it that evening, but it didn't go with my taffeta dress and borrowed rhinestone jewelry.) Their act was sensational. They sang all their hits, including "P.S. I Love You," "From the Vine Came the Grape," "I'd Rather Die Young," and my favorite, "Poor Butterfly." Their sound was principally Jimmy Sacca's lead backed up with a simple "doo-wah" harmony. In their sweaters and baggy gray flannels, they swayed from side to side in unison, sort of like cheerleaders. At intermission, I was allowed to go backstage to meet my idols, and during their second show they introduced me proudly to the audience. This may have been my defining moment—my mothlike entry into the ethereal realm of stars. I was transported, as if I had just sprouted wings.

In the second show, the Hilltoppers wore tuxedos. Afterwards, they bought my mother and me Cokes and potato chips. The Hilltoppers didn't drink, but they smoked and drove a Cadillac. They drove us back to the hotel in their sky-blue 1954 Fleetwood, and Jimmy Sacca gave me forty dollars to help operate the fan club. Mama was hooked. After that, we saved our berry money and took off to see the Hilltop-pers whenever we got a chance. Mama drove our little yellow Nash Rambler or the Willys Jeep, and we sang Hilltoppers songs all the way.

The next time we saw the Hilltoppers was in Vincennes, Indiana. Mama and I were walking down the main street from Woolworth's to our hotel there when we spotted the Cadillac. It was the Hilltoppers, arriving in town for their show. I waved at them, and the Cadillac pulled over. Jimmy was driving.

"It's us again!" Mama cried.

Jimmy hopped out and hugged us. While the other members of the group—more replacements—checked into the hotel, Jimmy took us to eat at a grill down the street. We sat in a booth and ordered pork chops with applesauce and French fries.

"Well, what did you think when you heard the news?" Jimmy asked us worriedly.

"I was shocked," I said lamely. I didn't know what to say. I had seen the newspaper: one of the various substitute Hilltoppers had been ar-rested for possession of marijuana. My mother and I had never heard of marijuana, so the news didn't really faze us.

"I was at the racetrack," Jimmy said. "And the P.A. system called my name. I had no idea he was using the stuff. I fired him so fast he didn't know what hit him."

"He wasn't one of the real Hilltoppers," I said loyally. I longed for the day when Seymour and Don would rejoin the group. I knew I would like them, because they looked like such cutups in their pictures. Jimmy and Don and Seymour and Billy, the original group, were all family men, with wives and children.

After we finished eating, Jimmy lit up a Pall Mall, and Mama said, "If y'all come to Mayfield I'll get you some free Tony Martin suits from the Merit."

"How will you do that?" I asked, surprised.

"Willy Foster will let me have them," Mama said confidently.

Mama was full of high regard for Willy Foster, the president of the company. He was a country person who had worked his way up from office boy. I remembered going to his farm for the employees' picnic—fried chicken and roasting-ears and washtubs of cold drinks. His farm was like a plantation—a magnificent place with acres of pasture and horses and a little lake with rowboats.

"We'd love to come to Mayfield," Jimmy said. "But you don't have to get us any suits."

"Well, you come, and I'll cook you up a big supper and get you some suits," Mama said. "I used to sew labels in coats, but the foreman told me to slow down because I was making more than the men. I could make a dollar an hour, I was so fast." She laughed. "But with all the farm work I don't have time to sew labels this summer."

"But you don't work there all the time, so they won't let you have any free suits," I argued.

"Oh, Willy's good to his workers," Mama said. "And if the Hilltoppers wore his suits, that would be good publicity."

"Well, gee, Mrs. Mason," Jimmy said. "That would be swell."

He bought us strawberry sundaes and then we went to the show.

Mama and I traveled many places to see the Hilltoppers. We went to Centralia, Illinois; Princeton, Indiana; Herrin, Illinois; Blytheville, Arkansas; St. Louis and Cape Girardeau, Missouri. Mama loved the trips, and I knew it did her good to get away. She was always glad to throw a fishing pole in the car and go fishing, and these excursions were something like that. We plotted our getaways. Daddy didn't object. I think he was somewhat wistful about our adventures, but he had to milk the cows and couldn't go. Of course there was something unreal about our outings. We felt as though we were on *Queen for a Day*.

The Hilltoppers always welcomed us. Don and Seymour got out of the Army and took their rightful places in the group. They were boyish, modest, and funny. I adored them. Being a groupie in the fifties was as innocent as pie. The Hilltoppers never even swore around me, except once—the day Jimmy forgot the words to "My Cabin of Dreams," which they lip-synched on a TV show. They took a protective attitude toward me, and they were crazy about my mother, who didn't put on any airs just because she knew some stars. "I think it's nice they've got that Cadillac and ain't stuck-up," Mama said. She kept talking about those Tony Martin suits and how good the Hilltoppers would look in them.

In a way, the Hilltoppers weren't real to me. They were stars. If they walked into my house today, I'm sure Jimmy Sacca would give me one of his big bear hugs and we would fall easily into joking conversation. We were friends; but even though I spent a lot of time with the Hilltoppers during my high school years I knew very little about them. I didn't ask about their backgrounds—their parents, brothers and sisters, schooling, and the rest. Background had no meaning to me, because I hadn't been anywhere; where I was going was what counted.

I finally got to Detroit when the Hilltoppers played the Michigan State Fair. I went by myself, on the Brooks bus, because my mother had just given birth to my brother, Don. She named him after one of the Hilltoppers, Don McGuire. In Michigan, I was supposed to call Mama's aunt Mary, in Pontiac. Her husband had died, and her brother Rudy was reported to have become a millionaire from working in a tire plant, saving his money, and living in a hut.

In Detroit that week, I stayed with a girl in my fan club whose father was a maintenance engineer at the Ford plant. They lived in a suburb in a gleaming new house with a guest room, and they fed me piles of tiny White Castle hamburgers and rich Hungarian cream cakes. I was so busy with the Hilltoppers, I kept putting off my telephone call to Aunt Mary. She did not know where I was staying or how to contact me. Pontiac was far away from where I was staying, and I didn't want to miss the shows at the fair. I was living in another world now—where the tall buildings were. And I appeared with the Hilltoppers on Soupy Sales's TV show. I remember answering questions about the fan club and someone throwing a pie. Eydie Gormé was also at the fair—before she married Steve Lawrence and they became Steve and Eydie. Eydie told me she admired my pixie haircut. Some weeks later, I saw her on TV and she had had her hair pixied. But the head-liners at the fair were Bill Haley and the Comets and Billy Ward and the Dominoes. My life was astir with such sounds that were emerging from the familiar old Saturday night radio show Daddy and I had lis-tened to for years; behind the roaring train of rock-and-roll, the Hill-toppers' style began to seem slightly quaint, a caboose.

I never got around to calling Aunt Mary. After I reached Mayfield, on the all-night bus, I learned that Mary had telephoned my parents, worried about me. It shocked me that a relative, planted far away and seemingly disconnected, would be so concerned about me. As it hap-pened, I never saw Mary again, and it was years before I gave any thought to her brother Robert, my lost grandfather.

The day my mother and I drove to a show in Blytheville, Arkansas, was the day the Russians sent up Sputnik. After the Hilltoppers' show, Don drove back to Mayfield with us in our Nash Rambler; he planned to get the bus to his home in Owensboro. As we rode through the night, listen-ing to Chuck Berry and Little Richard and Elvis Presley on an after-hours show from New Orleans, we were aware of Sputnik spying on us.

I noted the Sputnik launch in my 1957 diary:

OCTOBER 4. *Blytheville, Ark. Cotton Ball. Hilltoppers and Jimmy Featherstone Ork. Russian sattelite, Sputnik, launched.*
NOVEMBER 3. *Sputnik II.*
NOVEMBER 7. *40th anniversary of Russian Revolution. President Eisenhower's address to the nation. Senior rings.*
NOVEMBER 15. *UFO sightings increase.*
DECEMBER 11. *English theme, "National Security." A+*

That fall, when I was a senior, a girl named Janine Williams went with my mother and me to see the Hilltoppers at a ballroom in a little town in Tennessee. Janine made a great impression on the Hilltoppers with her teasing, flirtatious personality. All the crinolines she wore under her dress made her look ready for flight, for a trip into outer space. "My brother went to Louisville to the basketball tournament last year," she told the Hilltoppers. "He won the tickets, and he flew up there in an airplane. And he stayed in the same hotel as the teams."

This was an outright lie—I didn't know why she told it—but the Hilltoppers didn't know the difference, so I didn't know what to say. I was happy, though, showing off the Hilltoppers to my friend. Jimmy introduced both of us to the audience at a special moment in the show before the group sang "To Be Alone," in which Don did an Ink Spots–style monologue in his surprising bass voice and caused girls to squeal. (He had cherubic looks.) The Hilltoppers had a new record, "Starry Eyes," and I was disappointed when they didn't sing it. I was afraid their new record wasn't going to be a hit, and I was getting frustrated with the power of positive thinking. I hadn't told the Hilltoppers about the ESP experiments I had been trying (they involved sending telepathic messages to d.j.s to play Hilltoppers tunes). I was afraid they would laugh.

"What do you think of Elvis Presley?" Janine asked the Hilltoppers later. Elvis Presley was singing "All Shook Up" on the radio of the Cadillac as Jimmy drove us out to a café for hamburgers.

"He's great," said Seymour. "He has a fine voice."

"If I could wiggle like that, we'd make a million dollars," Jimmy said.

Don laughed. "Our manager had a chance once to manage Elvis Presley, but he turned it down. He said nobody with a name like 'Elvis' would get anywhere."

"I like Elvis," Mama said. "He can really carry a tune."

For me, there was something as familiar about Elvis as our farm, with the oak trees and the cows and the chickens. It was as though Elvis were me, listening to WLAC and then coming up with his own songs about the way he felt about the world. I tried not to think too hard about Elvis, but I couldn't help it. Janine had said to me, "If I got Elvis in a dark corner, I'd tear his clothes off."

With the arrival of rock-and-roll, the Hilltoppers had begun recording livelier imitations of black tunes—"The Door Is Still Open," "Only You," and Ruth Brown's "Teardrops from My Eyes." On some of the songs, you could hear a rock-and-roll saxophone or a boogie piano and even a bass vocal "bum-bum-bum" against the "do-do-do-do-do-do-do" background harmony. I was ready to embrace the new and outlandish, whether it was rock-and-roll or jazz or sack dresses—a hot style from France one year. (Mama made me one.) I was reading *The Search for Bridey Murphy, The Practical Way to a Better Memory, The Report on Unidentified Flying Objects. Reincarnation: A Hope of the World* impressed me. I was filled with philosophical questions, and I wrote a paper for English class on agnosticism. My teacher, Miss Florence, summoned me to her office and accused me of plagiarism. "Young lady, you have no business entertaining ideas like this," she said. "Where did you get such an idea?"

I quaked. "I read about it. I read lots of philosophy," I said, which was only partly a lie. Reincarnation was philosophy, sort of. I told her I had read John Locke, which *was* a lie. But I hadn't plagiarized. I really believed it was possible that God did not exist, and furthermore it seemed likely that there was no way to know whether He did or not.

Miss Florence had lavender hair, and she kept a handkerchief tucked in her sleeve. Now and then she daintily plucked it out and snuffled into it. She was a terrifying woman, much admired by the whole town. Everyone since the thirties, including Daddy, had been in her senior English class. Her sister, Miss Emma, was the teacher who had flunked Daddy in algebra.

"Take my advice," Miss Florence said, growing softer. "Give up these strange ideas of yours. Your field is mathematics. That's what you're good at. Stay away from these peculiar questions, because they're destructive. And stick with the Bible. That's all the philosophy you'll ever need."

I was silent, rigid with fury—too intimidated to speak.

"You have a lot of big ideas, but they will lead you astray," Miss Florence said in dismissal.

At school, the Hilltoppers were my secret. In Mayfield, I was an outcast, but in the greater world I could be suave and self-important. It was as though I could slip into a telephone booth and change into my National President cape, ready to assume my powerful role. When d.j.s interviewed me, I spoke glibly in *Billboard* lingo. "Well, Ed, this new platter is slated to be a chart-buster," I said to Ed Bonner on KXOK, in St. Louis. I had my own stationery, with a Hilltoppers logo. After Miss Florence's edict, I immersed myself in my presidential duties, publishing my bimonthly newsletter, *Hilltoppers Topics*. Running a fan club was expensive, but the Hilltoppers sent me ten dollars a week for expenses and fifteen dollars a week for myself. I saved all my money for college. I started hating math.

My mother had been serious about those Tony Martin suits. Shortly before my graduation, the Hilltoppers came to Mayfield, and Mama whisked them off to the Merit and got them measured. They picked out an off-white material with a subtle gray stripe in it. Later, when the suits were finished, Mama went to the Merit and personally sewed in the labels. That spring, I was a soda jerk at the Rexall drugstore in Mayfield, making fifty cents an hour, and after school that day I was drawing a Coke from the fountain for one of the regulars when all four of the Hilltoppers strolled into the store. It was my big moment. I could show them off. A classmate of mine, a popular cheerleader—an uptown girl who always made me feel like a shabby bumpkin—was testing nail polish at the cosmetics counter. I rushed over and told her I would introduce her to the Hilltoppers. "They're here," I said, pointing to the end of the counter, where I had served them Cokes.

"Oh, I don't think so," she said, flashing her cheerleader smile. "I wouldn't know what to say." With two fingernails painted Persian Melon, she hurried out the back door. The Hilltoppers scared her.

It was a triumph, sort of. I got off work early, and the Hilltoppers drove me home in the Cadillac. Mama made a huge catfish supper, with hush puppies and slaw and blackberry pie, and that evening my family and I all went to Paducah and saw the Hilltoppers sing at the National Guard Armory with Blue Barron's orchestra. It was a perfect day. "Your mother is an amazing woman," Don said to me.

The Hilltoppers were so conventional, such nice guys. I didn't know how to talk to them about the crazy thoughts in my head. I had just received a reply to my letter to George Adamski, the man who claimed in his book about UFOs to have been on a spaceship to Venus. He thanked me for writing and assured me that he had indeed been to Venus, but he failed to answer my questions about the spacecraft's interior and the landscape of Venus.

That summer, I picked blackberries in the early-morning dew with rock-and-roll songs like "Get a Job" by the Silhouettes and Eddie Cochran's "Summertime Blues" blasting in my mind, and in the afternoons I trudged down the dusty lanes through the fields with the current dog to round up the herd of cows. In the evenings, I worked at the Rexall. I went out with boys—boys who wanted to settle down and work in the new factories—but I wasn't impressed. I was always dreaming. From our house I could see the traffic on Highway 45, which ran straight south to Tupelo, Mississippi, where Elvis was born. I knew he had dreamed the same dreams.

Miss Florence refused to write me a recommendation to Duke University, where I wanted to study parapsychology with the famous Dr. J. B. Rhine, so in the fall I went away to the University of Kentucky, in

Lexington. I neglected my fan-club duties and failed to get *Hilltoppers Topics* out on schedule. I read *Brave New World* and *1984* and *Mandingo* and *Elmer Gantry.* I studied French and psychology and philosophy and volleyball. After hours, I still listened to John R jive-talking along with Ruth Brown and Little Walter and Jimmy Reed. Buddy Holly died that winter. Elvis was in the Army.

A year later, I saw the Hilltoppers for the last time, at a nightclub in Louisville, where they were performing with Mel Tormé. I had driven over with some girls from U.K. The Hilltoppers' popularity had declined drastically. They were being eclipsed by rock-and-roll. In their tuxedos or in their Tony Martin suits, they never really got the hang of it. I remember Don and Seymour sitting at a table in a corner with me that night in Louisville. They were as kind as ever—funny and generous, the way I always remember them. I had on a black cocktail dress with a taffeta balloon-hem. "Those U.K. boys better watch out," Don said, teasing me.

Shyly, I told them about breaking up with my boyfriend. He was going with some other girl and my life was in ruins, but I didn't go into detail. I apologized for letting my club work slip. The newsletter was two months late.

Don smiled. "It's about time you forgot about the fan club," he said.

"No, it's not," I said loyally.

"You'll have other interests," he said. "You'll get married, and have your own family."

"I don't know." I thought I would never get married.

"People change and go on to something else," Don said. "We won't stay with this forever. It's no way to live—one dinky ballroom after another. Traveling around all the time isn't what it's cracked up to be."

"Even in a Cadillac?" I asked.

"Even in a Cadillac," Don said, smiling again. "By the way, we'll drop you off in Lexington tomorrow."

"Thank you," I said. It was my last chance to travel in their Cadillac, I thought—a good way to end my national presidency. They had traded in the blue Fleetwood for a newer, black model. I imagine it even now, rushing through the night, unrestrained in its flight, charging across America.

It was after midnight when Mel Tormé finished his set, but the band wouldn't quit. The crowd was wild. Jimmy took the microphone again. He sang "I Can't Get Started," a droopy-drawers sort of song. He had had a couple of drinks, and he was in mellow spirits. Then he eased into "St. James Infirmary." As the deep sadness of the song emerged, he suddenly became real to me, not a star. "St. James Infirmary" was slow and bluesy, but it wasn't a droopy-drawers song. It was the meanest, low-downest, saddest song I ever heard. I thought I would die. It was after hours, way down South in Dixie. It was 1959.

Three

Clearing Out

....

13

Then came the sixties. The rolling stone of history knocked me down, rolled me over, and pushed me out. At the University of Kentucky I declared myself a math major, as Miss Florence had directed, then tuned out when calculus departed from charming puzzles to dull engineering applications involving bridges and water towers. I wandered among majors. Learning was like a buffet, and I wanted to devour everything. Indiscriminately, I sampled etymology, existentialism, the theater of the absurd, Shakespeare, French symbolists, realism, naturalism, logic, Jack Kerouac. Dada and surrealism followed my Rimbaud period. I didn't consult a guidance counselor. One of my primary traits—coming from the independent spirit of generations of farm people—was the refusal to seek advice or ask directions. I preferred to blunder along, exactly the way Daddy did on the occasions when he and Mama drove me to school in Lexington. Sometimes on the way home they would take a side trip, blazing trails. Daddy wouldn't consult a map.

No one told me what to do. Nobody talked about where learning was headed, what it was for. As far as I knew, it was meant to be nothing more than a reprieve from the necessity of labor. I knew I would have to get a job after college, and I had shorthand and typing from high school to bank on. I figured I would go to a city. I would not work outdoors. I would work in an office or a store. I couldn't imagine that anybody would pay me to read or write the kind of books I cared about. Still, after discovering Thomas Wolfe and J. D. Salinger, I switched my major to English. Miss Florence was not there to make me mind, so I rushed headlong into the dangers of literature.

And without a second thought, I moved to New York the day after graduation. I craved change and excitement—and all the tourist attractions. Going to the big city did not seem bold or brave to me. It merely seemed inevitable. New York had burned its authority into my brain long ago, when I watched Elvis Presley on *The Ed Sullivan Show* and listened to Martin Block's *Make-Believe Ballroom* from WABC, broadcast on an affiliate station. I had been to New York once, on a school trip my sophomore year at U.K. Our group toured the United Nations, the Bowery, and Broadway, and we heard beatnik poetry at a coffeehouse, the Gaslight. My college creative-writing teacher, Robert Hazel, insisted on New York. He booted his students right out of the provinces. "Get out of this backwater Podunk," he urged. "Go get some experience. You can't be a writer unless you've lived intensely." New York was the place.

Robert Hazel was a seductive personality, an engaging man who made all his students believe they could be writers. We fell for his romantic portrait of the artist. Professor Hazel had published books. His photograph on one of the jackets was a brooding, handsome profile. He emulated F. Scott Fitzgerald, who was my literary hero. For all of his writing students, Professor Hazel embodied the glamour of the writing life. He frequently talked about "Bill" Styron and "Phil" Roth, as if they were old buddies of his. He spoke knowledgeably of jazz and art. He would tell what Miles said to Coltrane at some bar in such a way that you thought he was in thick with them.

So I headed to New York. There, I thought, I could get a job in an office, working at a typewriter, while I checked out the Greenwich Village scene and gathered material—gritty street life, colorful characters—to write about. I knew I wanted to be a writer, but I thought I didn't have much to write about yet. In New York I would soak up life, as Robert Hazel—and Louisa May Alcott—had said, and take notes. In any case, I would not have to pick blackberries again.

I got a ride to New York with a Cuban woman who had been visiting her family in Lexington. In the trunk of her car, I stowed my matching set of blue Samsonite luggage and my long file drawer of notes. Several of my college friends planned to join me in the city within the next few weeks. I checked into the Hotel Taft on Times Square, and the next day I went straight to the Museum of Modern Art to see the fabulous paintings I had just studied in my art-history course. I was spellbound; the paintings really existed—Picassos and Cézannes and Pollocks. Professor Hazel had spoken knowingly of contemporary artists like Motherwell and Kline, as if he had been in their studios at moments of great inspiration. I was surprised that up close the paintings had so many blemishes and irregularities. Seeing them was like spotting movie stars without their makeup. At the museum café I met a man who promised to call me. That afternoon he had to go visit his mother's grave or he would have asked me for a date right there, he said. He did leave me a message later at the hotel desk, but I didn't return his call.

I knew no one in New York. I wasn't used to walking on sidewalks in high heels. My feet were killing me. A creepy man followed me down Broadway, muttering to me. He followed me into a shoe store where I bought a pair of low-heeled shoes. There, he became bored with me and drifted off. In my new shoes, I charged down Broadway, enclosed in a throng, with buses whooshing by. It was summer. The trash bins on the streets were painted gold that year, with Miss Rheingold ads.

I had no prospects, no contacts, not even a résumé or letter of introduction. However, I had one possibility. During one semester in college, *Life* magazine had hired me to write a weekly advertising column for the student newspaper. My column, "Bobbie Mason Looks at Life," previewed the coming week's *Life*. I hoped this would lead to a writing job. The Time-Life Building was my favorite building so far, with its fountains and breezy plaza. A brisk young woman in personnel told me that unfortunately Time-Life had no writing or editorial openings, but she talked to me for an hour, offering me guidance and job-hunting tips. "Call me if you need help," she said. People were exceptionally friendly in New York, I thought.

I studied the classified ads and went to a publishing house that advertised for an editorial assistant, but that position required two years of publishing experience. All the jobs advertised seemed to require experience. Although I had a stringbook of my college newspaper pieces and had minored in journalism, it never occurred to me to present myself to *The New York Times*. I was sure I needed more experience to write for a large newspaper.

I applied for several clerical jobs, then answered an ad for a secretarial job at a synthetic textiles (Acrilan and nylon) company. It paid a hundred dollars a week. The personnel manager was from North Carolina, and she was enthusiastic about me.

"Do you play Scrabble?" she asked.

"I never have. Why?"

"It's a prerequisite," she said with a smile. "All the girls play it at lunch."

She sent me in to talk to the vice president, a dour pear-shaped man with hair that fell onto his forehead in wads. He was dutifully garbed in his synthetics. He jabbered about his company for a while, and I pondered his dark surroundings. He reminded me of a groundhog in its hole. After reviewing my typing test, he offered me the job.

"We'll start you Wednesday at nine," he informed me. "May I ask you as an afterthought just what you hope to contribute to this company? What does the job mean to you?"

"I hope to get some experience," I said quickly. "I want to learn a lot so I can succeed. I'm interested in writing."

At that, he advised me not to work for him and dismissed me. "It seems clear this job is wrong for you," he said, shooing me from his burrow. "I want somebody I can rely on to be right here. I don't need high turnover."

When I left his office and explained to the woman from North Carolina what had happened, she tried to console me. "I was rooting for you," she said brightly. "Us Southerners have to stick together, you know? New York can be a hard place, honey, but you'll find something you'll like better than this."

I wasn't sorry I had flubbed the interview. I thought any fool could do the jobs I had applied for, so I was hopeful of finding something more agreeable. At Macy's, I applied to be an advertising copywriter. I had designed newspaper ads in a journalism class, those old-fashioned clutters of drawings of everything from hats to toasters strewn willy-nilly across a double-page spread. To that interview I wore blue mascara and a large black Panama-straw hat like the one Audrey Hepburn wore in the role of Holly Golightly in *Breakfast at Tiffany's*.

"How much salary do you expect from this job?" I was asked by a skeptical middle-aged woman with a lacquered hairdo like a hornet's nest. She glanced askance at my hat. Her Bronx accent sounded hard to me.

"Oh, a hundred dollars," I said breezily, thinking hopefully that was a typical amount.

"Sorry. This job pays seventy to start. Perhaps you should pursue your dream elsewhere."

Afterwards I learned that advertising copywriters could advance rapidly and make lots of money if they had a flair. Too late, I was sure I had a flair. Didn't my hat say so?

A friend named Lamar, another aspiring writer, was bringing me my hi-fi and typewriter from Kentucky. He was one of the dozen or so

U.K. graduates I knew who were moving to the city. He had already written a novel, and he had spent a year in Hollywood playing bit parts in movies—*Flaming Star* with Elvis Presley and *Tammy Tell Me True* with Sandra Dee. But he said he found the life in Hollywood hollow, so he had returned to school.

To my astonishment, I ran into Lamar on the sidewalk near Rockefeller Center.

"You're never going to believe this," he said. "I just got here today. I left the car for two hours, and when I got back it was gone." Bewildered, he waved his hand across his face, as if to block out the swarming crowd on the street. "Say good-bye to your hi-fi and typewriter! They were sitting in the backseat. I've already been to the police."

I was crestfallen. Life without a typewriter or a hi-fi looked bleak.

"Does your family have theft insurance?" he asked.

"I'm sure they don't."

"Call them and see."

"No, I'll give them a scare if I call."

"But it might be covered under their general policy."

"They don't even have health insurance."

Lamar insisted. He couldn't file his claim until he knew for sure. I knew my family didn't have insurance. All they had was burial insurance for their children. They paid twenty-five cents a week per child to the insurance man who came around and collected it. My parents had kept up the payments on me. No doubt, they expected to need the policy since I was off in New York and my body might be found in a gutter any day.

Reluctantly, I telephoned home. Long-distance calls always signaled disaster. My parents were disturbed by my news. Of course they didn't have theft insurance. They had known I'd get in trouble. They had expected this and worse. But they were glad to know I had arrived safely, at least.

"Do you have a job yet?" Mama asked.

"No. I just got here a few days ago."

"It hasn't rained a drop since before you left," she said. "The corn's drying up."

Briefly, I felt homesick. LaNelle was now ten, and Don was five. Mama and Daddy were like a pair of birds raising a second brood as soon as the first ones left the nest. I missed the little ones.

·   ·   ·

After a frustrating week of answering ads for clerical and editorial work, I signed up with an employment agency. The agency would take approximately the first month's salary. "What will I live on?" I asked Miss Rabinowitz.

Cheerfully, Miss Rabinowitz said, "Oh, people live on spaghetti."

Spaghetti? I had hardly ever eaten spaghetti.

Miss Rabinowitz found me an interview for an editorial-assistant position at a fan magazine group. I wore one of my Kentucky sun-back dresses and my Holly Golightly hat. The editor wanted two years of experience, but she was impressed that I had written for my college newspaper. She gave me an assignment. I had to write a story about Troy Donahue, a costar of *Surfside Six*. The editor gave me a copy of *TV Star Parade* as a guide, a headline ("Troy Donahue's Secret Date with Sandra Dee" or some such wording), and some clippings and photographs. I whipped up some fluff based on the material and landed the job. I was filled with relief that I didn't have to settle for a dull clerical or sales job—or worse, a slot in manufacturing. I didn't want to sit on a stool and sew. But I felt uneasy about working for a fan magazine. I'd left the Hilltoppers and fandom behind. Now my job—my future—would be like writing *Hilltoppers Topics*. *TV Star Parade* was the same magazine that had once listed my Hilltoppers fan club in its Betty Burr column. I learned that Betty Burr, who had once been an honorary member of my fan club, was only a name, like Miss Lonelyhearts. Part of my job at the fan magazine was to write Betty Burr columns about fan clubs.

Hoping for some alternative, I telephoned the Time-Life personnel manager who had been so helpful to me. "You're too nice a girl to work on such scandal rags," she said. "Go to a temporary service. Get odd jobs, and then you'll have time to look around and find something you really like."

But what would I like? I knew I wouldn't truly enjoy any job. I didn't want to work at all. I wanted to study at N.Y.U. or Columbia. But each course cost about three hundred dollars, and I would have to save some money to take a night class.

So I stayed put. Fan magazine work turned out to be easy, a leisurely job that left me little chunks of time to scribble a bit on my own. My colleagues kept a bemused, professional distance from the stars whose lives they ground through their editorial machine. At home, most people I knew were in awe of movie and TV stars. But this was New York, where people in the rural South could be dismissed as hicks—gullible customers for fan magazines. I tried not to think about this.

That first summer in New York, my wardrobe consisted of my Kentucky sundresses. New Yorkers wore long sleeves to work. I had never worn long sleeves in the summer. The editor, a pert, pixie-haired woman from Maine, said to me, "You may want to bring a sweater to the office, because the air-conditioning gets cold."

I moved to the Shelton Towers, a hotel on Lexington Avenue, where I could room more cheaply by the week. I sat in my cramped room and read *Heart of Darkness*. I tried to write in a notebook, but I had nothing to write yet. The words would flow better from a type-writer, I thought. Lamar found his car, empty, and he was eventually able to give me a little money from his insurance, but it was not enough to buy a typewriter.

In the mornings, I ate cereal at the hotel coffee shop. I ate hot dogs at Nedick's. I ate pasteboard blocks from vending cases at the automat. Sometimes I ate at Hector's, a cafeteria near Times Square. I was al-ways hungry. I grew very thin that year in New York. I walked more than I was used to. The horde of high heels rumbled along the side-walks like a regiment in battle dress. I wore tennis shoes to work, then changed into heels in the telephone booth in the lobby of my building. No one else did this. I was ahead of my time.

Mama wrote:

> *Your Daddy won't let you borrow the money for that employment agency. You was offered better jobs. He said with a college education you should have got a better job. Those agencies are just a racket. By the time you get them paid off you either quit or they lay you off and they grab another sucker. There you've been out all that money. Why didn't you go to the unemployment office and they could have placed you in a field of work you are qualified for? We've had to have lots of work done on all these old cars and truck since you were home. Our expense is more than your daddy makes, so we keep dipping into that Build & Loan fund until there's not much left. The money you left here with should have been enough to see you through till you got to working, if you hadn't signed up with that agency. If you see that you're going to be broke without money maybe I can send you a little money until you can get started. With no more than you will make, how will you ever get paid back now what you owe?*
>
> *How well did you know that boy that carried your typewriter and*

Hi Fi to New York? I don't want to think this, as he was nice enough to carry your things for you, but maybe he did something with them himself.

I didn't share her suspicions, of course. I could hear Daddy saying "You brought it on yourself, Rollo!"—a saying he had picked up from the Katzenjammer Kids. I remembered that Daddy had been stationed awhile in New York when he was in the Navy. His ship had been docked at the Brooklyn Navy Yard. He knew things about New York that now fed his intolerable imaginings about his vulnerable daughter up there alone in that sinful city. Murder, assault, rape—I'm sure such images must have haunted him. But it wasn't physical danger I feared in New York. It was smells and sounds and intimacy. Men breathing garlic fit snugly against me in the gut-wrenching roar and gnash of the subway.

I wasn't alone in New York for long. Soon after Lamar appeared, I connected with some other U.K. graduates, including my college roommate, Kyra. She and I found a studio apartment on the Upper East Side and furnished it from Goodwill. Kyra got a job on the fan magazine too, and we shared an office with our editor. At work, we wrote about TV stars on programs we never saw. (We had no TV.) We wrote about Dick Chamberlain (*Dr. Kildare*) and Vince Edwards (*Ben Casey*) and Mike Landon (Little Joe on *Bonanza*). A fan magazine piece was a concoction of news angles, speculation, and file clippings. The editor would buy a set of photos from a traveling salesman. The pictures could be of young TV stars Susan and Dan walking on a beach together. The editor would dream up an idea about these pictures, based on something in the news—their new TV series, perhaps. Then she would write a provocative headline: "The Scary Secret Susan Shared with Dan on a Lonely Beach." The art department would create a layout, placing the photos and sizing them, with the provocative headline, space for subheads, and a block of lines designated for the copy—usually only a couple of paragraphs. The story would be continued in the back of the magazine. My job was to write the story, including a tantalizing come-on about the scary secret, enough to carry the reader to the jump page. The secret would turn out to be something innocuous: Susan is nervous about her new TV show and worries that she will fail, as her mother did at the same stage of her own career. Before this is revealed and worked out, the reader gets a rundown on the star's mother's mental illness, her father's fatal car crash, etc.—all the familiar facts from clippings in the files. Fan magazines then were not the lurid tabloids of today. They were relatively wholesome, chatty glimpses of stardom, exaggerated but faithful to the facts, and written with the purpose of making the reader finish the story with a feeling of satisfaction and consolation. Elizabeth Taylor was good copy because of all her scandalous marriages. At the end of the stories about her, the reader felt superior because fame was tough and Liz couldn't have children.

Sometimes we actually talked to TV and movie stars. Richard Beymer (*West Side Story*), Robert Vaughn (*The Man from U.N.C.L.E.*), and Robert Goulet (Sir Lancelot in *Camelot*) stopped by our office. Goulet got us tickets to *Camelot* on Broadway. The young Greek in Elia Kazan's *America, America* flirted with me and telephoned me later, but I missed his call and he returned to Greece. I went to lunch with beach-blanket bunny Annette Funicello and her publicist, and Annette said she envied me because we were the same height—five three and a half—but I was five pounds lighter.

Fabian, a singer in the Frankie Avalon–Annette Funicello bubblegum pantheon, was very cute. And he was very polite, which surprised me. We met in a ground-floor apartment that had an office, where his publicist arranged our talk. The movie magazine didn't run interviews the way a newspaper would. These meetings were just P.R. chitchat, so it didn't matter what we talked about.

"I just got out of college and I'm saving money to take some more courses," I told Fabian.

"I wish I'd gone to college," he said. "I'm trying to educate myself a little." He showed me a book he was reading. It was lying open and facedown on a desk: *History of the Peloponnesian War*. I was impressed that he was reading something that sounded like a college course requirement. I also liked his grin.

"I read *The Catcher in the Rye*," he said. "That was good."

"Oh, have you read *Franny and Zooey*? Read the stories. Read 'A Perfect Day for Bananafish,' " I bubbled along. I thought we hit it off. He was only a year or two younger than me.

Naturally I waited for him to call me, but he didn't. It must have been the ordinary seersucker shirtwaist dress I had worn, I thought. I couldn't afford any new outfits. Sometime later I learned that Fabian had married a former Miss Rheingold.

•   •   •

My year in New York was a hodgepodge of discoveries and indulgences, with a backdrop of scrounging. I brought egg salad sandwiches to work and ate at my desk, leaving my lunch hour free for rambling through Peck & Peck, Korvette's, Arnold Constable's, Lord & Taylor. I glided up the old wooden-slatted escalators at Gimbel's. Sometimes I went to the public library and looked up Salinger stories in old *New Yorker*s. On weekends, I went with Kyra and our friends from Kentucky to museums and movies and to bars on Third Avenue where you could get a draft beer for fifteen cents. We yearned for something enthralling to come our way, something glamorous that would lift us out of our lives. We were deliriously hopeful. When I review the letters I wrote to friends during that period, I am embarrassed by the gushing accolades, the naïveté, the youthful diatribes, the rampant hyperbole. The letters verify the state of mind that accompanied me on my sojourn in the city—and the endless walking, the search for satisfying food, the hungry drifting through the racks and racks of fashions in the Fifth Avenue stores. We saw *The Night of the Iguana* on Broadway, *The Fantasticks* off-Broadway. We went to art galleries, the Museum of Modern Art. We went to live TV shows and Atlantic beaches. At the Coney Island beach we gazed, incredulous, at huge women with elephant legs. My legs were slim and hard from all the walking I did around the city.

According to my diary, I saw one hundred and forty-three movies in 1962. I saw *Mondo Cane, Hatari!, Lolita, Jumbo*. Sometimes I went alone to a double feature at the Apollo on Forty-second Street. Once, I sat in the balcony in an empty row; a man sat snugly next to me, and he followed as I kept moving away. The romantic alienation of Antonioni and Fellini was hip. I wallowed vicariously in all the European angst. Fellini caricatures swarmed around me on the streets of New York. I was drawn to the fabulous hairdos of the vacuous, elegant women in *La Dolce Vita*. People kept calling to the main character, "Marcello!"—as if he could be retrieved, but he could not get a toehold out of the orgy. It was the way I felt in high school, that sense of being swept along in a current and wanting so much to attain something better. Maybe it was the way Fabian felt about wanting to go to college. The music in *La Dolce Vita* was lilting and sad and sweet, the perfect tone for the haunting feel of the sweet life and its hidden sorrow. "Marcello!" they called from the street.

Kyra and I wanted the sweet life, but we felt disqualified. Once, we were booted out of Bergdorf Goodman's soon after we entered. We just didn't look right. We had no money and no class. Besides, we were giggling, knowing how out of place we were. We were always self-conscious about our Southern accent, even though people seemed to like it. When I interviewed Ann-Margret at the Sherry-Netherland Hotel, she said to me, "What a sweet little accent." She was starring in the movie of *Bye Bye Birdie*, and she was preparing to make *Viva Las Vegas* with Elvis Presley. She was wearing a smashing kelly-green outfit with an overskirt. Immediately, I went straight to Bloomingdale's and bought two dresses with overskirts. Both Kyra and I, and some of our Kentucky friends, kept searching for the sweet life. On New Year's Eve we drank champagne out of our shoes. In subzero weather, we clattered along the streets in our champagne-soaked spike heels. Some of our friends who stayed out later than we did crashed a party where some Broadway stars were present.

I borrowed a typewriter from a U.K. graduate, and from time to time I filled up pages with Thomas Wolfe–inspired meditations. I thought about Big Tom—striding through the city, brooding and spewing adjectives. I tended to write in jerky fragments that I had to knit together. One day I lost a large manila envelope of typed pages, including notes for a story about a young woman—smart and tall and attractive, with a sense of fun—who comes from the South to New York and works on a fan magazine. I didn't miss the envelope until I got a call at work from a public relations director at a midtown firm. He had found it, with my work address on it.

"I found it on a bench in Washington Square," he said. "I realized you'd really want to have it back," he said pleasantly.

"Oh, that's where I was last night after work," I said. "I hadn't even missed it."

"It sounds as though you're a long way from home."

He had read everything. He knew my intimate thoughts. I tried to remember what I had written. After work the day before, Kyra and I had wandered through the Village before going to see *The Eclipse* at the Waverly. I remembered sitting on the bench in the park and sucking Italian ice from a fluted paper cup. The bench was so near the checkers tables that we could hear the players, old men in wide-brimmed hats, speaking what sounded like Portuguese.

The man on the telephone sounded nice, like someone I might want to know, but I didn't have the nerve to strike up an acquaintance. So he mailed the envelope to me. When I reviewed its contents I was mortified. I had written "Her tears flowed over the hot earth like rain" and

"O, lost, and the wind lost, and the typewriter lost, and gone is the music." And "She glinted like strewn money."

Whenever I passed Scribner's on Fifth Avenue, I glided virtually on tiptoe, out of reverence for Wolfe and Hemingway and Fitzgerald.

Kyra was bright and hopeful, and she had flair. She embraced New York with a Southern innocence that was bolder than mine. It made me fear for her safety. She was friendly with everyone, attracting men easily. She would go out with a construction worker she met on the street, but she was just as likely to fall in with a company vice president. She met a man who sent his chauffeur to bring both of us to his penthouse for a visit. Kyra called him "the Prince." He claimed to know President Kennedy, and he supplied details of campaign trips he said he had been on with J.F.K., whom he called "Jack." The chauffeur brought us a load of takeout cartons from an expensive Chinese eatery; we ate amid the Prince's statue-and-greenery decor, viewing the East River. The Prince told us that Jack Kennedy often left the White House in secret and traveled by helicopter to the Carlyle Hotel in New York, where he would surround himself with "girls." The Prince talked as if everyone knew about Kennedy's affairs. I did not know what to make of the Prince's revelations. At work, Kyra and I had written a special issue about the Kennedys. It was called a Kennedy "one-shot," the magazine equivalent of a TV special. We wrote stories about the tragic older brother; the sad, hidden Rosemary; heroic Jack the sailor; Rose the matriarch; fashion-box Jackie.

Kyra and I got our notions of meeting men directly from *Breakfast at Tiffany's,* where Audrey Hepburn casually paraded around in elegant dresses and jewels provided by rich men she met and innocently entertained. (They gave her fifty-dollar bills for the powder room.) I didn't meet guys easily, being reserved and careful, but I met one man who took me for a drink at a midtown place called the Pink Poodle. He told me I could be a glove model because I had nice hands. He claimed he had a contact. I didn't follow up. Then I met a self-described millionaire named Fred, who took me to lunch. He said he had a sort of harem of models and a yacht and a place in what he called "the islands," wherever those were. He talked like the synthetic-textiles man who had hired me and then fired me. He said he liked all his girls—he meant his models—to wear girdles. He asked me to meet him for a drink at a certain bar with a nautical theme on Madison Avenue, so I went there after work, trussed in my girdle. Apprehensive, I waited about ten minutes, eyeing the porthole view of the street, then split.

I always chickened out. Something would stop me. I led a charmed life. Mr. Cotton, the publisher I worked for, took Kyra and me under his wing. He was a Southerner who flew home to Tennessee each weekend in his own airplane. Snarling heads studded the walls of his office, which sported a tiger rug and footstools made from elephant feet. Mr. Cotton had personally bagged all these himself in Africa. In his chauffeured car, he took Kyra and me to dinner at the Eden Roc, where he dined nightly. We ordered filet mignon and green turtle soup because we had never had either. We felt safe and privileged with Mr. Cotton, an older gentleman.

I behaved myself in New York. But I knew four women there who had illegal abortions by the same doctor. One nearly died from infection; another would have had twins. The doctor was arrested eventually. While I was in the city, a transient was arrested in Central Park in connection with a crime that had occurred in Lexington while I was still at U.K. A student had been murdered, strangled with her bra. Clippings about the case were found in the transient's possession. And while I was in New York, a young career woman named Janice Wylie was murdered by an intruder into her apartment. The case was sensationalized because she was writer Philip Wylie's niece and she had worked at *Newsweek*.

Granny got sick with her nerves as soon as I left home. Late that summer, when I had been in New York a few months, she wrote me in a halting hand:

> *I thought I would try to write you a little. I don't seem to get much better, not able to help your Mama do the work or anything, she has practically spent the summer in the garden. I can't see to read much and the days are all so long. LaNelle and I watch the mail for your letters and we are always so glad to get one. She usually reads them to me, and I think she is a bit disappointed when you fail to mention her. She is precious anyway, and so good to me.*
>
> *Well, you seem to be having a very exciting time. How many days do you work a week, and how many hours a day? I think we were all disappointed because you took that job instead of some of the others. There is just so much sin, strife, and immorality in movie business. We hate for*

you to be making a study of it or even remotely connected with any of it in any way. I wish you would take time to go to some of those churches there so you could tell me about them when you come home, you know the book says "Remember the Sabbath Day to keep it Holy," and staying up all night before and sleeping all day is not doing that you know.

Janice makes good grades in her school and keeps the little car on the road between times, LaNelle will start to school 5th Sept. Then I am going to miss her I know. Bob has been sick but is better now, I don't know whether you can read this or not. I can't see much but thought I would try. Don't forget us here at home and be good always. I pray to Him every day to guide your thinking and your heart in the right way. We love you. Granny.

I cherished letters from home, but I wouldn't take my grandmother's warnings seriously. My job didn't seem to threaten to plunge me into sin; instead, it offered me fresh glimpses of human nature. Letters came into the office, letters to movie and TV stars from fans. They were not forwarded, but dumped in the trash can. I rescued some of the letters, searching for topics to write about. They sobered me. Most were from harmless pubescents agog over Johnny Crawford (of *The Rifleman*) or Mike Landon or Richard Chamberlain. Others were from women—troubled, lonely, mistreated, empty. Widows wrote frequently. ("I was spiritually drawn to your magazine in a grocery store.") They wrote that they kept pictures of Mike Landon or Lorne Greene of *Bonanza* because they reminded them of their dead husbands. The widows sent snapshots picturing the husband and the *Bonanza* substitute together on the mantelpiece or on top of the TV. Some wrote that they preferred the TV heroes to their late husbands.

It was unsettling to get these glimpses into people's hearts. Most of the letters were from people like those back home, people I knew who watched images on the screen and often confused the actor and the role. Most weren't obsessive—they expressed an innocent if naive pleasure. I could see stories in these letters, like something I imagined writing one day—stories of disappointment and desire.

At the office, for the first time I heard a woman say "fuck." She said it as casually as if the word were perfectly normal to say. In her mouth, it was an angry word. That anger could be expressed so openly was as shocking to me as the word itself. Frequently, I saw people maundering in the street, like the precursors of nineties talk radio. In the city it was not clear to me what mental health was, much less good manners.

I was thinking a lot about sanity, wondering what it would take to send someone out to rant along the streets or in letters flung haphazardly at the world. My grandmother had another nervous breakdown not long after I received her letter. This time Granddaddy committed her to the state mental hospital in Hopkinsville, what was loosely called the insane asylum. She had grown increasingly nervous and tearful, and my parents feared a relapse into the helpless condition of 1950 that had sent her to Memphis. Mama said in her letter that Granny was afraid she was going blind because she had cataracts. I imagine Granny was also worried about me. I had never seen her raving, and I could not truly think of her as crazy. But I could imagine her fears growing into a huge, paralyzing knot of worry. I remembered how she had loved learning and had once wanted to teach school. And I could picture her sitting in a corner, tortured by nightmarish visions of New York, the modern sister of Sodom and Gomorrah.

The week Granny traveled to Hopkinsville, the Cuban missile crisis erupted. The day of the crisis, I was walking up Sixth Avenue in midtown among lighted skyscrapers, just about dark. It was milking time, I thought. It was a brisk October evening in that early-dark, melancholy preview of winter. I would find that after-work time of day depressing for as long as I held a nine-to-five job. I was cold. I identified with the moody isolation of Monica Vitti walking through a desolate landscape, often with her back to the camera, in another one of those Italian movies. My information about Cuba and Castro was spotty, but I had a feeling of hovering doom. The tabloids shouted nuclear war in 144-point type. I had known Cubans at U.K., students whose parents had been high government employees but were forced to work at menial jobs after coming to the United States. The Cuban woman who gave me a ride to New York early in the summer told me that her family had escaped a totalitarian evil, and now I could feel its threat palpably in the air. The Time-Life Building, which at that time had almost a block of elbow room, could fly apart in millions of pieces. As I walked past this blue tower, I imagined all those bright lights to be smithereens already—a foreshadowing of the horror. Still, I had a sense of detachment and disbelief, as if whatever might happen were all part of a show that I would be privileged to witness.

The next day, another letter arrived from home. My sister Janice had gotten married. My mother's letter seemed distracted and helpless. I saw marriage as a trap, especially in Kentucky, and I wondered which would be worse, marriage or the insane asylum. Janice and I were four years apart and had not shared interests since childhood. Now it was as though she had been spirited away, but I hoped she was happy. As the early cold spell chilled me that autumn, I felt my family shattering, the way Mama's paperweight was supposed to have done when Daddy tried to crack it. Mama wrote little detail about Janice's new life or about Granny's condition.

When my parents and my grandfather committed Granny to the Western Kentucky State Hospital, the administrators told them to take her things back home. They would be stolen if she kept them there in the ward, where she would have two or three roommates. Granddaddy returned home with her good clothes, her brush and mirror and hair combs, her gloves and scarves.

The doctors ordered shock treatments to blast Granny's self-involvement into oblivion and uncoil her nerves. She pleaded with them not to do it, but they insisted. The following Sunday, the family went to visit her, carrying food to her because the meals at the hospital were unpalatable. Children weren't allowed in the building, so Daddy brought Granny outside to visit with Don and LaNelle. The family sat with her on benches on the lawn while she ate biscuits and some cold fried chicken and vegetables Mama had cooked. She was calmer after her first treatment, and she was glad to see faces from home.

The place spooked Don and LaNelle. Don, a mischievous and hyperactive child, gamboled across a flower bed and peeked in a barred window on the side of the building. He jumped back, screaming.

"What did you see?" Daddy said, but Don could not stop bawling. He was trembling. Daddy peered through the window and saw a naked woman tied to a chair, howling.

"Don't look in there again," Daddy told Don. "You oughtn't to see that."

"What was it?" Mama asked, as she held Don close to her.

"A crazy woman tied to a chair," Daddy said. "Not in her right mind."

"One night I woke up and saw a mean fat woman standing over me," Granny said. "It liked to scared me to death."

"But they told us they put people like that in quarantine," said Mama. "They don't let them out."

"I ain't crazy," said Granny, gazing at her lap.

"Nobody said you were," Mama said.

"I've got to go home. The chickens need to be fed, and I need to do my washing."

She was frightened by the sensations assaulting her. The unfamiliar and the unbalanced were the same to her. But the doctors, one of them a woman, insisted to my parents that the environment—the erratic behavior of the patients, the noise, the misplaced identities—would shake Granny out of herself.

The next time the family visited her, they found her more placid and open, but forgetful. She repeated herself and seemed not to remember that they had been to see her before. Again, they went outside, sitting in lawn chairs.

"These young people that are locked up here," Granny said sadly. "It's such a waste." She was almost seventy-five years old.

Seeing the young people tore at her heart. She saw wild-headed, suicidal, babbling teenagers thrashing and flailing in straitjackets. She saw them herded into holding chambers and electric-shock rooms. She said they were tied up in their beds and could not get out to relieve themselves. She knew that people like that had once been kept in people's attics, chained. She said it was better to have them at home, even in the attic, where they could be with their people, than in a public place, among strangers. She could not bear the pitiful sight of those raggedy-haired young people, thrust out of their homes, away from their parents and their brothers and sisters. She begged to go home. The shock treatments were so dreadful, she refused to complete the full course. Finally, she contrived to come home a few weeks earlier than recommended by insisting on having her cataract operation.

"She came home a different person," my mother wrote me. Mama worked closely with her to bring back her mind, just as she had done in 1950. Trying to stimulate her memory, Granddaddy talked with Granny endlessly about their life together when they were young. "Now, Ettie," he would say. "Think back to that buggy ride down to Spence Chapel when we were late to the singing that time. It commenced to rain. And Old Peg eat up that ground like a twister."

14

The literary life began to wink at me through the clouds. At the start of 1963, while I was still in the city, my creative-writing teacher from the University of Kentucky, Robert Hazel, accepted a teaching job at New York University. He had lived in New York during the forties, and now he returned with the fanfare of a homecoming. He summoned his Kentucky pals, inviting us to hang out at his "pad" on MacDougal Street, the center of Village bohemian life. At the San Remo Bar, he introduced us to noted poets and artists we'd never heard of. They talked over my head, while I sat mute and bewildered but eager to be in the scene. The allure of the literary life was as delicious as the rum-raisin ice cream at the Figaro. Bob Hazel had hobnobbed with Allen Tate and John Crowe Ransom, names that sailed luxuriously through the air like winged maple seeds. "You can't be a writer unless you work among, and associate with, other writers of your time," Bob told me.

He was disdainful of my movie magazine work. He sneered at my journalism background—fatal for a writer, he said, as if my writing for the college newspaper had already caused permanent damage. But I told him I was grateful not to be sewing labels in Tony Martin jackets or canning tomatoes in a hot kitchen with brats underfoot.

"You were pretty dumb in Kentucky, sitting on your ass in that journalism building," he said. He had a way of delivering cutting remarks with a little dip of his head, eyes lifted, coquettishly assuming forgiveness. He dressed in brown—trench coat, twill pants, V-necked sweaters over plaid shirts. His brown hair had a flipped forelock like a horse's. Back in Lexington, he had been dazzling—handsome, electric. But now he was beginning to fade, like a worn-out couch.

We attended lectures on French painting and Federico García Lorca at the New School. He took me to N.Y.U. to hear Lawrence Ferlinghetti rave repetitiously about death, to the beat of a jazz tune. I lumped him with the beatniks, which Bob told me was not exactly right. Distinctions were important to him. He could talk about "hip" and "cool" and "beat" in precise terms. He wasn't beat himself, but he was exceedingly hip. In college, I had yearned to wear black tights and chant poetry at a coffeehouse. I owned some bongo drums. I didn't drink coffee, but I liked jazz, which was essential to the beatnik scene. I was vague, though, about exactly what the beatniks were rebelling against.

I know Bob introduced me to Ferlinghetti after the reading because I jotted down the meeting in my diary, but evidently the poet wasn't as impressive as Fabian because I have no memory of our encounter. To me, poetry was like layers of wet lace stuck together. But Bob was a serious poet and was recognized as a good one; he aspired to the mantle of Hart Crane. Bob was at the end of the twentieth-century wave of celebrating and romanticizing the alienated artist. He was a problematic figure, around whose center I wavered uncertainly. He had been fired from the University of Kentucky for a dalliance with a student (her father had complained to the dean). Earlier he had attempted such a dalliance with me. I recalled how he'd put the moves on me back when I was in his writing class my junior year. And here he was again. As soon as he turned up in New York, he began flirting with me again. I could have avoided him, but he was the nearest thing to *La Dolce Vita* I could find.

At U.K. in Professor Hazel's class, unlike any other literature class I took, we read some works by writers who were still *alive*. We read *Goodbye, Columbus* and *Lie Down in Darkness* and Flannery O'Connor stories. From Professor Hazel we first learned of cocktail parties, European cafés, Greenwich Village, and the Brooklyn Bridge. He lectured the class against women's magazines, melodrama, and Henry James. He eschewed bourgeois values. His poems juxtaposed the lyrical and the cynical, and he admired the brutally physical and sordid. His novels were lurid. In one of them, rats ate a baby's face in a New York apartment. Authenticity was essential in that period. Everyone was reading *Nausea* and trying to use "existentialism" in a sentence.

He was an egregious flirt. At the time, I didn't imagine that his come-ons were anything but normal, since his romantic vision of masculinity fit sweetly with all I knew of seduction from high school, songs, and the movies. I was in his class, and I was flattered and elated by his attentions, since he was a handsome, worldly man—a writer.

I had been in Professor Hazel's class about two months when he invited me one Saturday to go out to the country to shoot mistletoe out of a tree. Mistletoe, an evergreen parasite with gummy white berries, grows so high up a tree you have to bring it down with a gun. In the South, it is traditional for a man to go out shooting mistletoe on Christmas Day. Professor Hazel had a .22 rifle. After he blasted down a couple of mistletoe bunches from a tall ash, the farm family who owned the land asked us in for some cornbread and beans. Professor Hazel said there was nothing he loved better than good cornbread and succulent beans. He seemed right at home with farmers, which seemed odd to me, as if this suave professor who had lived in New York secretly hankered to hitch up some mules.

With the mistletoe in the backseat of his car, he drove me to his place in Lexington. He was renting the downstairs of a brick antebellum manor house with a circular drive and Doric columns. An art professor and his wife lived upstairs, but they weren't home. The house was dark and shabby, furnished with antiques. I noticed manuscripts lying around casually, worn books stuffed with papers, original artwork (by the upstairs professor) on the walls. Professor Hazel laid a jazz record on his turntable and pricked it with the needle. "Progressive jazz," he said, and he told some story about New York and a jazz club and Gerry Mulligan. I took all of this in, heavy with the weight of its authority.

Holding the mistletoe above my head, Professor Hazel asked me to spend the night with him. He said something like "Your charms require you to stay here in my bower until morning." Or something less lame, more acutely modernist.

I wasn't sure about my charms—or his, either. I was scared of a person so old. He was about eighteen years older than me, divorced, and he was my teacher. His marriage had fallen apart not long before. I wanted to please him, but I wasn't sure what the rules were. I hadn't expected such a bold advance from him.

"Will you do me the honor of spending the night?" he asked.

"I can't," I said. "I have curfew."

He seemed genuinely disappointed, as if he were lonely and carried a sorrow that was too adult for me to understand. He returned me to my dormitory, but he wouldn't get out of the car and walk me to the door—as etiquette required on a college date. He said he didn't want to be seen.

After that, Professor Hazel's overtures toward me cooled, which disappointed me. A mystique hung over him like a purple wine haze, and I signed up for the second semester of his course. I loved the way he made his students feel privileged to get a glimpse of his literary domain. Commenting on our work, he would say "That scene puts me in mind of Hemingway" or "When I read your story I thought of what Dylan Thomas said on one occasion when I was with him in New York." He made his students believe that writing was a calling; a writer was much like a preacher receiving his personal summons from the Lord. This was a notion his wide-eyed students found irresistible.

In the second semester, I wrote a story that featured Professor Hazel as a character—renamed Tom or Bud or something. It included some suggestive remarks that he had made to me at a party, lines such as "Where do we go from here, baby?" The day I was to read the story aloud in class, I became nervous and withdrew it. I had encountered him in the hallway just before class. He said he had read the story, and he handed it to me with a mock flourish.

I couldn't look him in the eye. I stuffed the story between the covers of my notebook, as if to hide it. "I can't read it in front of the class," I mumbled.

He didn't seem surprised. He nodded. "That story has *some* things going for it," he said. "But there are others you may want to think about." He gave me an enigmatic smile, which I loaded up with significance.

In confusion, I retreated. I had always got my lessons dutifully, but I did not write any more stories that semester. He gave me an A in the course anyway. No doubt he sensed my bewilderment, and perhaps he felt guilty about his part in it. By then he was in deep with the student whose father later got him fired.

He cultivated a coterie of young male followers. When these protégés visited his house, he fed them whiskey and steaks, and they brought their manuscripts and stayed for hours talking about writing. Four of these students—one right after the other—had won prestigious creative-writing fellowships to Stanford University. I wanted to apply to Stanford too, but I had not completed enough work to make a strong application, so I decided not to try that year. I had never before ended a class on a note of inertia. It surprised me, and I did not know what to do.

When Robert Hazel appeared in New York, we did a cautious little dance around each other. I safely distanced him, but he was still my guide, my foil to Miss Florence. He had a boozy complexion. I didn't know what cigarettes and hard liquor had to do with writing, but I inferred that a certain school of male writers—the romantic degenerates—depended on them. And there were rules about food. It had to be authentic, such as Spanish peasant fare, with wine. Writers like Bob found their European cuisine in cafés. I figured they just didn't know how to cook. But Bob invited my roommate, Kyra, and me over once for fresh asparagus. He panfried it in cornmeal, the way Hemingway's character Nick Adams might have fried up a fish over a campfire. Asparagus and Scotch were the entire meal. I didn't like Scotch. I'd never had asparagus; it was all right, but not enough to fill up on. I was still hungry.

On another occasion, Bob invited me out to one of the cafés on MacDougal Street. He ordered veal scallopini marsala and wine.

"I have an offer to make to you," he said, looking up at me with his familiar dreamy-eyed come-on gaze. "Let me seduce you, and I'll make you happy. I'll make you happy for the rest of your life if you'll be my mistress."

Mistress? What an adult word! And dirty sounding. In the Italian movies, mistresses were commonplace. Maybe the word occurred to him because we were in an Italian restaurant, I thought. I picked at my pasta.

"That doesn't sound like me," I said. Mistress of the house. I envisioned cooking and cleaning.

He had a little mean streak. After a while, he said, "Three things, if you're going to be a serious writer." He held up his fingers to tick off his list. "You've got to hold back youthful enthusiasm, and don't emulate that mediocre sludge on television, and avoid sentimental shit about dear old grandparents."

He finished the veal scallopini, spearing the mushrooms and mopping up the marsala sauce with a hunk of Italian bread. He ate sloppily, drunkenly.

I didn't know where this was going. I had been feeling that my job and my ambition and my background were all a jarring and jerky mix, like Mondrian's *Broadway Boogie-Woogie*. At my job, I was exploiting people who romanticized the movies, but Bob Hazel exalted the very kind of people who loved the movies and TV—farm folks, laborers, working people—while condemning what they felt. My parents were at home watching *Gunsmoke*. Bob Hazel would have sneered.

"I've spent my life getting away from my rural Indiana background," Bob explained when I tried to ask what for me were central questions about a writer's material. "My family thought writing was sissy, even though I was a quarterback on the football team." He slugged down some more wine. "You'll have to resist sentimentalizing 'good country people' if you're really going to be a writer," he said. "They're too nice. You need to get tough."

"Does that mean I can't write stories about where I come from?"

"It means that you have to stop going to those shit movies and think about what Randall Jarrell said."

I don't remember what he said that Randall Jarrell said. It was indistinguishable from what he said that Allen Tate said and John Crowe Ransom said and Wallace Stevens said. On the subway, I reread *Lie Down in Darkness*, about a Southern girl who went off to New York and eventually committed suicide. It was written from her father's point of view. None of it applied to me.

Bob Hazel invited me to Poughkeepsie one winter weekend to visit his brother and family. From the train window I saw trees, whole forests, deep in snow. I hadn't realized how much I missed trees. Vividly, I recalled the ice-covered twig I had broken when I was a child, the act that stung me with guilt. These trees seemed so calm and beautiful, so necessary in the landscape. As we rode along, Bob spotted a teddy bear left out on a fence, and he pointed it out. Maybe he wrote it down. It was the sort of thing he would put in a poem, he said.

There was a party that weekend, dozens of professional, nonliterary people in their thirties. I wore my black cocktail dress with the taffeta balloon-hem, the dress I had worn the last time I saw the Hilltoppers. It was still stylish. Bob said to me, "How does it feel to be the most beautiful woman in the room?" I was twenty-two. The others were all old. He was forty. He thought I was beautiful because I was young.

I returned to New York on an afternoon train on Sunday, in time to meet Kyra and rush to Rockefeller Center for *The Jack Paar Program*, a weekly television show. Someone at work had given us tickets to the taping. George Burns and Pearl Bailey were guests. I knew I didn't belong in New York. And I knew I shouldn't be building a career based on TV stars. Before long I began searching for a different job. I went to an interview at an address on Fifth Avenue, on the sixteenth floor. I knew that the Empire State Building was in that vicinity. Afraid of heights, I had always avoided going there. It was only after I was far down the block, after the interview, and glanced back that I realized I had been in the Empire State Building. For a long time that trivial irony impressed me. It seemed like the teddy bear on the fence.

By then, it was trees I needed. The occasional trees I saw in the city's concrete landscape leaped out at me like images in a 3-D movie.

I could not imagine my future. I thought I would be alone, but not lonely. My farm background had taught me to take what comes—drought, cattle disease, dead dogs. I had thought that if my life were to change, some opportunity had to present itself to me, so I should keep bumbling along until this cosmic accident occurred. But now I came to realize I had to take my life in hand. I had to ask myself what I really wanted. I knew I wanted sanity and clarity, and I knew I didn't want to waste my life. Bob Hazel started me on my true course, but he yanked me backwards, too. Then I yanked loose. Later, I saw that for all his shining facade and sad romanticism, he had been utterly serious. He was a genuine poet, and I was still young, unformed.

In 1963, only weeks before President Kennedy was murdered, I left for an upstate school to take a graduate assistantship in literature. Bob warned me that academic study was anathema to a writer, but I knew I had plenty to learn before I could write. In Binghamton, the trees were blazing autumn colors on forested mountainsides. I had never seen trees perform so brilliantly. Back home, the predominant oak trees made the autumn brown and gold. But this Northern landscape was full of fire; the trees were flames.

15

When I went away to New York City in the summer of 1962, I left many of my college books at home. Mama stored them out in the junkhouse. Why keep books in the house, where they would be in the way? Two years later, during a visit home, I learned that Granny had found the books soon after I left, and she had read a few of them. She read *The Old Man and the Sea* by Ernest Hemingway and *Anglo-Saxon Attitudes* by Angus Wilson. And she read my copy of Henry Miller's *Tropic of Cancer*.

"Such as that is awful," she told me. The books were stacked on her wicker lamp table, on a white doily. Her hands worked nervously along the edges of her apron.

A pervert looking for filthy books could have searched the whole University of Kentucky library and not found anything naughtier than *Tropic of Cancer*. It's raw sexual adventure. It has the word "fuck" in it. I had left that book behind and taken *The Great Gatsby* with me. As far as I was concerned, *Tropic of Cancer* was a reject—too sordid and lacking literary style—while *The Great Gatsby* was a treasure.

I knew I had caused my family worry, but I did not dwell on the possibility that I had sent my grandmother to the nuthouse. She seemed better now, and I was immersed in my studies.

Later, when Granddaddy got sick again, I was studying James Joyce. I came home for a long stretch—from Thanksgiving to New Year's. The weather was mild, and I sat outside at a picnic table in the oak woods by the house, reading *Ulysses*. Dutifully, as I had always been taught to study, I was following a guidebook, annotating the pages of the novel. There was a comfort in plunging deep into this methodical task while trying not to think about what was happening with my grandparents. Fourteen years before, when Granny was at the hospital in Memphis and I was certain she was dying, I had been deeply afraid. Now I had annotations to do. Joyce had used the kidney as the dominating organ of the Calypso chapter. Copying that in my book didn't seem at all wacky to me then. I kept notebooks of system and design. Joyce's art was too dazzling to question. I consumed, I regurgitated.

No one in the family knew about James Joyce, and I would not tell them anything. Anyway, they didn't ask. I wouldn't tell them *Ulysses* had been banned, or that Joyce and Henry Miller might have crossed paths in Paris. I didn't know how to explain a writer who had taken years to write six hundred pages about a day in the life of an Irish ad salesman. I couldn't tell my family what pure pleasure was in this book, surely of no relevance when it came to stocking the freezer for the winter. Mama had wanted to follow my studies with me in high school, and we began with the Latin text, but she was too busy to keep up. After a few fitful starts and stops, she had to quit. Now, at a school of higher learning, I felt guilty that I was soaring out of sight, into the arcane—and often inane—intricacies of scholarship.

Granddaddy died in January, 1965, a victim of ulcers, his stomach lining gnawed away from years of secret worry about Granny's delicate health. The day before his surgery, I was in his hospital room. He unzipped his leather change purse from the bedside drawer and counted out several coins.

"Go get me some cream," he said.

At the drugstore across the street, I bought two dips of vanilla ice cream in a waxed pasteboard cup. I was aware of his dignity, his precision, his intention to pay his way, and his love of ice cream. He was very much alive. I didn't consider that he would not survive the surgery.

The evening after his funeral, I was watching Marilyn Monroe in *River of No Return* on TV. Granny said, "How can you watch such trash at a time like this?" That night in bed I was afraid of childhood ghosts; I pictured my grandfather rising from the grave. The thing I had feared throughout my childhood had finally happened. A family member had died. I could not bear to think about it. For several years afterwards, whenever he came to mind, I deliberately switched him off. Eventually, I realized I could hardly remember anything about him except the time he spit tobacco juice into my eye. I was about ten. He was walking toward me on the driveway behind his house, and when he got close, he spit toward me. He was probably absorbed in thought and didn't see me, but when I howled with pain, he kept walking, ignoring me. This heedlessness of cruel effect—this harsh, blind innocence—was a trait I also saw at times in my father.

Daddy had promised his father not to leave Granny alone at night, so he brought her to live at our house, in the tiny back room. Even though her house was only a few dozen yards away, it must have seemed a hundred miles to her. She didn't have her kitchen, her things, her own home. Everything was wrong. She found fault with Mama's cooking. Don and LaNelle were young and troublesome. Her husband was dead.

LaNelle's records blared out of her room. The squawks sounded to Granny as if a fox had got in the henhouse. In the spring, while the Beatles blasted throughout the house, Granny sat outside in the car to escape the sound. Granddaddy's car, a green boxy Dodge, was parked in the woods behind the house. Granny stayed there for many hours, in her bonnet, head lowered, studying her plight. She had never learned to drive. She had not learned the areas Granddaddy had handled—the finances, the livestock trading—just as he had not learned to patch pants or work up preserves. Now Daddy was in charge of the manly jobs. She often called him "Bob" by mistake. When she talked to anyone, she repeated that the funeral expenses were $1,294.75 and the hospital bill was $1,048.45; she told how much money she had left, and how her house was deteriorating with no one in it.

After six months of listening to Granny's litany of complaints, Mama and Daddy and LaNelle and Don moved to her house with her. With grim resolve, my mother stored much of her furniture and belongings in one of the outbuildings. She did not fight the move, because she did not see any alternative. Besides, she figured Granny would not live long.

Granny's house had a large living room, a dining room, a kitchen, a closet, a recently installed bathroom, and a new gas furnace. But there were only two bedrooms. There was a large, closed-off attic, but it did not occur to anyone to remodel that space to make more bedrooms. My parents placed their bed in the living room. They stowed Don in the front hall, on a small bed, just inside the glass-paned front door. He had nightmares there, fearing ghosts and the legendary man with the hook for a hand. LaNelle occupied the north bedroom, with its high ceilings and cold drafts. Outside, long-armed spirea bushes scraped menacingly across the windows.

The house was uncomfortable and old. The floorboards bounced. The kitchen faucet dripped. Granny's clock struck every hour. Mama hated the clock, but Granny could not sleep without its regular announcements of time's trek.

Once again, my mother was living with her mother-in-law. She didn't know what her life was going to come to now. She had sent one set of children out into the world, and she had another pair yet to raise. It was exhausting. She had little time or energy to take Don and LaNelle to the lake or the show, and she paid scant attention to their schoolwork. She was often needed in the fields, and her garden grew larger each year. To earn cash, she sewed for people, working into the night on elaborate suits and dresses. In the cramped kitchen, Granny was at Mama's elbow, trying to direct the cooking and insisting on her scummy lye soap for the dishes.

I imagine Mama felt she was drying up, disappearing like a pea vine in the fall. Daddy, however, began to bloom after the death of his father. He began frequenting flea markets, collecting old gun parts and piecing together collectible antique guns, which he then sold. He still enjoyed trading; it was in his nature and his history. He was curious about the world, sociable within his own class, and now he began to emerge from the slump he had suffered when Don was born. He bought some beef cows and some machinery. He was truly the man of the place now. Granny continued to call him Bob. Her nerve medicine, from Hopkinsville, fuzzed her mind. For the rest of her life, she took Thorazine to calm her nerves and to keep her head from swimming.

Daddy rented our little white house in the woods to Janice and her husband. He installed a water heater because Janice had a new baby, her second. He had never put in a water heater for Mama. She had always heated our bathwater in her largest stewpot on the kitchen stove. A few years later, Janice and her family moved to a place in town, and our little house became the trashing ground of a series of renters. It caught on fire once—a cigarette on a mattress. Large families stressed out the septic system.

I usually came home at least twice a year, but I didn't fully appreciate the strain the family lived under. I didn't see their day-to-day life, so I didn't realize how, for them, my visits were celebrations. Mama made cakes, and we played cards till midnight. I played games with LaNelle

Bernice Christianna Lee as a teenager in the 1930s.

Christy Lee Mason, 1940s.

Christy Mason (third from right) eating watermelon with her factory pals at a park, about 1938.

*Christy and
Wilburn, 1945.*

Wilburn Mason, 1945.

*Bobbie Ann Mason,
at an early age.*

Robert Lee (Bob) Mason, with his brother Bee, at the turn of the century.

Bob Mason, center, with his sisters and brothers—
Daisy, Bee, Dove, Roe—1930s.

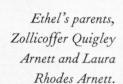

Ethel Arnett, age thirteen, in about 1900.

*Ethel's parents,
Zollicoffer Quigley
Arnett and Laura
Rhodes Arnett.*

*Ethel's grandfather
William P. Arnett
(1821–99).*

Bobbie Ann Mason's birthplace, above, the home of her grandparents Ethel and Robert Lee Mason (Granny and Granddaddy).

Ethel and Bob Mason behind their house.

*Wilburn Mason
and his cows,
1950.*

*Mary Lee and
Christy Mason
with buckets of
blackberries, 1962.*

Bobbie at Cuba School, Grades 1 through 5.

Bobbie and Janice Mason, 1950—the book is
The Bobbsey Twins at School.

Hilltoppers Topics

VOL. 1 - 1957   MARCH-APRIL ISSUE   NUMBER TWO

From The National Office

Hi!

First of all, I would like to say thanks so much for the splendid cooperation and success we have had with the first 'edition of our newspaper. So many swell people have expressed their enjoyment of our efforts in publishing the HILLTOPPERS TOPICS that it really makes us feel good and we are hoping that we will be able to do just as well in future issues. We want to remind you to write in with your suggestions for the betterment of the paper and ideas for the contents. We want to print just what you, the fans, want to read.

Second, we want to mention the Hilltoppers' tremendous success with their latest disc, MARIANNE. It is amazing the way this record has caught on. To date it has hit fifth position on the national surveys and has sold over 400,000 copies. Daily orders exceed 20,000. The Hilltoppers have asked us to express to you their appreciation for all you've done to further their popularity. They are really happy about it!

Did you catch the 'Toppers on the Steve Allen Show? We know you will agree that they were just terrific.

You will notice by comparing last issue with this that the name of our secretary has been changed. Last issue was listed Miss Frances Brogan. Now secretary is

Hilltoppers Entertain At Casa Loma In St. Louis

Hilltoppers on stage at the Casa Loma Ballroom in St. Louis.

CALYPSO BECOMES COMMERCIAL

(Reprint from Cash Box Magazine)

The record business has a trend--calypso.

It's still much too early to just how far it will go but of a sudden the whole business is interested in with a calypso beat.

The trend started with " Oh Cindy" broke out for and has been followed u such other records as "J Farewell" and "Banana Song."

Now everyone is look one.

We certain

The swinging, singing collegiate quartet known as the Hilltoppers made their sixth return engagement at one of St.Louis' biggest night spots, the Casa Loma Ballroom, on the weekend of November 30, December 1 and 2. Jimmy, Karl, Lou, and Eddie made nightly appearances including a matinee on Sunday afternoon. On opening night several hundred fans were present in spite of the fact that the performance had hardly been advertised. At first the Hilltoppers were in for only Saturday and Sunday, but a last-minute change did in no way affect the crowds which are typical of the Hilltoppers' response in St. Louis.

After the show on Friday night, which received so many encores ran out of songs,

Jimmy, Bobbie, and Ed Bonner at KXOK.

rant. The place was packed and everyone enjoyed seeing and hearing the Hilltoppers tremendously. Afterwards, the boys went to radio station KXOK and spent than an hour with Ed Bonner jockey.

Chuck Norman Hilltoppers at suburban restaurant.

rd in the new trend. And it's accepted axiom of merchan-

Bobbie with Jimmy Sacca and d.j. Ed Bonner, KXOK, St. Louis, 1956.

THE HILLTOPPERS
Dot Recording Stars

The Hilltoppers, 1954.

Bobbie with the Hilltoppers, 1959.

One of Bobbie's columns in The Kentucky Kernel, *the University of Kentucky newspaper, 1960.*

Kyra Hackley and Bobbie Ann Mason, roommates at the University of Kentucky, 1960.

Bobbie Mason

looks at LIFE

LIFE magazine this week is beginning a series of debates on America's "national purpose"—whether we lack one, whether we need it, and if so, what it should be.

It is clear that America's original "purpose" has degenerated. It has become so diversified that there is no longer a single thread called unity which the people can or will follow.

On this assumption, there is need for revision. What the revision should be is not so much a problem as how it can be done.

Is it possible to stir the vacuous public mind toward one common, well-defined goal?

'Completed Society'

Walter Lippman wrote a few mont'   critical
weakne··   people
                                          vanting
                                          ive. to
                                          te. We
                                          y, one
                                          t busi-

                                          Com-
                                          :ed to
                                          tional
                                          yone
                                          pose
                                          et of
                                          nant
                                          at's
                                          nee

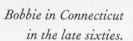

Bobbie at TV Star Parade *in New York, with TV starlet Eva Six, 1963.*

Bobbie in Connecticut in the late sixties.

Marriage of Bobbie to Roger Rawlings, April 12, 1969, Storrs, Connecticut (photo by Frank Cantor).

Bobbie and Roger in their first garden, Connecticut, 1970 (photo by James Baker Hall).

Granny in her garden in the 1970s.

Christy and Wilburn Mason's fiftieth wedding anniversary, 1986 (photo by LaNelle Mason).

Wilburn and Christy on the farm, 1987 (photo by Lila Havens).

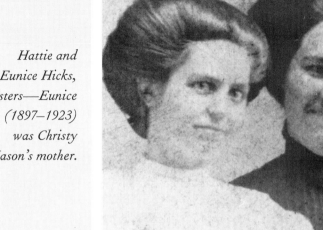

Hattie and Eunice Hicks, sisters—Eunice (1897–1923) was Christy Mason's mother.

Christy with Peggy Rea on the set of In Country, *1988.*

Robert E. Lee with his two daughters and two grand-daughters at the Lee homeplace, August, 1944. From left to right: Thelma, Christy, Janice, Bobbie, Robert.

The Lees: James F. (Jimmo) and Mary Lue Lee (seated) and their children, Rudy, Mary, and Robert, August, 1944.

Jimmo Lee, Detroit, 1947.

LaNelle, Bobbie, Janice, and Don Mason, 1970s.

Christy and Bobbie in Christy's garden, 1996 (photo by Guy Mendes).

Christy Mason fishing at her pond, 1980s.

Bobbie at work with feline assistant, Kiko, 1990s.

The Mason home, where Bobbie Ann Mason grew up (painting by Christy Mason).

and Don and drove them to the lake. I watched TV shows with Daddy. We always had a great time. Granny clasped my hands tightly when she greeted me, and she wept when I went away again.

Although in some ways I had renounced the South, I could not lose the ties to my immediate family. But I did lose touch with the kinfolks at Clear Springs. I saw them only infrequently. Over the years, Grand-daddy's sisters and brothers all died off, almost without my knowing it. I forgot about his sisters—Little Daisy, whose high-pitched voice was always cheerful, and Dove, whose strong jaw and husky voice startled me as a child. And Granny's ancient aunt Etna, whose mile-high, featherlight angel food cakes were renowned in Clear Springs. Years later, at my parents' fiftieth anniversary, Daddy's cousin Herman accused me of "going off," as if it were a sin to leave. "You forgot your kinfolks," he said. I realized it was true. I didn't think of them when I was away. I was free to adventure, while my loyal parents kept a place for me. I was loyal to them too, even though I was too busy to inquire into farm prices or Granny's nerves or Mama's burdens. I was devouring Homer and Virgil and Chaucer and Shakespeare. The sweep of Western literature offered pleasing abstractions—such as the journey theme and the quest-for-the-father theme. Was Telemachus looking for his father as much as he was looking for an idea of his father?

In Binghamton, New York, in a small apartment with pink walls, I listened to Motown and the Beatles on a late-night Boston station and wrote papers on Milton's *Paradise Lost* and Yeats's Fergus poems. To earn extra cash, I typed term papers. I bought my first car, a 1952 Chevrolet.

Working on a fan magazine had hardly prepared me for the rigors of postgraduate education. The English department had sent me a reading list of books I should know before arriving. There would be no exam, just an expectation of mastery. The list was a daunting array of over a hundred books, ranging through Western civilization. *The Decameron, Humphrey Clinker, Tristan and Isolde,* Augustine's *Confessions.* Previously, I had read a handful of books from the nineteenth century, but hardly anything farther back in time. Earnestly, I labored over the list as if I were laying up a woodpile for the winter. I was stranded at a small, isolated institution in the snow belt. The snow was deep, engulfing, like my innocence.

At Harpur College, my professors—all very large men—were tweedy impresarios. Professor Bernard Huppé spun his students through the dim beginnings and dark ages of England. Being in his class was like drifting past dioramas in a museum: Beowulf fighting Grendel; the wars of the Angles and the Saxons against the Danes; sassy pilgrims on donkeys hightailing it to Canterbury. Professor Huppé, whose white forelock bounced along with his enthusiasms, guided us on our journey through the history of the English language with joy in his heart. Professor Seymour Pitcher spent a trimester toiling over his translation of Aristotle's *Poetics* with us. "Was this word a happy choice?" he inquired. The exact word for what is usually translated as "catharsis" troubled him throughout the term. What was a catharsis anyway, I wondered. Does art make us feel blown out and purified, as from a purgative? Or is it intended to have a calming effect, like that of cows chewing cud in a more complex digestive process?

I wasn't ready for the elusive and false trails of advanced learning. From the depths of the roaring river of illusions and prismatic images of literature, I was expected to gig a metaphorical frog, color it, name it, and defend it—all out loud, with a Northern accent. There was no joy in that challenge, in that realm of territorial skirmishes—scholars clashing on a darkling plain. I loved books, but I didn't want to argue about them. Instead of embracing what they read, other graduate students, in their competitiveness, rejected. They would say "Fitzgerald's vision was limited by his status consciousness" or "Nabokov's introverted style prevented him from being universal." How could a novice blithely quibble with greatness? How could anyone even hint at superiority to those supreme artists? I balked. There seemed no room for genuine admiration in this new game. Bob Hazel had revered the great writers; he invited his students for strolls through the pantheon. I began to see what he had meant about academic study. It was adversarial. It assumed no heroes. The pressure to speak up made me feel, not for the first time in my life, that the cat not only had my tongue but had eaten it. Everybody was smarter than I was! I was sure this was so, since I couldn't think of what to say. I had had no practice in debate and discussion. Other students spewed out opinions, stating positions in the time it took for me to say, "Huh?" I felt soft-headed, like those tiny soft-shelled eggs that hens sometimes laid by mistake. There I was, in the North—disoriented, out of my element, but determined to plow through.

From the South I brought an ingrained sense of shame. The mannerisms came with me—the disingenuous smile and "the down look," the lowered eyes of self-effacement. My overconfident self, forged on the farm and at Cuba School, shattered in that Northern intellectual climate. I was invisible, voiceless, stupefied by my naïveté. All around me were Yankees, the foreigners of the Little Colonel books. If they noticed me at all, they gazed at me penetratingly, pinning me on the spot as if I were a specimen of bug. My accent betrayed me.

Worst of all, I was expected to teach. I was a teaching assistant, assigned to conduct a freshman survey of Western literature from Homer on up. In sweet little wool suits and breakneck heels, I faced a classroom of fiercely bright kids from New York City. Some of them were only sixteen or so; they had skipped grades. They dressed sloppily, they wore long hair in the Medusa mop-top style, and they were glib and serious. I had had no teacher training, but suddenly I was supposed to be a guide to the great books of Western civilization. My students zigzagged around me like the Jets from *West Side Story* as I stumbled and bumbled in incomplete sentences, trying to recall my diligently prepared notes.

The professor I assisted tried to share his passion for the Greeks with me, so that I could stimulate this sharp gang of valedictorians.

"I read Plato's *Republic* to my wife on our honeymoon," he said. "There are parts of it that are so beautiful."

I couldn't *imagine* reading Plato on a honeymoon. I couldn't think of what to say to the professor. I studied *The Republic* assiduously. Plato said throw out the poets. He said nothing—a table, a refrigerator—was real, but it had an ideal form somewhere. I pictured the ideals in orbit, like Sputnik.

I had the wrong gear for this venture. I was like one of those catfish that can sort of walk on land—awkwardly, using their whiskers like elbows. Previously, I had floated from one enthusiasm to another, and I had often been in charge, with the illusion of power. Now I felt like Granny in Hopkinsville, or Daddy in the Pacific. I was in alien territory and there was a war on. But I persevered, while trying to lose my accent.

After the dramatic snow season, I expected daffodils and forsythia. Nothing happened. The days continued cold and gray. I yearned for the long, languorous springtime of Kentucky. I craved the mellow air that seemed to caress every pore. I wanted tulips and redbud and dogwood blossoms.

Except for my frivolous year in New York City, I spent the decade of the sixties in school. I didn't know what to do except to continue my plodding pilgrimage toward a teaching career. But graduate study at Harpur College was monastic, and I had little awareness of what was going on in the world beyond those wooded mountain ridges along Route 17. I was getting restless, worried that I faced a lonely future teaching at some junior college. I wanted some action—or at least a boyfriend. So I transferred to the University of Connecticut, a much larger school with less intellectual pretension and more mating possibilities.

But in Connecticut, I found myself wading into a maelstrom. Everything—even the worth of literary study—was in question. The growing youth rebellion against middle-class values gathered me up and whipped me around like a wind ripping into sheets on the clothesline. I had aspired my whole life toward such amenities as central heat and running hot water, and suddenly they were the wrong goals. The new goals included living in a yurt or a dome, dressing in ragbag fashion, randomly coupling, and just plain grooving. The Vietnam War twisted everything around. The prized became trivial, and the ordinary became exalted. The war itself seemed distant to me. I didn't know a soul in it, and I still had no TV. I listened to rock-and-roll on WBZ and subscribed to *Newsweek* and *Life*. The images of mud-spattered, grungy G.I.s with their M16s, dazed or lying dead in a jungle, seemed unreal. Yet those soldiers were the same age as my freshman students, the same age as all of the vociferous, long-haired students around me. These kids looked dazed, too.

But not all of the shooting was overseas. Images of racial violence and bigotry flooded the newsmagazines—ugly scenes of beatings and murders, especially in my homeland. More than ever, I felt ashamed of being from the South. I feared that when people saw me, they imagined a walking, mute mannequin of Southern Gothic horror in high heels and a beehive—or worse, a baton twirler with a police dog. I was afraid my teachers and colleagues thought of hillbillies eating Moon Pies and swigging moonshine on the way home from a lynching. I remembered one of Daddy's cousins talking once about the significance of the date August 8. "That was the day Abe let the niggers go," he said, as if he actually remembered the emancipation. I didn't want to be Southern anymore. But my metamorphosis wasn't forthcoming. I was caught in a paralyzing culture shock.

It was stopping up my mind. I couldn't think. I questioned my intelligence, my sanity, my identity. I believed wholeheartedly in my own inferiority, and people treated me accordingly, like a wadded-up dishrag. A few defining episodes stick out among memories I'd like to banish.

I became involved with a fellow graduate student I'll call Larry. He was one of those guys whose soul was too sensitive for the Army to make use of him. He was an artist, passionate about what was tasteful and genuine. When he scoffed at the curtains I'd bought at a discount place, I saw instantly, through his eyes, that they were inauthentic, like something in Lucy Ricardo's kitchen. The design was tasteless, the colors too loud.

"I want to show you my quilt," I said to him a few days later, when he came over to my hopelessly bourgeois apartment for coffee. I brought out the star quilt I had helped Granny make when I was a child. It was supposed to be my marriage quilt, but she had given it to me when I left for college, perhaps to celebrate the opportunity for education that she had not had for herself. I had washed the quilt until the edges were frayed. I laid it across my bed. I wanted to impress Larry because he seemed to like things that were lovingly crafted. (He threw pots on a wheel.) But instead he was taken aback by this simple creation with its five-point stars, pieced from the print dresses I had worn as a child.

What Larry said was "Ugly!"

"My grandmother made it," I said in a faltering voice. Of course I could see, now that he mentioned it, how crude and primitive it was. Granny hadn't been to art school. I had so much to learn.

There was another contretemps with Larry. I made supper for him. In a new casserole dish I had obtained with Green Stamps, I baked chicken thighs and sliced potatoes in mushroom soup. My cooking was part imitation and part intuition. After we finished eating, Larry lifted the empty dish and walked around with it, talking about how he would have made the dish differently on his pottery wheel. We stood on a little balcony that extended outside my kitchen door, looking onto a lawn in front of birch trees. Larry held the dish out over the balcony railing as if he were trying to consider it as part of the landscape.

"I wonder what would happen if I dropped this dish," he said in a contemplative voice. He was regarding the dish, turning it, judging it. Clearly, he disapproved of it.

"Why would you drop it?"

The dish fell from his hand, as if it had dived of its own accord. I watched in disbelief as it cracked on the concrete patio below.

"The dish won," he said with a little blurt of laughter.

I was confused and hurt, but I didn't show it.

"That's all right," I said. I dismissed Larry's act, feeling I deserved to have such an inferior dish broken, even though it was hard-earned and very useful. But Larry was testing me, cruelly and deliberately. I realized later that I was supposed to get angry, show some fire. I was supposed to be real, authentic. But Southern girls aren't taught to be real. I had learned modesty and submissiveness, the veneer of my rebellious streak.

None of that was clear to me at the time. I grew ever more withdrawn and hesitant, fearful of saying the wrong thing. I learned, to my distress, that what was expected of me now was precisely the opposite of what I was equipped to do. Instead of expecting me to conform and please, people here expected me to be myself. But what was that? I seemed to have lost sight of who I was; I was only a vague presence. I felt I was judged for being a Southerner and then judged all over again for trying not to be a Southerner. Where did that leave me?

Then, at a particularly low point in my desperate postgraduate career, somewhere in the middle of American Romanticism 469, John and his girlfriend Carolyn appeared unexpectedly at the door of my apartment. I had attended a few gatherings at their apartment for anti-war discussions, and I admired them exceedingly. They were a striking couple, both lean and intense, with passionate ideas and appropriate hair. I especially loved Carolyn's long, straight sheet of blond tresses that trailed nearly to her waist. I had gotten a Beatle haircut just before it became apparent that I should grow my hair long. I knew Carolyn had been sleeping with an undergraduate, but this fact did not seem to matter to anyone, even John.

John and Carolyn marched onto my hooked rug in their snowy Army surplus boots and came straight to the point. John said, "We've decided we can't be friends with you anymore because we don't think there is anything underneath the surface. You don't reveal yourself. We feel you're playing games with us."

That was what Larry had said when he told me we shouldn't see each other anymore. The same wording. "There's no tension with you," he had said. "You always try to agree with me."

Grasping for something tangible, I petted my cat Blackie while John went on. "And so we don't know where we are with you. We thought this could be a productive friendship, but we're not getting much out of it."

"You don't assert yourself," Carolyn said, casting a disdainful eye around my nondescript apartment. "You don't take a stand on anything."

"It's a matter of honesty," John said.

"You're just not being honest with us," Carolyn said.

I didn't throw them out of my apartment. I nodded. What they said was true: I didn't speak up for myself. Inside, I couldn't even find myself anymore. Mumbling, I tried to explain how Southerners expressed themselves differently, but John and Carolyn were impatient with my mealymouthed defensiveness. Most of my real explanations came later, silently, in lucid afterthoughts. It struck me then that Southern behavior was devious, depending on indirection, a fuzzy flirtation that relied on strategic hinting. But it didn't occur to me to wonder how I could let John and Carolyn form such a solid wall against me when they weren't even faithful to each other. I admired their self-possession and style too much to question their motive for attacking me. At the time, I didn't know they were both seeing psychiatrists and that their smug union would soon shatter.

This rejection, on the heels of Larry's rebuff, threw me into despair.

Meanwhile, at home, my mother wrote me about the garden and the weather and broken machinery. She wrote, "You told about reading about that guy that built a cabin at a pond. Well, he didn't have to raise a family and so he had time to write down things he saw. He had an education, so he should have been able to get somewhere. And you wrote in your letter about the environment, but don't forget you can't solve the whole world's problems."

Mama coped. She dealt with what was handed her. Yet I didn't realize that I was behaving just like her. In my own style, I was subservient, bowing to authority. Yankee culture sat on me like the rocks Mama set on the lid of a pickle crock to hold the pickles down in the brine.

Still, I paddled bravely along in an uncertain current. I talked to a psychologist in West Hartford a few times. He said, "Don't you feel somewhat disoriented, being so far from home?"

"Oh, no, not at all," I insisted. I believed I was meant to be in New England, in Carolyn and John's sophisticated world. I couldn't live in the South, where so much ignorance and prejudice persisted. I thought he was suggesting I should go back home.

But when I told him about Carolyn and John, his response worked like a brain corrective, like electroshock.

"They sound shallow," he said. "Why would you let them treat you that way?"

That was a revelation. I felt as if he'd given me a happy pill.

I was afraid of drugs, but the psychedelic revolution—mainly through music—was transforming everything around me, fracturing objects and ideas like a light show at a concert. The bizarre juxtapositions, loss of context, and random acts of hallucinogenic vision seemed familiar—that was my life. Rock-and-roll musicians were leading the way. Once again, as it had when I was a teenager, music grabbed me and shook me up with a vision of truth. Perceptions were shifting, precisely what I needed. I had to unlearn "supposed to" and "should ought to"—all fatalistic agricultural imperatives. Instead of making hay while the sun was shining, I had to see the sunshine. I needed to see as a child again. It became important to stop and gaze at a toad-frog as if it were the first one on the planet. A flower petal restored childhood's magic; the infinitely reverberating sound of a sitar had an undertone of shifting colors, with the smell of patchouli; the spidery veins of glazed ceramics mapped inner landscapes. One night in my apartment some friends and I hopefully baked some banana peels and smoked them, taking our instructions from Donovan's "Mellow Yellow."

The counterculture saved me. I wasn't really capable of sustained despair anyway. The world was too interesting, and I hadn't truly lost my naive enthusiasm. I had already done things my grandparents could not have imagined. I had bought a Volkswagen at the factory in Wolfsburg, Germany, and driven it throughout Europe; I had joined a peace march in New York; I had seen the Beatles at Shea Stadium (both times, 1965 and 1966). Now I was ready to let loose. I remembered Granddaddy's advice: "Don't be contrary." But I always was. I plunged into the trappings of the revolution with the same industriousness I'd applied to puzzles and studies.

I painted my old gray Zenith radio bright orange. The next day the Rolling Stones were singing "Paint It Black," so I painted it black. I made clothes from cotton Indian bedspreads. I wore beads, bellbottoms, sandals, the works. I bought the regulation paraphernalia (paper flowers, Indian cowbells, buffalo-hide sandals) from Azuma on Eighth Street in the Village. In the summer of 1967, the sounds of *Sgt. Pepper's Lonely Hearts Club Band* followed me everywhere I went. In Toronto, where I visited friends from Binghamton, the sounds and symbols of peace were spilling over the streets of the Yorkville area.

The language of the period was seductive. Go with the flow; be here now; do your own thing; it's your bag—concentric circles spreading from a pebble in a pond, washing away time and money and respectability and status. I didn't need money, didn't need television, didn't need a washer and dryer. Who needed television when we had Bob Dylan? My Toronto friends and I pored over the collage of icons gathered at a mock funeral on the cover of the Beatles album. We cut out magazine pictures and pieced our own collages. If we paid too much attention to surface details, it was because they were shared symbols of our inner story. That summer I was thrilled to be liberated at last from pseudo-Chanel suits and high heels. In bluejeans, the garb of country people, I had come back to myself.

I hadn't been home for an entire year. At the end of 1967, when I arrived for Christmas, I saw immediately how much my mother had aged. She was only forty-eight, but her face had begun to sag and her hair was turning gray. I noticed her tight, grim expression whenever Granny interfered in the kitchen. Mama dashed outside with her cigarettes at every opportunity. She didn't want Granny to know she smoked, but the telltale aroma swished throughout the house.

Don still slept—and had nightmares—in the chilly foyer, and I shared LaNelle's bed in the north room. LaNelle, who was by then in high school, was going steady with a boy Daddy disapproved of. I was afraid she would try to escape from that cramped household by leaping into an early marriage. She was worried too, but not about that. She told me she was afraid that if the war kept on, Don would have to go. Although he was only a child, Don would be of age in a few years. "The boys ahead of me are getting drafted right after graduation," LaNelle said. "Unless they go to college." She didn't say whether she was worried that her boyfriend might be sent to Vietnam.

Daddy sat quietly in his easy chair as the reports from Vietnam were broadcast on the network news. He would not speak of his own fears. When some antiwar activists came on the screen, he said, "They ought to round up all them protesters and put 'em to work. Make 'em shuck corn." He laughed. I did not want to argue with him about the war. Mama, hurried along by her own immediate duties, seemed to pay no attention to the war news.

Shortly after Christmas, Mama came home from a doctor's appointment. She entered the kitchen. It was almost dark. She shoved groceries onto the table and stood motionless. She didn't remove her coat. I laid down my book and turned on the kitchen light. I could see the alarm in her face.

"He got the results of my test," she said. "It's cancer."

Her news plunged through me like a heavy stone. I could not believe it. I could not lose my mother—that was absolute. When I was a child, I wasn't afraid my parents would die, because it seemed impossible. Now I didn't know how to tell her my feelings. I tried to say something reassuring, but my heart was pounding, and I thought she could hear it when we hugged.

"They say worry brings on cancer," Mama told me glumly. She fumbled for her cigarettes in her pocketbook and slipped outside again into the coming dusk.

For the first time in his life, Daddy had to borrow some money. Mama had to have an expensive operation, a hysterectomy. She came through it well, except that her smoker's cough jiggled her stitches painfully. After a week, with Mama still in the hospital, I had to return to school. Daddy drove me to the Greyhound bus station at midnight. We waited for the bus in his truck, with the heater on, and talked about how we could not go on without Mama. "I don't know what I'd do," he said.

LaNelle and Don, left in Granny's care while Mama was recovering, were hungry. "We were just kids," LaNelle told me recently. "We were used to cramming junk food, but Granny begrudged every bite. She tried to cook for us, and it would be a little dab of this and a little dab of that, and if we tried to eat leftovers, she'd say, 'No, save that for supper.' "

After her surgery, Mama was supposed to rest for two months and not exert herself for a year, but the household was helpless without her. "Everybody stood around and gawked at me," she said later. "That made me so mad!" Within a few days she was up, cooking chicken-and-dumplings and fried pies and improvising a peach double-knit pantsuit for a woman who exceeded the extra-large pattern.

Late that summer, I traveled home on the bus. It was a miserable thirty-six-hour journey. I took Dramamine so I could sleep. As the bus neared the Jackson Purchase, it stopped in Hopkinsville, and a dozen soldiers—just boys—boarded. They were in their working uniforms, carrying duffels. I stared at them. I was used to seeing long hair, but these guys were like plucked chickens. They wore dusky green, their pants ballooning above their combat boots. I would not have been surprised to see M16 rifles, but they had none. I tried to concentrate on the book I was reading for my modern poetry class.

A boy threw his duffel bag overhead and sat down beside me. "Hey," he said.

"Hey." I averted my eyes.

"You go to college?" His voice was deep Southern. I saw that his eyes were light blue.

"Yes." I clutched my book.

"I thought you did 'cause that looks like poetry and don't nobody read poetry unless they have to—that is, except me."

"Oh, do you like poetry?" I asked, surprised.

"I like poems. I write a poem now and then, just to express myself, you know? Everybody laughs at me, but I just keep on. I like to do it. I don't care what they say. Do you write poetry?"

"No. I'm not very good at that. I like to write, though."

"Well, you could write me a letter, then. I bet you're good at writing letters."

He grabbed my book of poetry and saw the poet I was reading. He said, "T. S. Eliot—never heard of him."

"Backwards, it's 'toilets'—almost, anyway."

He grinned but seemed embarrassed, and I remembered that in the South "toilet" is a dirty word. I was self-conscious about my peace-and-love duds, which suddenly seemed as much a uniform as what he was wearing. My hair was long and straight, and bell-bottoms shrouded my ankles. Hadn't Daddy worn bell-bottoms in his war?

"Did you get drafted?" I asked.

"Yeah. But I said I'll go and get it over with."

"Then what?"

"I'll go in business with my brother, I reckon. He's running a gas station back home—Jackson, Mississippi."

"Where are y'all going?" I asked, indicating the group of soldiers.

"We're shipping out tomorrow morning," he said without emotion. "Vietnam."

I didn't know what to say. It was hard enough for me to grasp the magnitude of the war when I heard about it on the radio or saw pictures in magazines. But now, for me, the war came down to this—this breathing, actual boy, who liked to write poems. My main thought: he could *die*. Was that his main thought too, or was he eager to go over there? He didn't seem like a warrior. Why hadn't he gone to school instead? Why were some boys in school and some in the war? I squirmed. It seemed worse to send a boy who liked poetry. But what did that mean? That he was too special to die?

The soldiers got off at Fort Campbell. As the boy next to me gathered his gear, I began to cry, but I forced back my tears and said goodbye to him—faintly. He was my only tangible link with the Vietnam War. I couldn't bear his innocence. Indeed, I couldn't bear to imagine my innocent little brother in just a few years in that same uniform going to that same place. I wished I'd gotten the soldier's name. I should have said I'd write to him.

And then I was home for a week. Mama looked healthy and rosy, and she was working as hard as ever. One evening while she was cooking supper, Daddy and I sat watching police clubbing demonstrators at the Democratic National Convention in Chicago. The war protesters were screaming, and reporters were hustling. Daddy cheered for the police, who were handcuffing the demonstrators, mostly students, and tossing them into paddy wagons. "There's another one dragged off," he said, as if he were keeping score.

"You don't really mean that," I said. "*I'm* a student. That could be me." But I didn't quarrel with him. I was frightened by what I was seeing on TV. The world seemed to be separating into two camps, and somehow I belonged to both. I didn't want to believe my father was serious; he liked to be contrary.

"If those protesters had done that in Russia, they'd have been shot by sundown," he said.

"I thought Americans didn't approve of Soviet tactics," I said.

He grinned.

"I caught you in a contradiction, didn't I?" I said. He grinned, and I relaxed.

Mama said, "Y'all come on in here and eat before this grub gets cold."

Granny had eaten early and had gone to bed. She still went to bed at dark and never watched TV. After supper, we crowded into the living room–bedroom to watch the convention, but Mama hunched down over her sewing machine. She was making a pleated dust ruffle for one of her customers.

When I returned to Connecticut, I thought about that soldier I had met, and from time to time I wondered what happened to him over there in the jungle. My mind turned, like Daddy's tractor flipping clods in the fields in the spring. With the plow hitched behind the tractor, he broke the ground first, then disked it. Then he pulled a harrow over the ground to break up the clods and smooth the dirt. My thoughts swiveled. I began to write a novel. It was a story about the Beatles, in experimental, psychedelic, Donald Barthelme–inspired prose. A VW busload of hippies travel cross-country from California to see the Beatles at Shea Stadium. It was Jack Kerouac in reverse, through a mirror fractured by sound. Actually, it was sillier than that. But I was hopeful.

Finally, I met someone who felt so much as I did that we recognized each other as kindred spirits. He was a loner, too. I was a Southern girl trying to get over my culture; he was a Northern middle-class boy trying to get over his. He wore plaid flannel lumberjack shirts and jeans and plow shoes—like one of the Future Farmers of America at Cuba School. In the past, I would have been embarrassed to be seen with a guy dressed like that. But now I was changing.

I was conditioned to expect rejection. But Roger, the guy I fell in love with, didn't berate me for being Southern, or being coy, or playing games, or having cockeyed ambitions. Roger wasn't truly a Yankee. He had midwestern roots. Also, he was funny and could sing. "I could have been a Beatle," he'd say playfully. He brought me tulips on our first date. He had picked them from the university president's yard. We went to see *Finnegans Wake*. Roger drove an old light-blue Rambler with rust spots. One day he painted it a peculiar bright forest green, using an old paintbrush and a can of paint he happened to have on hand. The brush strokes gave the job an interesting oil-painting texture. Within the next few months, we spotted nine haphazardly painted vehicles in the area, all that same odd shade of green.

We married in Connecticut. It didn't occur to me that going to Kentucky for the wedding might be important. I had never been to a wedding in my life and was familiar with the trappings only in the movies and on the society page of the *Mayfield Messenger*. (Writing the social notes was one of my summer jobs during college.) Daddy planned to send Mama and LaNelle. "But I'll have to put them on different airplanes," he told me on the telephone. "If there's a crash, I don't want to lose both of them at once."

In the end, they decided that the trip would be extravagant, but Roger's family came from Long Island. They expected a real wedding, so—since they were Lutherans—we enlisted a Lutheran church. The minister chain-smoked. His name was Eddie Fisher. We had a breezy chat with him in his office about commitment. I went to a florist to order a bridal bouquet but was appalled that it cost twenty-five dollars, so on the morning of the wedding I bought a bunch of Shasta daisies for two dollars and fifty cents. I wound a rubber band around them and carried them with the wet stems exposed. I wore a short, white, leather-bodiced dress that I had bought on Carnaby Street in "swinging London" in 1966. A photographer friend created some arty photos, with my face overlapping Roger's, and the ring on my hand overlaying our faces. The ring was enamel, with painted flowers on it. Eddie Fisher, in a white robe like the choir robe I wore at Calvary Methodist as a child, read the service we had written and then a James Joyce poem we liked; we skipped music because we couldn't pay for the church organist.

My grandmother had begun her household with fine things she had tatted and embroidered and pieced as a girl and young woman. My mother had had nothing when she and Daddy eloped. I didn't have much except books, records, a few Corning Ware dishes (minus a casserole dish), a stereo, my black radio, and a blue electric typewriter. Roger owned a hand-painted car, a reel-to-reel tape recorder, and a TV.

We rented an old New England farmhouse with a warren of small spare rooms upstairs that we painted all colors. We played Scrabble and listened to the Beatles and Dylan and the Doors. We accumulated cats. We sat reading in front of the stone fireplace, which had, improbably, a heart-shaped stone above the mantel. We had no expectations of china, silver, or kitchen gadgets. Mama sent us a double-wedding-ring quilt she had made, and I was pleased when Roger admired it. From a salvage shop, we bought beautiful etched champagne glasses for twenty-five cents apiece; we bought nineteenth-century photographs and daguerreotypes for pennies. Driving past a fraternity house, Roger found a discarded, blue-painted plywood STOP sign. He put legs on it and created an octagonal coffee table. He fashioned a desk—legs on a door; and he made a dining table—legs on plywood. I made curtains of dark corduroy, which the sun soon faded. We hung whimsical mobiles we constructed from art paper. We painted, and I sewed and crocheted.

"Well, you're finally grown up," Mama observed. "Now that you've taken an interest in sewing." We decorated our clothes with Magic Markers.

"I heard Bobbie married a hippie," Cousin Datha told Daddy.

Daddy bristled and told her off, although in truth he had no idea whether Datha was right, since he hadn't yet met Roger. His greatest worry about hippies was that they wouldn't work. But actually we were both full of energy. Through Roger, I discovered coffee. With the coffee and a new blitz of confidence, I finished my degree—the logical conclusion of my graduate days. I had made it to the arbitrary goal I had set for myself. A while later, my thesis was published.

All around us, young people were discovering land, gardens, organic methods. We read *Walden* and *The Whole Earth Catalog*. We were on the cusp of the back-to-nature movement, the natural look, the real thing. I was ready to hoe. Roger didn't know a shelly bean from a marigold, but ambitiously we launched into growing a garden. We bought a radio to scare raccoons from the corn. In late summer, when the corn grew ears, a loud argument woke us up in the middle of the night. A man and woman were yelling at each other about Woodstock. It was the radio, a talk show blasting out in the wee hours.

By hand, we broke sod for our garden. When I plunged my hands into the black New England soil, I felt I was touching a rich nourishment that I hadn't had since I was a small child. It had been years since I helped Mama in the garden. Yet the feel of dirt seemed so familiar. This was real. It was true. I wheeled around and faced home.

16

Toward the end of the sixties, LaNelle, unhappy over Mama's servitude in Granny's house, told Mama, "I'm taking Don and we're moving back down to our house." The house was empty, the most recent renters gone.

Startled by LaNelle's determination, Mama agreed to move back with LaNelle and Don. She needed that push, and her own home, standing forlorn and unoccupied in the woods, must have beckoned to her. In deciding, Mama stood up to Daddy for once: she forced him to choose between her and his mother.

Of course, he agreed to the move. He fixed the roof, while Mama repapered the walls and repainted the woodwork. But I know Daddy was torn, because he had promised his father not to leave his mother alone at night. He had to honor that promise somehow. Consequently, throughout the seventies, while Granny lived alone, Daddy went to her house after supper. She went to bed at dark, while he stayed up and watched TV. He slept on a narrow bed in the dining room. Mama and LaNelle and Don slept in their own beds in the little white house.

The arrangement was anguish for both my parents. But they felt they had no choice. It was unthinkable to put Granny in a nursing home. It was unthinkable to fail to care for her. And it was unthinkable to flout the kinfolks. Tongues would wag if Mama and Daddy neglected Granny. But no one would say a thing if Mama were left virtually alone, her marriage divided. Duty to elders was primary; a wife's wishes were secondary. And Mama would not have thought of divorce or separation or striking out on her own, starting some career. My parents were prisoners of an old order.

Although I was increasingly aware that Granny was a burden on

Mama, my devotion to my grandmother persisted; I always loved her. Every time I came home, I banged at the screen door of her back porch until she came to unhook the door. In cold weather the metal hook rattled its familiar song against the plastic sheeting tacked to the doorframe. She was proud to see me, her gentle smile welcoming. We sat close to the stream of air flowing from the gas furnace through a large floor grate in the dining room. Visiting was always awkward, as we slipped around on a veneer of small talk, like the slim notations in her old diary. There wasn't much to say. She was concerned about where Wilburn was at any given hour. "What's Chris a-doing?" "Has the mail gone on?" She wanted to know what work was being done, what needed to be done now, what could wait.

When LaNelle announced that she was moving back home, Mama acquiesced in part because I was bringing home my Yankee husband, and there was no place for us to sleep in Granny's house. Besides, she surely felt shame at the awkwardness of the family's arrangement, especially because Roger was from New York. People in Kentucky had an inflated image of New York folks. If someone from New York was expected to visit, it might be necessary to wallpaper the living room, paint the house, or blacktop the driveway.

One day during Roger's first visit, Granny made a special dinner for us. She was still nursing her grief over Granddaddy's death. She undoubtedly felt abandoned when the others moved out, but she may also have felt the relief of masterminding her own house again. She was still able to cook and keep house and work in her garden. She had a few chickens.

That particular day, she welcomed us warmly into her kitchen. From her dish cabinet, she brought out her good dishes, including her better bowls—the china floral ovals with scalloped rims. Carefully, she laid them on a muslin tablecloth with a tatted edging.

"I was always proud of this set of dishes," she said, caressing a white, gold-bordered plate. "I always thought they were fine."

She had fried a spring chicken and made biscuits with milk gravy. She gave us English peas with little new potatoes, and she also served white field peas, which I preferred to the brown varieties. She had Waldorf salad with apples, walnuts, celery, and minimarshmallows. She chopped the ingredients very fine; her salads were always as richly textured as her embroidered dresser scarves. Dessert was damson pie. I was aware that I still hadn't really learned to cook and wouldn't have the patience to chop anything into such tiny bits. But I was starting to see more value in her ways, I thought, as the kaleidoscope twisted another turn, bringing the past into a new configuration.

Daddy was outside mowing. He mowed and manicured the place incessantly, even though his lungs suffered from the pollens and molds the mower stirred up. "I don't want anybody driving past to think trash lives here," he always said. His enemies were precisely the shiftless, impoverished ne'er-do-wells that he feared Roger had expected. Daddy was fighting against anyone ever getting the impression that such low-lifes lived here. He collected the trash discarded from speeding automobiles, and he trimmed borders with his Weed Eater.

"Tell Roger what it was like when you were growing up," I urged Granny.

"Tell us what kind of school you went to, Mrs. Mason," Roger said encouragingly.

Granny was bashful with Roger. "He won't find it that interesting," she said, looking at me.

But at my insistence, she brought out her old speller, her Bible, and her arithmetic book. The pages smelled musty, like the old books at the Merit Clubhouse library. The bent-backed Cornell speller contained recitations. As I turned the pages, which were falling loose from the binding, I realized that the old method of memorization was based on sensitivity to sound, groupings of similar-sounding words: blunderbuss, incubus, nucleus; ulcer, cancer; suffer, pilfer. And the sentences seemed like quaint poems:

The farmer hatchels flax; he sells corn by the bushel, and butter by the firkin.
The farmer fodders his cattle in winter.

I wondered about hatcheling and foddering with firkins.

Roger told Granny about our garden in Connecticut. "We have a radio to scare away the raccoons."

Granny laughed at that. "Do tell! I never heard of anybody playing the radio for coons!"

"They like the late-night blues shows best," Roger joked.

I told Granny I'd been reading nature books. "They got me to thinking how I missed the garden and the fields and the cows," I said.

"We have neighbors who are organic gardeners," Roger said. "They've helped us out some."

Granny removed the bowls from the table. She set her enamel dish-pan on the gas stove to heat water. Alternate ways were of no interest to her. There was only one way to hill up beans, to set a hen, to make damson pie.

Later that year, Mama came to Connecticut to visit us. For the first time, she traveled on an airplane, ate cheese fondue, drank some wine, and went fishing out of state. While Roger and I were busy teaching freshman English classes, she upholstered our old chairs and made me a corduroy military-style coat with epaulets. She wasn't used to taking a vacation, and she claimed she didn't sleep for the entire two weeks she was with us. The strain of the four years at Granny's house had wrung her out. She couldn't relax.

"But you're living in your own house now," I said. "You've got it fixed up again."

"I don't know how I'm going to make it," she said.

She was only fifty years old, but she spoke wearily, with resigna-tion. She said, "I don't have but ten, or maybe twenty, years left." She cried, and at first I thought she was crying because she believed her life was nearly over, which hardly seemed credible, but then I realized how troubled she was. She saw her life being extinguished, her identity faded out like the pale moon in the evening. She was in the prime of her life, but it was being taken from her. Her own husband left her at night to stay with his mother. I talked Mama into extending her visit another week, thinking more time away would do her good. I was happy, a newlywed, and I was optimistic. Mama had always been strong, and I could not imagine her any other way, despite the strain in her face. When a friend remarked to me that my mother was the same age as his mother but looked much older, I bridled. My mother had al-ways been young and beautiful, and to me she still was.

After Mama had gone back home, I tried to put her tears out of mind. Her letters brought the comforting familiarity of home, with nothing really surprising—just a steady coping that seemed timeless. She wrote that she was making a George Washington suit for a little boy, and that there was a man-eating catfish at Kentucky Dam. But she also wrote, "Wilburn hasn't been fishing in eight years. He thought one of us should stay around here with Granny." She wrote that he might have to quit selling milk—the smaller milk companies were going out of business. She wrote that it was getting dangerous to stay in the house in the woods without Daddy there. And she sent me instructions for making blackberry pie.

Again and again, throughout the seventies, as Granny grew feeble and inactive, I tried to get her to tell me about her early life. She had so much hidden knowledge. I wanted to know where we came from, who we were, and why. I wanted to penetrate her mind. Why had she had those breakdowns? Wasn't my mind a lot like hers? I pleaded with her to tell me about her youth. Could she have ever been young and sexual? I wondered. I didn't always know the right questions to ask her. I probed and teased, assaulting her with my queries.

"There's not much to tell," she would say. She seemed to have no belief in the uniqueness or worthiness of what she harbored. Her mind was balled up like yarn. Her silences were extraordinary, as she sat in her rocking chair with her head down, brooding. I had no gift for drawing her out, but I plunged ahead insistently. What was Clear Springs like when you were little? What were your parents like? What games did you play?

She told me that she and her sister, Maud, made little houses in the woods, out of sticks, with roofs of bark and moss. "We'd use acorns for cups and leaves for tablecloths," she said. "We'd lay moss all around. And feathers."

I was enchanted. Later, I heard someone call such playhouses "fairy shelters." I begged her to show me her family photographs—an album and some loose pictures in a box.

"Can I write their names on the back?" I asked as she began identifying the people for me.

"But I know who they are."

She didn't notice me jotting their names with a pencil.

"That's Floyd Arnett," she said, of one handsome young man.

"Who was he? What was he like?"

She thought for a minute. "He was a farmer." Her knobby fingers fumbled with the pictures. "Here's one of me when I'm about thirteen," she said.

In the photograph, she looks older than that. She seems ladylike, in a white blouse with simple frills, with her hair piled up. She looks innocent, hopeful, unaware of her attractiveness. She has an eager countenance, but also a dignified reserve. Her ears stick out a little.

One of her photographs shows Granddaddy sitting behind a pair of horses in a buggy, with his younger brother, Bee. Bob Mason is a handsome youth with dark hair and sharp, well-defined features. I'd say he is about to trot right into a rip-roaring Saturday night. He's holding the reins confidently. He and Bee are parked in front of a white house with an awning. In a later generation, he might have been a young stud at the wheel of a Mustang convertible.

But Granny would not divulge her feelings about this hunk with the buggy who courted her for thirteen years before she finally married him. I suspect that in her mind her sixty-three years with Bob—years when he changed from youthful suitor to aged invalid—were a complex swirl, with no separable phases. She and Bob still were those young people in the pictures.

She told me her mother was named Laura Rhodes, and she married an Arnett.

"Where did they come from?"

"North Carolina, I believe. Or Virginia, or somewhere over yonder." She pondered. My questions demanded a grasp of distant fog. "There were three Arnett brothers who came here—way back," she said, waving her hand at the past. "But one of them went on to Texas and wasn't heard of again."

"One of the brothers was my grandfather," she said. "My father was Zollicoffer Quigley Arnett." She pronounced the name with a smile. It was a mouthful. "He was named Zollicoffer for a general and Quigley after a lawyer. They called him 'Z.Q.' or 'Coff.' "

After more of my probing, she told me, "My grandfather was in the Confederate army. And his brother was in the Union army. But they got together at home and there was no hard feelings. The ladies in Paducah made quilts for the Union soldiers. And pies. And they brought all the quilts and pies in a wagon to where the boys were camped."

She chuckled softly, but these revelations exhausted her. She heaved a sigh, directing it back across time. How could I know what these people were like, with such slim clues? They sounded impossibly far away, but I liked the names. I said them over and over to myself. "Arnett." Pronounced *Arn*-it, the same way Southerners said "iron it." For weeks afterwards, during waking moments, the name "Zollicoffer Quigley Arnett" would spring out of my head like a jack-in-the-box.

My mother spent the prime years of her life in the service of her mother-in-law. From 1965 to 1981, as her health declined, Granny depended on Christy and Wilburn to take care of her. We children broke the rules. Recklessly and hopefully we grabbed at change as if it were a white sale at Penney's. We didn't stay around to help. Our flight was especially hard on my parents because the family was so small. My parents had no brothers and sisters, so I had no aunts and uncles, no first cousins ("own cousins"). Granny's kin, the few who were left, were out in Clear Springs.

I had wanted to return to Kentucky after graduate school, but Roger and I couldn't find teaching jobs there, so we settled in northern Pennsylvania, where he accepted a job teaching English at a small college. We bought an old farm and planted a garden and some fruit trees. I was in the snow belt again, near Binghamton, where spring refused to come. I began writing a novel, and I grew to love snow. I still went home to Kentucky twice a year, and I traveled other places too, but my mother, with the responsibility of caring for Granny as she grew more feeble, was tied to the family farm as surely as Daddy had always been by his cows. She didn't even go to church much. Toward the end of the seventies, after both Don and LaNelle married and left home, our parents once again abandoned their home and moved in with Granny. She had gotten too unsteady to stay alone. For some time Mama had been carrying her meals to her, after discovering she wasn't eating anything but cereal and fried toast. They moved in, halfheartedly, and once again they rented out their own house.

Mama's letters were troubling. She wrote about having to listen to both Granny and Daddy moaning "Oh, me" to get attention. "Wilburn's nerves are getting worse all the time. He use to set down by work—he was lazy. Now he has to keep on the move, just wears hisself out in a long run. He can't sleep. He's going to be just like Granny. She's just about got me drove up the wall and now I have him to deal with. My nerves are shot." Later, she wrote, "Granny won't get up out of her bed. I made her an angel food cake for her birthday. She just strings food on her bed. The health nurse was here and said the only thing wrong with Granny was her laying in bed and not taking any exercise. She quit trying to use herself. Why she quit—it hurt. She just lays in a ball, that way she don't hurt, that's the way old people does."

Granny's nerve medicine muddled her mind. She thought strangers were living in the north bedroom, the one my parents had occupied at the beginning of their marriage—the room where I was conceived, the room they returned to now. Granny kept asking questions about the couple in that room. She slept with her pocketbook under her pillow.

At times she didn't seem to realize she was in her own home, because my parents had made so many changes. They redecorated the house, putting up dark paneling and painting the woodwork brown. There had been a special on brown paint, and paneling was an easy fix for much-papered walls.

"I don't want the woodwork painted brown," Granny told her son. It had always been white, with lace curtains on the windows. Now the large, airy rooms became dark and claustrophobic. She said, "I never liked brown. I never even had a brown dress."

My father had always been forbearing with her, but he was getting more easily annoyed. He said harshly, "We're taking care of you, so we'll paint it any color we want to."

He had never stood up to her like that in his life, but by now he was overwhelmed by the sacrifices he and Mama had made for her. Abashed, Granny didn't persist. She told Mama, "He talked so awful to me."

Mama heard one of Granny's nieces say to her, "You better watch what you say, Aunt Ethel. Or they'll put you in a rest home."

Daddy teased his mother in a gruff way and reported their dialogues to me like jokes.

"Where's Chris?" Granny wanted to know.

Daddy replied, "She went to mess and the hogs eat her up."

"Did Bobbie go with her?" Granny asked.

Daddy had the freedom to get in the car and go to town, but Mama had little time to run around. She did all the cooking, washing, housekeeping, gardening, canning, and freezing. She supervised Granny's medicine and fixed her meals. Usually, Granny ate on a TV tray beside her bed. When I visited her, I couldn't bear to stay in the room while she ate because of the rattling of her ill-fitting false teeth. I would often stare at the raised blue veins in her hands, wondering if they were hard, like iron pipes.

Although she became bedridden, Granny had no severe medical problems. Apparently her heart was strong, in spite of hardening of the arteries. She had few visitors; most of her kinfolks were dead. Mama took her regularly to the local mental-health clinic, where doctors from Hopkinsville chatted with her and renewed her Thorazine prescription. They told her to get out more, go for rides. One of the doctors asked Mama, "How are *you* doing?"

Mama said, "I'm not the patient. *She's* the patient."

The doctor said, "And I asked you how *you* were doing."

Mama told me later, "He knew she'd drive me crazy."

Daddy had slowly been selling off his dairy herd as milk prices dropped. Mama wrote me, "Wilburn sold Pumpkin Seed. It like to have killed him. It's the first time since the Masons came here from Clear Springs that the farm didn't have cows on it. He was five when they moved here. He misses feeding her and packing water to her. I would be glad of that in the winter time. He went to an auction and bought fifty-one snuff boxes full of jewelry and a box of old odd shape glass bottles and jugs." Daddy took a new job, driving a bus for a work center for the mentally disabled—a job he enjoyed immensely. And Mama escaped now and then. She played Rook with a group of women much older than she, but she said she felt she was their age. She also went fishing whenever she could. This was still her favorite pastime; there was no pleasure quite like reeling in a fish, worrying and working a large one toward shore until it was weak enough to bring in. When she was fishing, she felt that her life was her own. She went fishing at the lake once with a woman whose husband had made a boat out of car hoods.

In 1979, as Granny grew even worse, Mama wrote, "She was out of her head yesterday, talking in unknown tongue. Today I got this potty chair for her. She didn't think much of it and kept wanting me to hide it behind the door. I wouldn't do it. I said if she could walk that far she could go to the bathroom. She asked me four times in about fifteen minutes to put it behind the door and I wouldn't. So the last thing she said before I left, she asked me to move it again. I just turned and walked off. So she hasn't used it yet. _Oh!_ She wants to be petted and made over. She still thinks of me as a child and she should be boss. I don't take it anymore and she can't take that. _Oh!_ While I was cleaning up yesterday, she found out it was Sunday. She got up walking around, going to the table. She's not as bad as she makes like she is. She's just using me. Wilburn won't fool with her."

Even though my mother didn't laugh much anymore, I was pleased to see traces of her humor in the little "Oh"s that always infused her letters. But I was afraid. The main note in her letters now was pain. For the first time, I began to see that my move to the North meant an abdication of responsibility. There was no solution I could see to my mother's burdens. I felt helpless.

Limited home-health visits were covered by Medicare, so Mama enlisted a nurse to help with Granny. But when the nurse tried to bathe her, Granny refused to cooperate. My mother wrote me, "She hauled off and slapped that nurse halfway across the room. She wouldn't have it!"

By custom, only family should attend to personal matters. The nurse did not return.

Too late, Granny tried to show affection and gratitude to her daughter-in-law. Grasping Mama's arm, Granny would say, "Don't let me die."

With her pocketbook hidden under her pillow, Granny lay in bed, adamantly clinging to shreds of life. Perhaps her tenacity lengthened her life. Month after month, year after year, she held on. But eventually she wore down. She died in 1981, when she was almost ninety-four.

It was not until the night of her death that my parents spent a night alone together, in either house, in all their married life. They had stayed at motels a number of times, but at home there had always been children around, or Daddy's parents—since 1936. The magnitude of this moment is staggering for me to contemplate. By then they were formed by habit, and I don't imagine they felt liberated at first. I picture them sitting silently in front of the TV, stunned by the finality of Granny's passing, drained by the ordeal, numbed by grief.

"No matter how ready you think you are, you're never prepared to see somebody go," Mama told me.

Only gradually had I realized what those trying years were doing to Mama. Her spirit seemed broken. She was fearful and uncertain—after being pushed around so long and uprooted on two occasions from the little house she and Daddy had built. Witnessing her shatter—quietly, far away—left me disconcerted and guilty. Mama had told me how bad her nerves were, and Daddy had complained a few times too about Mama's growing fearfulness. They had not gone anywhere together in years, and after Granny died, Mama refused to ride in the car with Daddy at the wheel. "His driving makes me nervous," she told me. She lost confidence in her own driving and would not dare venture onto the busy highway to Paducah.

My gentle grandmother had been such an unintentional tyrant. She hadn't demanded privileges. Instead, she denied herself, hoarding scraps and silences. As matriarch, she was upholding a way of life—frugality and kinship loyalty—and her whole personality represented the force of this ideal. But a tyranny can be formed from silence—the things that go without saying, the inexorable ways and rituals and expectations that form an unspoken law.

It was only after Granny died that my parents used the word "depression." Mama acknowledged, "She was depressed, and she just gradually got worse, a little at a time." Recently Mama told me that when Granny had been institutionalized in Hopkinsville, one of the doctors asked her, "Have you ever thought about suicide?"

"Yes," Granny replied. "But I didn't know how."

Her silences were stultifying, even after she was gone. I wondered if her problem had been caused by a chemical imbalance, or if it arose directly from the psyche—an extraordinary capacity for worry, or maybe just excessive timidity. I could imagine that her failure to reach out of herself was like my own when I went to school in the North and froze in culture shock; the mental block that stopped up my mind may have been like the barrier in hers. I wondered what was going on in her imagination when she read Henry Miller—maybe something so tempestuous that only shock treatments could quell her rampaging nerves. She seemed to possess dignity and strength in her quiet, imposing, stern way, as long as she was in charge. She was self-possessed and strong until something violated her control—a worry, a foreign intrusion. Then she came apart.

When Granny had her breakdowns, was she brooding over some strain of mental illness that ran in her family? Was she dwelling on some shameful secret? In her time, a simple human error—like an unwed pregnancy, or a son who "turned out wild"—could cause a trauma that colored a lifetime. It was disgrace, shame, the sense that everything one worked for and believed in and hoped for was ruined by a single misstep. One of Granny's aunts had "turned out bad" and had left Kentucky. The family disowned her.

What was Granny really so depressed about back in 1950? If her nerves were so fragile, why didn't she break down again when Granddaddy died, in 1965? Would the sounds of the Beatles really have wrecked her nerves if she hadn't fled to the car in the woods? What could she bear? What were her limits? Thorazine altered her, blurred her.

Of course, having only one child made Granny overprotective and fearful. And evidently giving birth had been traumatic for her. Mama told me, "The doctor told her not to have any more children after she had Wilburn. She nearly died from a kidney infection." Granny survived the childbed, but she probably wouldn't risk it again. This must have meant no more sex. "I never heard them carrying on after the light was out," Mama told me. She couldn't quite imagine it either. I thought about my young, handsome grandfather with his horse and buggy. I remember how he would tease Granny, saying, "Buss me, Ettie," and she would draw back in embarrassment.

When Daddy was away in the Navy, Granny's worry about him might have equaled my mother's, her potential sense of loss just as great as ours. Even though he came back safely, did she sense something changed in him, something lost that she would never get back? Did the aftermath of World War II—he was out there when they dropped that big bomb—simply fester until 1950, when her nerves snapped? The threat of war had not vanished. She may have feared that her son would at any moment be sent to Korea.

Granny's 1950 breakdown was enclosed in silence. She apparently worried herself into a black hole but couldn't explain. She revealed only one clue. In the ambulance to Memphis, Mama kept asking her, "What's bothering you? Tell us what's wrong with you so we'll know what to do about it."

Finally, Granny uttered one sentence. "A year ago the doctor told me I have an enlarged globe in my heart," she said.

That was all Granny would say. Apparently the doctor had not explained. She didn't know whether she had a serious heart condition that needed treatment. She probably would not have returned to the doctor to ask questions or have him listen to her heart again. It was more common to let well enough alone, in case the doctor said something you didn't want to hear. But from the moment the doctor spoke, she had probably imagined her enlarged heart bursting out of her chest, exploding. It could happen at any moment. What would become of her husband, her son, the family, the garden, her hens? Everything was involved in the silent storm of her worry. The whole world as she knew it revolved around the size of her heart—a heart she had thought was tight and stingy. But her heart was too big. She had to hide it, as the men hid the bull's amorous swelling from little girls' eyes. She had to contain her heart. She felt it beating, each beat threatening her. She could see the throb all the way to her navel. It fluttered and patted her pendulous, unsupported breasts beneath the peach ribbed-cotton camisole she wore. She could remember her heart beating like that— in excitement, in anticipation, when Bob came courting, as he had done for several years. In 1910, five years before they married, Bob was twenty-eight, and she was twenty-two. He came on Sundays and took her riding in his buggy. She was living with her parents and her brother and his stunningly beautiful new wife. In the night, Ethel heard noises: her sickly parents moaning in pain; the newlyweds moving together in their four-poster bed, entwined in each other's arms; and in the cot in the annex to the kitchen, the heavy breathing of Winston Tucker, the boarder, who labored on the farm. Winston was eighteen. She could hear him stir in the night. She slept lightly.

It was so cold going across the breezeway early in the morning to the offset kitchen to cook breakfast. The boarder had to be fed first, so he could get out to feed the animals and milk the cows. He saw her in the mornings, fresh from bed. She hastened to pin up the falling strands of her hair. Silently, she dipped water into the kettle. Sometimes he would have the fire started. Winston Tucker had few prospects. She, of course, couldn't form an alliance with a hired hand. Her father—Zollicoffer Quigley Arnett—was a respectable blacksmith and carpenter and farmer. He was an invalid, and her mother was not well either. Ethel took care of them. She did not dare leave them. She needed to tend her parents. She wanted to teach school. She kept putting Bob off.

I imagine Granny through her twenties, living in the same household with the dark, muscular boarder, getting up at dawn and traipsing in her nightgown to the cold kitchen to build the fire and start the biscuits. I imagine the fire of her youth, burning so slowly and so deeply that she was hardly warmed by it. Maybe she wasn't as passionate as she should have been about patient Bob. Maybe the real love of her life married someone else, unable to wait while she cared for her parents.

When she was twenty-six, her father died, and she married Bob a year later. I wonder if Ethel insisted on waiting until after her father's death. Did Z.Q. disapprove of Bob? Was she too embarrassed or frightened in the face of his grim authority to make the sexual leap into marriage? When he died, maybe her mother, Laura, mindful of the biological exigencies, urged her to plunge ahead. Perhaps it was her mother's encouragement that enabled her to leave home finally, to join her long-suffering suitor. But what if Ethel had still wanted to teach school, which she couldn't do if she married? Did Laura push Ethel into marriage against her desires?

Ever since my grandmother's death, I have pondered the mystery of her mind. I remember my own mind during late childhood and adolescence. I was afraid of fire and brimstone, afraid of death and the dark. My mind is hers, in part. The imagination connects me with her as surely as eye color and hair texture. I see myself in Granny's face. I can almost imagine her feeble, bedridden last days, as she lay in silence replaying her life, retreating, reliving her dark secrets.

Recently a photograph of her parents, Laura and Zollicoffer Quigley Arnett, came to me. I had never seen their likenesses before. Laura is big-boned and upright; Z.Q. is thin, delicate, fair-haired. He is sitting in a straight-back chair, and she is standing beside him like a porch post. I can see my grandmother in Laura—her will and strength; the fine, upswept hair. Granny had her father's large ears.

Laura and Z.Q. are buried together in the Arnett family cemetery. When I went there not long ago, I discovered a small stone next to theirs. It is the marker for Granny's little brother, John. He died when he was four. I never knew Granny had a younger brother. She didn't tell me about him when I was so full of questions. My mother, who was part of Granny's household for forty-six years, did not know about the child, either. So here was one more secret. Maybe, I thought, a big one. Granny was eight when her little brother was born. At that age, she would have had a large role in the family—learning the household chores and helping to care for him. She would have felt pride as she washed the baby's dresses on the washboard and helped to feed him spoonfuls of potatoes and beans she had mashed up. She might cream some chicken too. Maybe she would sing songs to the baby while she watched out for him, to see that he didn't burn himself in the fireplace or fall into the cistern or eat bluing or caustic soda.

He didn't live long enough to get his ten-year cake. I don't know how little John Arnett died, but losing a little brother must have been traumatic for my grandmother, who was twelve. And it is conceivable that she blamed herself for whatever happened to him. My imagination seizes the bare fragments of names and dates, with their tantalizing implications. I fill in the colors, the way I did in my coloring books long ago. Maybe John fell into a vat of boiling water while she was supposed to be watching him. Or maybe he died of one of those deadly overnight fevers that swooped in on children so often in those days. That would not be her fault, but she could have found a reason to feel guilty anyway—especially if she had let him get a chill because she took him outside on a rainy day. Her mind, always busy, could concoct outrageous scenarios.

But my mind wants a grounding, a few facts to anchor my imaginings. Nosing around for more clues, I came upon the obituary of Granny's father.

> Z. Q. ARNETT, aged about 58 years, died Thursday morning at his home, three and one-half miles east of the city. Mr. Arnett, who was a well-known farmer, had been an invalid for twelve years, suffering from locomotor ataxia, but a few days ago he developed pneumonia and his death came quickly. He was born and raised near where he breathed his last and is survived by a wife and three children.

> —*Mayfield Messenger*, September 12, 1913

The past jumped out at me. I had heard that Z.Q. had gout—he used a cane and passed the time sitting on his front porch. Now my imagination took a stunned, ninety-degree turn. Locomotor ataxia, a painful hardening of the spine, is a condition associated with the third stage of syphilis. Years after infection, syphilis comes to rest in some area of the body—the spine, the heart, the brain. The siege can go on for years. Victims of locomotor ataxia typically are thin and have sad-looking faces. I remembered that Z.Q. was said to weigh a hundred and twenty-six pounds. I looked back at the photograph. Yes, his face is sad. He seems so delicate and uncertain. But his wife stands tall and staunch, her hand on the chair behind his shoulder.

So my grandmother spent the bloom of her youth dutifully caring for her father, who suffered from syphilis! I could hardly take in the thought. Did her mother contract it too? Wouldn't Z.Q. have infected his wife? Laura looks fit and strong in the picture. But I had heard that she walked with a crooked stick and that the doctor came to the house once and used a red-hot poker to sear her spine.

What of the little boy, John? My earlier speculations are knocked aside, replaced by more terrible possibilities. Perhaps he died from congenital syphilis—passed on through his mother. Against my will, I imagine him with scabby, sore eyes; chronic sores in his mouth and nose; knoblike bulges on his legbones and head. He could have been deaf or blind. I'm horrified—I want to reject the images. Maybe Laura had gotten past the infectious stages of syphilis before the little boy was conceived.

I could find no more traces of Granny's little brother, but I located the death certificates for both Laura and Z.Q. The disease is confirmed for both of them. Laura had it for eight years. Her death was precipitated by starvation, after she refused to eat for fifteen days. She was fifty-seven years old.

Their suffering, and my grandmother's burden, are almost too much for me. I shudder at Granny's pain and dread. Probably no one ever told her the specific source of her father's illness—a trip to Cairo? a whorehouse on some back street behind the stockyards in Mayfield? an assignation with a diseased widow in bucolic Clear Springs? Granny wouldn't have known the facts—but she knew the shame of his sin. The family's shame, although shrouded in silence, must have been stark and heavy. And it must have preyed on her inflamed imagination. Z.Q. apparently contracted syphilis after she was born, for she and her older siblings were not infected, but maybe she didn't realize she was free from the sickness. She might have feared that she would inherit the spinal malady her parents endured, that it would visit her in her middle age as it had them. Maybe, years later, she thought her enlarged heart was the terrible disease flaring up at last. She must have felt haunted, doomed. She may have spent her life waiting for her horrible fate to overtake her.

Syphilis! My God. Granny's story—her worries, her silences, her breakdowns—rearranges itself completely in my mind.

Silence fell over the family when Z.Q.'s troubles began. Kinship loyalty came first, and young Ethel Arnett struggled to hold her suitor, Bob Mason, at bay while she tended to her parents' hideous affliction. The household depended on her, for Z.Q. was incapacitated as a farmer and Laura was too poorly to keep house. Yet—whether or not he suspected the origin of the illness—Bob waited for Ethel, cheerfully pitching his woo. Ethel, fearing the taint of evil, put off her own sexual fulfillment until she was twenty-seven. Even after her marriage, she maintained a stubborn silence. Stiff, secretive, she never confided in Bob or anyone else. Her troubled heart expanded and palpitated as she ate it out from within.

At the cemetery where her parents are buried, the fecundity of her family is celebrated. William P. Arnett, Z.Q.'s father, had three wives and fifteen children—fifteen after he reached the age of thirty-five. Who knows how many others came before? He remarried each time he lost a wife in childbirth, merrily reproducing until he was sixty-seven. On a monolith at the cemetery, William P. Arnett's photograph—a vacant-eyed man with a gray, pointed beard reaching down to his breastbone—presides over a portion of his progeny. His countenance is remarkable. His long hair is swooped up and pinned into a topknot, and on the sides it is swirled into large pin curls. He and his three wives are marked by creek stones. Z.Q. and Laura and little John lie nearby. They lie together in a row, like spectators of the future.

17

It is a sad truth that we were all relieved when Granny died. A weight had been lifted. Before long, Daddy had a lighter step. He told Mama he realized he should never have allowed her to be burdened all those years, but he hadn't known what else to do. His mother's unbending will and his promise to his father had been like the commandments handed down to Moses.

Daddy set out to make it up to Mama. He was sixty-five, Mama was sixty-two. It wasn't too late to enjoy their lives, he told her. "Do you want to move back home?" he asked her. She did, but the little house, built in 1944, would need extensive repairs. It was good enough to fix up for renters, she said, but not for themselves. They discussed building a new house. Finally, Mama decided that Granny and Granddaddy's old house was good enough for them to live out their days in. "It would cost too much to build a new house," she declared. With this observation, she initiated the final direction of their married life.

Granny had saved her Social Security checks for sixteen years, and my parents inherited everything. With the bounty, they splurged. They redid some of Granny's cabinets and installed a new sink. They covered the kitchen linoleum with a dense brown rug, and they laid dark, textured carpeting throughout the house. They finished paneling all of the walls and lowered the ceilings. They enlarged the dining room. Daddy replaced the shower with a tiny bathtub and built a cabinet and pasted down some linoleum. He bought a vanity with a built-in, fake-marble sink. Mama hung up an amusing set of plaster figures—a woman in her nightgown marching with a lantern to the outhouse under the moon. They redecorated the room where Granny died.

They were tickled with their handiwork. They were acting like kids: this is how they should have started out their marriage in 1936, I thought. They began going to yard sales and auctions, picking up knickknacks and antique furniture. They stuffed the house with their gleanings. Daddy acquired a school bell from an old one-room school-house, and he set it on a post by the junkhouse.

He built a small deck out back. From the deck they could admire the fields—and the new pond, his pièce de résistance. He had hired a bulldozer to create a pond for Mama, so that she could go fishing whenever she pleased. The pond was a pocket at the intersection of two creeks. It caught the flow of one creek and spilled to the other. He worked industriously on a levee, fortifying it with heavy rocks. He battled weeds, mowed paths, manicured the banks. He stocked the pond with catfish and bream and bass.

For himself, he fashioned a shop in the junkhouse, where he worked repairing antique guns. Sometimes he created little explosions by mistake. He had been trading antique guns for some time, locating the parts he needed to restore guns for collectors. The old trade days had now become flea markets. He found it entertaining to see what junk people would buy and how much they would pay for it. He knew a man who had peddled a bushel basket full of "Indian arrowheads" he had chipped out of flint while he watched television.

Mama joined the senior-citizens group in town. Daddy would not consider joining such a group. "I ain't old," he said. But Mama needed friends. At the senior-citizens center she took an art class and began painting still lifes and copying paintings from magazines. She painted a portrait of him they both thought was eerily realistic. She did a paint-ing from a photograph of the old dairy barn, which had burned a few years before—a cigarette from a passing motorist. She painted fruit bowls and flowers. Daddy was amazed at her talent. Before long, they found that they were talking, discussing things, sharing their day. They were starting over, with the privacy and the honeymoon they'd never had.

Mama still wouldn't ride in the car with Daddy at the wheel, but she went traveling with the senior citizens on chaperoned tours. Daddy stayed home. He told me that fools were everywhere and he didn't need to go out of his way to find them. And he did not feel comfort-able spending the night away from home. "I want to get back to my an-imals," he told me. "And sleep in my own bed."

"Wilburn, you're crazy!" some of the kinfolks told him. "Spending two thousand dollars on one of them trips! You're liable to need that money someday."

"If Chris wants to spend *nine* thousand dollars on a trip, it's all right with me," he replied. Guilt over the sacrifices she had made for his mother gnawed at him, and he was pleased to see Mama blossom, to hear her old laugh returning. He even bought her a diamond ring at a pawnshop.

She went to Hawaii. She went out West, through the Badlands and across the Continental Divide. She cruised to the Virgin Islands. She toured Nova Scotia and New England. She traveled through Europe. There, she got a kick out of the various styles of commodes. In Germany she noticed the women working in the fields while the men lazed under a tree. She wasn't surprised. The scene seemed familiar. The Swiss Alps scared her and the Italian heat smothered her. She hated European bread. "That bread would yank your teeth plumb out," she said.

When she went on the New England fall-foliage tour, the trip included a two-day stopover in New York City. I traveled from Pennsylvania, where I was still living, to join her at the St. Moritz Hotel. It was the dinkiest hotel she had ever seen, she said. "The rooms ain't big enough to cuss a cat in."

"Space is scarce in the city," I said. I thought for a moment about my cubicle at the Hotel Taft, when I moved to New York after college.

I went along with the group to see the Statue of Liberty. As the bus traveled down Fifth Avenue, our guide pointed out Saks Fifth Avenue, St. Patrick's Cathedral, Rockefeller Center. My mother was trying to write all the names down in her notebook. I had encouraged her to keep a journal of her trips, but now she wasn't looking at the sights. She was writing.

"I'll write it, Mama," I said. "You *look*."

By this time, I had become a writer—belatedly, after many twists and turns while I looked over my shoulder at my childhood dreams and shook my head to get out the nightmare residue from my journey north. I had discovered that I could draw on my true sources in order to write fiction. How could I have failed to recognize them? They had claimed me all along. So much of the culture that I had thought made me inferior turned out to be my wellspring. And my mother was my chief inspiration.

A friend of mine in the city was eager to meet Mama, so she had invited us to the Four Seasons restaurant, in the dark tower of the Seagram's Building, a landmark that appears in *Breakfast at Tiffany's*—one of the movies that had originally lured me to New

York. We strolled past the Picasso and Rothko paintings in the large foyer. The coat-check person wanted to take care of our parcels. "No," Mama said, clutching a plastic Kmart bag she carried. "I want to keep this with me."

The bag contained a painting she had done in her senior-citizens art class. She was going to present it to my friend Amanda.

The dinner was extravagant and dreamlike. We were aware that Amanda had the menu with the price list, while ours showed no prices. Mama, who tends to order the cheapest thing on a menu, was clearly uneasy at not knowing what the food cost. Nevertheless she indulged herself by ordering raw oysters.

"What do you cook at home?" Amanda asked.

"Fried chicken, ham, peas, slaw, green beans, shell-beans." Mama named her garden crops.

We talked about her garden and her travels. Amanda is lively and brisk, and she speaks in what at home we call "a New York minute." She has a joyous laugh that could rival Mama's. She got Mama to laugh.

At the table next to us, a young woman was being celebrated by her parents for her promotion in a public-relations department of a major firm. She was giddy with her success. Amanda told me later in detail the conversation she had overheard. A businesswoman who herself moves in powerful circles, Amanda said, "There I was wedged between two worlds, and I heard those people talking about this big-deal promotion, and I asked myself, what was all the excitement about? *What?* So what? Your mother was more real than anybody there."

"I don't see any catfish on the menu, Mama," I teased. We had been talking about her pond.

"I've never had catfish," Amanda said.

"You don't know what you've missed," Mama said.

We ate leek soup and crabcakes and hazelnut rice and swordfish and Linzer torte. Following Amanda's lead, Mama drank a glass of kir.

"I don't drink, but I had champagne on my cruise," she explained. "It bubbled up my nose."

She opened her Kmart bag and presented the painting, a bowl of flowers, to Amanda.

"I love it!" Amanda cried.

Afterwards, we walked down Park Avenue a few blocks. The lights were magnificent—from my skewed viewpoint a bit surreal. The Cuban missile crisis flashed through my mind. I frequently carry contradictory realities in my head. Amanda too was seeing the lights and the buildings in a new way, through heartland eyes.

"Aren't they amazing?" she said.

"Well, Mama, what do you think of New York?" I said. "We're on Park Avenue."

"It's about what I expected," she said, not terribly impressed. Then she explained, "I've seen tall buildings before—in Detroit."

Mama hadn't wanted Amanda to think she was provincial. As for me, I was remembering my younger self, spinning along Park Avenue in my Holly Golightly hat.

The trouble with walking on Park Avenue was that I couldn't see the stars for all the lightbulbs, and there weren't any fascinating bugs. It was time to return to Kentucky for good. For some time, voices from home had been calling to me in clear, beckoning tones—their speech unspoiled by P.R. consultants or professional jargon or the rules of grammar. Through the voices of my family, I heard the voices of my grade-school classmates who formed my first impressions of the world outside the farm. When I began to write stories, their lives were the ones I came back to.

I wondered what happened to the boy who fell on the icy steps outside the fifth-grade classroom and knocked his front teeth out. I wondered about the poor girl who never had a dime for the traveling show and wore drab plaid dresses but had a beautiful head of hair. I had heard of the girl who grew up to become a hotshot executive in Atlanta, and I had heard that Howie Crittenden and Doodle Floyd, the basketball stars, had declined to stay with the pros because the big city wasn't for them. I knew about the smart boy a grade ahead of me who got a Ph.D. and had a nervous breakdown. I wondered about the others. What did the ones who stayed behind do for a living? Farm? Work at the tire plant? Of course I was wondering about the kind of life I might be leading if I had stayed.

I wrote about a preacher's wife who escapes her unhappy marriage by playing video games at the church retreat; I wrote about an unemployed ex-trucker; I wrote about a guy who drives a bus for mentally disabled workers, as Daddy did; I wrote about a woman with breast cancer who falls for a devious flea-market trader. It seemed to me that the characters I imagined were slightly off balance, trying to comprehend their place in a changing world that appeared to have no room for them. But they were hopeful. I identified with their sense of jarring dislocation and also with their sense of possibility. It seemed I had to write their stories in order to try to find my way back to my own place.

Some of the voices haunted me because I was still preoccupied with all the guys who went to Vietnam. Six young men from Graves County had died over there. A novel began growing in my mind. Writing was like remembering, an act of retrieval. I wrote the story as if my family had lived it. It was about a young girl whose father had been killed in Vietnam just before she was born. She had never known her father. Now, in 1984, she was graduating from high school, and she was beginning to ask questions about him—just as I was increasingly asking questions about my family. She was among the first of the children of the war to come of age. The voices of the veterans whose accounts I read flipped me back into the sixties, and then back to the farm. I thought of farm boys shipping out to war, as my father had done a generation before. I remembered the Fort Campbell soldier I had met.

It was as though I were summoning voices from the past to undo the silences in my own family—my grandmother's fears, my father's reticence about his war, my mother's mute pain as she was caring for her mother-in-law.

While I was writing this novel, Roger and I visited the Vietnam Veterans Memorial. On a cloudy Sunday, we strolled down the Mall from the Capitol, past the Washington Monument, toward the hidden black gash in the earth. As we walked, I began to hear the characters in the novel, as if they were talking on a tape in my head. I could hear what they would be saying if they were ambling along beside me, on their way to the memorial. I could hear Emmett, a Vietnam veteran, speaking nervously, but holding back his feelings. I could hear the girl, Sam—scared though eager to find her father's name engraved on the wall. I could hear Sam's grandmother, a country woman far from home and too heavy to move fast. Her son was named on that wall. I could hear the grandmother say, "I'm afraid we won't find his name. It might not show up good." In Sam, I saw my younger self. I knew what all three characters would be feeling. I was trembling with their anxiety.

It began to rain. Roger and I had umbrellas, and we lifted them. It rained harder. We reached the wall, where streams of people, almost oblivious to the rain, were poring over the names on the wall.

We walked along a low section of the wall, gazing at the names, with the rain drizzling down over our reflections on the shiny black face of the wall. We had no particular name to look for; our eyes hit the names randomly. We saw a man and woman pause. "There it is," the man said. The woman touched the name silently, mouthing the words. We moved on. The names ran before us with the water.

Suddenly I saw my own name. Bobby G. Mason. My name, changed only slightly. A young guy with that name, my name, had died in Vietnam. I choked up. I couldn't tell if my face was wet with tears or with rain. The rain freed my tears. As the rain washed over the wall, I was aware that I was seeing it in several different ways. I grieved for Bobby G. Mason, and for Dwayne Hughes—the fictitious soldier whose name my three characters were seeking. Everyone's name, I thought, was on that wall. The soldiers we sent to Vietnam were not the only ones who went. We were all there. And we all had a long journey to make together to get back home.

The rain was overdoing it, I realized later. Too melodramatic for fiction.

The Hilltoppers had disbanded long ago, but lead singer Jimmy Sacca had kept a group on the road for years, especially during the nostalgia craze of the seventies. Don McGuire, one of the original Hilltoppers, had been a school textbook salesman, and now he was selling real estate in Lexington. I had been in touch with him a few times over the years.

"I want to buy a piece of Kentucky," I told Don on the telephone from Pennsylvania in the mid-eighties.

"Mason, you're being called home," he said. "Was it 'My Old Kentucky Home' at the Kentucky Derby that got to you? Did that song speak to you?"

"More or less," I said.

One bright fall day Roger and I visited Don and his wife, Maxine, in their large plantation-style home in Lexington. Their house had a room devoted to Hilltoppers memorabilia: autographed photos of artists the group had worked with—Johnnie Ray, Perry Como, Steve and Eydie—and photos of the Hilltoppers performing at the Chicago Theater and on Ed Sullivan's show. The walls were covered. Hanging above the piano was a gold record, an old 78 r.p.m. platter of "P.S. I Love You."

"We want a place with fields and forests, far from town," I told Don.

"You're looking for a hoot-owl farm, Mason," said Don.

He took Roger and me riding in his black Lincoln Town Car in search of a piece of land. We went out to the Kentucky River, lined with magnificent limestone palisades that harbor endangered species of plants. We drove along a country lane, searching for the farm listed for sale.

"This is like a national park," Roger said when we explored the place, which had caves and cliffs and giant boulders. The man who owned the farm loaded us into his pickup truck and we rode through fields of ironweed and goldenrod, festooned with the orbs of large golden garden spiders. I had not realized the geography of Kentucky was so varied and so beautiful. When I battled my way out in my youth, I felt fenced in by cornfields, uninspired by landscape.

That farm was beyond our means, but eventually, in a different part of the state, Roger and I found another place we loved. We had always lived in the country—first in Connecticut and then in Pennsylvania. Now we would claim a little corner of my homeland. I had unfinished business there. I had mercifully escaped the hardship of the old ways—no lye soap or washboards, no hog-killing. I wouldn't have to carry water. I wanted blackberries, but not the cruel, thorny ones; botanists had developed better ones now. I had grandiose visions of an asparagus bed. I was optimistic, just as I had been when I moved to New York years before. Now I could rediscover and celebrate the Kentucky springtime. Thomas Wolfe said you can't go home again, and I was wary of contradicting his wisdom. I wanted to return, but not relapse. Still, it would be a relief to live in a part of the country where a restaurant marquee might say CHICKEN GIZZARDS—ALL YOU CAN EAT. I wanted to be where people got together to play cards on a Friday night and didn't wait till nine o'clock to eat supper. Yet I didn't want to conform. Finally, I thought, I could live there now on my own terms.

Daddy came to inspect our land. When we walked straight up a steep hill, I was surprised at his stamina. He was now seventy-two. Without having to say so, he passed judgment on this hilly patch of ground that was poor cropland, so full of rocks we couldn't dig a well.

"Are you going to set out some tobacco?" he asked. "If a tobacco allotment comes with the land, you can raise tobacco."

"I don't want to raise tobacco."

Daddy nodded. "Good. Smoking liked to killed me," he said. "But I quit."

"Good. Now let's get Mama to quit."

We reached the top of the hill, where Daddy paused to catch his breath.

"Why didn't you want to come back and live where you were raised?" he asked.

"I wanted to be near an airport," I said. I realized that without even considering it, I had chosen not to go all the way home. The land we bought was a long way from Mayfield. I had to keep some distance, keep my options open.

Roger and I had the land we wanted, but it would still be a couple of years before we could leave Pennsylvania to live in Kentucky. The next time I saw that land, I had an anxious, bittersweet thought: maybe this would be the place where I would die.

18

The movie of *Gone with the Wind* came to Mayfield when my mother was pregnant with me. A few years ago, Mama told me that Granny wouldn't allow her to see the movie because Clark Gable said the word "damn" in it. Granny was afraid hearing dirty words might cause Mama to have a miscarriage. "Or it might mark the baby," she said. But I had already been subjected *in utero* to the unclean spirit of Biloxi and New Orleans when Mama went on the factory excursion.

I had never been interested in reading *Gone with the Wind*, but when I learned as an adult that the movie had been censored for me in the womb, I hurried to the video store and rented it. I hated the Southern-belle wasp-waisted view of the world so much that I couldn't sympathize with Scarlett O'Hara's loss or celebrate her courage in fighting to regain Tara. The Hollywood happy-humming-slave background of the movie reminded me of the Bobbsey Twins' cheerful servants, Dinah and Sam. Scarlett seemed pathological in her obsessions. Her whole world smelled strongly of the kind of small-town aristocratic pretensions that had made me feel like an outcast in high school.

Daddy's retreat from the movies into television was complete. He followed world news and sports and comedy shows. In the eighties, when he got cable, he roamed around the world from his La-Z-Boy chair. He was fascinated with human behavior, but his favorite shows were the animal programs on the Discovery channel. In general, animals pleased him far more than people did.

His piles of paperback mysteries and Westerns had long ago disappeared into the junkhouse. But in 1986, when William Faulkner's *As I Lay Dying* was banned at Graves County High School (the consolidation of all the county high schools, including Cuba), he suddenly showed a surprising interest in literary matters. He said it was ridiculous to ban a book by an important American writer like William Faulkner. He fumed and stormed—and laughed. Some of the parents had complained that the novel referred to abortion, used God's name in vain, and called a horse "a pussel-gutted bastard." Letters to the *Mayfield Messenger* deplored how depressing the book was—how blasphemous and nasty. One said it was unfit for children's sensitive nerves.

A former high-school classmate of mine named Juanita wrote a letter to the paper blasting the book ban. In her letter she mentioned—with some pride—my name as a local author, and Daddy called her to thank her. He hardly ever used the telephone; he would rather drive all the way to Paducah to buy a car part than call ahead and possibly save himself a trip. Daddy and Juanita struck up a friendly dialogue about the book controversy and telephoned each other with new tidbits and revelations. The topic of book banning had touched a nerve in him. Underneath it all, of course, he was defending me, his literary daughter.

Daddy and I began talking on the telephone more. He read me the letters to the editor. He guffawed. Some of the letters advocated returning to the good old days of wholesome reading—good books like *Mrs. Wiggs of the Cabbage Patch*.

"*Mrs. Wiggs of the Cabbage Patch*!" Daddy scoffed. He couldn't stop laughing.

As the news of the ban spread, a second wave of letters questioned the school board's decision. Wire services sent the story across the nation. In Oxford, Mississippi, a bookstore staged a marathon reading of *As I Lay Dying* in support of Faulkner—their own boy—and freedom of expression. Sales of *As I Lay Dying* boomed in the Paducah bookstores.

A peculiar scene entered my head. I had learned that in 1950, the year Granny was sent to Memphis for shock treatments, Faulkner was being treated for alcoholism and depression at the only psychiatric facility in Memphis. I don't know if that was the place where Granny underwent shock treatments, but it seems likely. I couldn't help imagining my Granny and William Faulkner conversing in the solarium—she almost catatonically reserved but finding something to say about banty hens maybe, and he saying odd things, about the mysteries of time perhaps. I tried to imagine Granny's interior monologue as she lay dying. Would the imagery in her mind have been as dense as Faulkner's prose?

Eventually, the complaint against *As I Lay Dying* was dropped, but not because enlightenment prevailed. The school and the town were being ridiculed, and that didn't look good.

"You'll have to read Faulkner's book now, since you've gotten so involved in it," I said to Daddy.

"Oh, I've read it. It's the one where that dead woman in the coffin in that wagon has them holes bored through her forehead."

It turned out that he had read *As I Lay Dying* years before, back in the forties. The vivid image of Addie Bundren's last journey in the wagon stayed in his mind.

"I'm very familiar with Faulkner's work," Daddy said. "And Hemingway's work."

This was stunning news. I thought his head was full of football games and sitcoms. But he was familiar with works of the imagination that I had thought were my secrets. I knew he was probably overstating the breadth of his reading for my benefit, but I wondered if he had read some of those books I had left behind, as Granny had. I was afraid to ask if he had read Henry Miller.

We were both well aware that my novel *In Country,* which had been published the year before, was too racy for local high school classes. It was almost too risqué for *The New Yorker,* where excerpts from the novel had appeared. The magazine's sensitive editor, William Shawn, ruefully acknowledged that the raw language of the characters who were Vietnam veterans was appropriate and inevitable, and I became the first writer to use the word "fuck" in *The New Yorker.*

My novel was not generally known in the Jackson Purchase, but then something surprising happened. Hollywood came to town. In 1988, emissaries from a movie producer appeared, with the intent of filming *In Country* right there in Mayfield. Scriptwriters asked my parents a thousand questions and snapped Polaroids of their stable and fields and the barbecue places in town and the courthouse. Later, P.R. people arrived to woo the mayor. Then location scouts showed up, searching for a modest old house with a good climbing tree in the yard. They drove up and down every street in town until they found the house they wanted. Then they knocked on the door and informed the shocked residents that their place had been chosen for a movie set. It was as though the family had won a home-delivered sweepstakes.

Everyone in town wanted to be in the movie, it seemed, even though there was an undertone of suspicion that the movie would portray the region in typical Hollywood possum-and-grits images. The whole town, apparently, was involved in the progress of the movie—following the movements of the crew, anticipating the appearance of the stars, gathering to watch the filming on the streets of Mayfield. A thousand townspeople stayed up late one night to watch Bruce Willis climb a tree and cuss God in a thunderstorm scene that took all night to film. A severe drought was on that summer, so the magic rain may have been the real attraction.

Always tangential to the life of the town, my family and I were now conspicuously absent. Maybe everybody thought we were too busy hobnobbing with movie stars at fancy restaurants in Paducah. Actually, Mama was working in her garden and fishing in her pond as usual, and Daddy was doing his regular farm-maintenance work. And I wasn't anywhere around, except for a couple of visits from Pennsylvania, where I was still living. My sister LaNelle, who got a job working in the art department, was the only family member directly involved in the production. She worked on set details, such as locating the correct period wallpaper for the interiors. In search of authentic props, she brought the set decorators out to my parents' house. They borrowed some of my mother's paintings and family photographs.

Then the film people realized it wasn't just the pictures and antiques in the house that were authentic goods—it was Mama herself.

The script called for a damson pie. LaNelle called home. "Mom, they want to know where they can get some damsons for a pie. Are they in season?"

"Well, they ought to be coming in about now."

"I told them you might be able to round up some."

"Well, I get them at that orchard east of town. They let you pick them for six dollars a bucket."

"Could you get some? They wouldn't know a damson from a Cheez Doodle. I told them you were the authority."

"I reckon I could go out and pick some. I've been wanting some for the freezer. But they might charge six dollars and a half this year."

"This outfit can probably afford it," LaNelle said.

Obligingly, Mama went to the orchard and picked a bucket of damsons for the movie crew. She paid six dollars for the damsons. The pie had to be the real thing, they said.

One of the film's stars turned to Mama, too. Peggy Rea—a woman of large dimensions—had played Boss Hogg's girlfriend in *The Dukes of Hazzard*, my parents' favorite TV show in the 1970s. When Peggy learned that her role in *In Country* was partly based on my mother, she came to the farm to meet Mama. She brought along a photograph of herself in her *Dukes of Hazzard* outfit, with a white cowgirl hat. Mama and Daddy would have been embarrassed to spend time with silk-shrouded Hollywood stars who couldn't milk a cow if their lives depended on it. But Peggy was delightful. She was down-to-earth, full of fun. After that first visit, she came back often, and my parents enjoyed her company. Daddy wasn't afraid to kid her about her size.

During one of my own visits home, Peggy came over for one of Mama's fried chicken dinners. We ate outside on a rickety picnic table that Daddy had reinforced by wiring a gun barrel onto the frame. LaNelle and I sat down on the built-in benches, and the whole structure wobbled. As we watched Peggy and Mama approach with their plates, LaNelle said under her breath, "This is not going to work."

Peggy saw the precariousness of the situation immediately and laughed. She said, "I'm afraid if I sit there, we'll all end up on the ground." Quickly, LaNelle found a chair for Peggy.

Mama said, "Well, if I didn't forget to bring my tea, then I'm not here."

"That's my line!" cried Peggy with a roar of laughter. "In my scene tomorrow I have to say, 'If *she* didn't wear her high heels out in the pasture, then *I'm* not here!' "

Peggy and my mother became friends. They were about the same age, and Peggy was in high spirits because her *In Country* role had reenergized her flagging career. "Out here, I feel I'm in the world of the characters," she said. Mama was pleased.

Peggy invited my mother to the set one morning. Mama was late because she had to go get her hair fixed. (She had won a hula contest at the senior-citizens center, and a hairdo was the prize.) When she arrived at the old house in town where the filming was taking place, she found the streets blocked off and enough trucks to haul a circus congregated around the house. The crew had reinforced the floorboards of the porch, slapped a new roof on the garage, and then punched a hole in the roof to make it look shabby. The greensman on the crew had painted the drought-browned grass green. Mama's hanging plants, which the company had borrowed, were lined up on the front-porch overhang.

"Those plants need watering," Mama observed.

In the scene being filmed, Bruce Willis, as Emmett, the Vietnam vet, is digging a ditch alongside the foundation of his house after a rain. Emily Lloyd, the teenage British actress playing the lead character, Sam, comes to the door and greets her grandparents, who drive up in a truck. Willis digs on the ditch during the scene. "He didn't really dig that ditch," Mama told me later. "He just shoveled on it when the camera was on."

In the scene, Peggy gets out of the truck carrying the damson pie.

"It was a double-crust," Mama explained to me. "I like to make a damson pie like a cobbler, with the top open some. Why, you couldn't see a damson in that pie. They could have put prunes in that thing and you wouldn't know the difference. I told Peggy they could have substituted a cow pile. She got in and out of that truck with that pie a hundred times. I knew that pie wouldn't be eat. I knew it would go to waste."

Mama had lunch with the movie crew in the gymnasium of the senior-citizens center, which the crew had rented. The caterers served Cornish hens. "You could have all you wanted to eat," Mama reported to me. "I never saw so much good stuff."

Emily Lloyd was cute and friendly, Mama said. "But she jabbered so fast I couldn't make out half of what she was saying. She could talk right when the camera was on, though."

Most people in town adored Emily because she didn't put on airs. But the general opinion was that Bruce Willis wasn't friendly because between takes he retreated to his black camper-van with his wife, Demi Moore, who was expecting their first baby. Late in the summer she gave birth to a baby girl in Paducah. As part of her job, LaNelle created an oil painting of the courthouse square, a commemorative of the Mayfield summer, to welcome the new baby.

One Sunday I was at home, spending a slow afternoon with my parents and LaNelle. Peggy was visiting. Mama fried a chicken and cooked some vegetables from the garden. She spread the table with one of Granny's nice tablecloths. Daddy wouldn't eat with us because he was watching a football game on TV.

That morning he had found a lesser horned owl dead alongside the road. He had set it down on the concrete floor of the milk house.

"I know a taxidermist who might want to do something with that," Daddy said when he showed me the owl. "That owl is something. It sure is beautiful. Wonder what happened to him."

The owl had feathered horns and a catlike face. It had been lying beside the road without a mark on it, as if it had had a heart attack and simply fallen from the air, making a soft but fatal landing.

Later in the afternoon, we all strolled to the pond, and while Mama fished we admired Daddy's ducks. Peggy admired Oscar. "He looks just like my little dog, Becky."

"Have you ever seen such an ugly dog?" Mama said.

"Why, Oscar's not ugly!" Daddy protested.

"Well, Becky and Oscar would probably hit it off," Peggy said. "But she's having a high old time living at her friends' house back in California."

Daddy liked Peggy because she had a sense of humor, but he wasn't impressed by the shenanigans in town. The parade of trailers and sound trucks was disrupting traffic; the cast and crew were throwing money around like chicken feed.

I wondered what Granny would have thought about the extravagance. It was only in the last decade or so of her life that she ever bought meat at the grocery, and then she saved the molded foam trays the meat was packaged in. She saved the twist-ties from bread bags; they lay mangled in a jar like the fishing-worms I collected as a child. She saved all the Christmas wrapping paper. I remember how Granny would never turn on her single kitchen lightbulb in the evening until it was completely dark. One of the lights on the movie set was enough to illuminate a church parking lot. Warner Brothers spent about twenty-three million dollars making *In Country*, pumping about five million into the local economy. Much of the movie budget was spent trying to conjure up an illusion of old-fashioned authenticity—quaint old things like those from Granny's time. Instead of filming at McDonald's, the crew chose a cozy diner with a giant rooster on the roof. For the filming, they replicated the diner, rooster and all, in a vacant lot across from what had been the Merit, where my mother had sewed labels.

In the late summer, the light on the dark-leaf tobacco that is special to the region was a soft glow. The film crew marveled at the way the light hit the dilapidated old corncribs and tobacco barns in the landscape. They adored quilts. Bruce and Demi were spotted emerging from an antique store with armloads of quilts. The crew—in their trendy industrial safety shoes with colossal toes—favored a certain late-night dance place in Paducah where white people didn't normally go. They descended on it and danced through the night. They hated the alcohol ban in Mayfield. Mayfield had been dry for time out of mind. Yet some of the men said the Mayfield women who went out with them drank more than anybody they'd ever seen, as if they were desperate for excitement.

. . .

Toward the end of the production, I was invited to watch a scene being filmed, and I drove out to the set—a snaky swamp, with cypress trees growing from the water. Trucks lined the lanes leading into the swamp. Apparently a jumbo wardrobe trailer was required to dress two actors in jeans and flannel shirts.

When I arrived, the filming was in progress. Near the end of the novel Sam runs angrily to the swamp to face her questions about what happened to her father, who died in a Vietnamese jungle. She has found his diary, and its revelations are horrifying. She spends the night in the swamp. The next morning her uncle Emmett finds her there. Emmett scolds Sam for thinking she can learn what Vietnam was like by camping out in this comparatively tame wilderness. But as he scolds her, his own emotions about the war erupt and the two reach out to each other.

The cameras were rolling. But it wasn't Emily Lloyd and Bruce Willis I saw. It was Sam and Emmett, my characters, standing there before me, their backs to me. Their flannel shirts looked slept in. Sam's camping gear was there, her sleeping bag, her snacks, her radio. I crept along the margins of the scene until I could view it from the front.

Emmett was leaning against a tree, gazing into the distance.

Referring to her father's diary, Sam said, "The way he talked about gooks and killing—I hated it."

Words I had written rose in the air as my heart rose in my throat. Sam, my creation, the closest I had come to having a daughter, materialized before me for this brief time in this swamp, a place I had visited with my father, where we'd spotted cottonmouths and great blue herons. I came close to crying.

The scene was supposed to end with an egret taking wing as Sam and Emmett walk arm in arm out of the swamp. The bird hired for the scene was not a common egret, but a snowy egret, a member of a dwindling species, wheedled away from Disney World (and probably FedExed to Paducah). At the appropriate time, it was released from its cage. Sam and Emmett walked away from the campsite. But the fluffy-plumed bird strolled about slowly, getting its bearings. The prop master slammed a clapper together, but the bird would not take flight. It pecked around nonchalantly, like a chicken scouting for bugs. The prop master fired a stage pistol. The egret ignored the sound. It refused to follow the script. It would not wing its symbolic arc gracefully through the scene. Apparently, no one had realized that in hurricanes egrets are the last birds to leave before the storm hits. The more the commotion, the steadier their nerves.

The next day, to their surprise, the camera crew discovered an enormous flock of egrets in the next cove. The birds may have been there all along. This was the kind of irony that amused Daddy. When I told him about it, he said, "If they'd asked you about it, they wouldn't have had to go all the way to Florida for that bird."

"But I didn't know there were egrets at the swamp," I said.

"You could have asked me. I've seen them over there time and again. Big flocks of them." He laughed, enjoying his bit of superior knowledge. "Sending all the way to Florida for a bird!"

Near the end of their three-month stay in the area, the film company returned the family photographs they had borrowed from my mother. I was present when a young man on the prop crew came to the house with the box of photos. Mama went through them, discovering that three of the most special ones were missing: a portrait of Daddy in his Navy uniform, a picture of herself when she was young, and a family photo of Granddaddy with his brothers and sisters.

"We can pay you for them," the young man said. "I'm sure I got all the pictures we had. I don't know what might have happened."

Mama said, "I don't want money. I want the pictures."

"I'm afraid there aren't any more. I brought all the pictures on hand."

In his van, he had the hanging baskets of ferns and airplane plants the company had borrowed. The plants were leggy and brown. He hung the plants up for Mama on the porch, and then he gave her some extra plants he had.

"I'm sorry about the pictures," he said. "I'll look again, but I'm sure I brought all I could find."

Mama was upset, but she wouldn't say so. She examined the plants, trying to remember all those she had loaned to the crew. Her abashed silence reminded me of my casserole dish sailing off a balcony years before.

"Anybody could have taken the pictures," LaNelle told her later. "There were so many people around. A lot of people are dying to have antique pictures."

Mama asked LaNelle again to inquire about the six dollars the company owed her for the bucket of damsons she had picked for the pie. "I wish they had those damsons stuck you know where," Mama said.

LaNelle investigated, and a few days later she reported, "When you see how much money they're giving you for borrowing the plants and the pictures, you'll shut up about those damsons."

Mama was flabbergasted when she received a check for eleven hundred dollars. "Well," she said after a moment. "But it won't take the place of those pictures."

In Country premiered at the mall in Paducah a year later. My family and I dressed up and went. A limousine was reserved for us, but I declined it, knowing it would make my parents uncomfortable. Daddy would snort and mock if he saw anyone riding around the courthouse square in a limousine, so he would have been humiliated to be seen in one himself.

I was acutely aware that some attention had come to me that we could not quite accommodate. I was afraid Daddy was disappointed, fearful that I had somehow moved into some other realm, rejecting his world. I thought he knew I wasn't likely to move to Hollywood and start throwing wild parties, or whatever depravity Granny had warned me against when I was in New York. But it wasn't corruption Daddy feared so much as falseness. Yet there we were at the premiere, all duded up.

The movie began. One of the first scenes was set in a Paducah park. Loud whoops of recognition erupted. It seemed that the audience couldn't concentrate on the plot because they were so excited about seeing familiar places on the screen. The movie was dotted with Mayfield landmarks—the courthouse, the Dairy Queen, a cemetery. Our town was on celluloid now, and we were authenticated.

In an interior scene, I glimpsed one of the photographs Mama had loaned to the company. It was a portrait of me as a sophomore in college, in my pixie haircut. The picture was standing on a piano. I was a shadow of Beth March.

After the premiere, at a reception, my parents were too tongue-tied to speak when introduced to the director. Daddy would not congratulate him on his achievement. I was sorry for his embarrassment, and I felt guilty for causing it.

Later, at home, my parents wouldn't tell me what they thought of the movie. They seemed uncertain how to express what they felt. But they hadn't said much about the novel either. I remember being at home shortly after the novel was published. Daddy had read all but the final scene. He opened the book (he always marked his place by dog-earing the corner of a page) and sat down beside me on the couch to finish reading it. He read the few pages quickly, closed the book, said nothing, and went outside to mow. I would have been hurt, but I understood his silence. A few years before, he had written me a letter. In it, he said he often got up at three or four A.M. (a habit from his milking days), made his bacon and eggs in the microwave, and then read my stories while the sun came up. He said he read them over and over because they meant so much to him. He wrote that he could express himself better in writing than he could in talking. He told me he was proud of me. I couldn't stop crying when I read the letter. He had had the courage to express himself to me, more courage than I had. I could not reply. I never replied adequately to his letter.

In Country did have a Hollywood ending, off screen. My sister LaNelle fell in love with one of the set designers she worked with. When the filming finished, she left with Craig Edgar for California, taking along her two cats. Daddy approved of Craig, who had good character. LaNelle and Craig returned to Mayfield several months later for their wedding. And then they went to Australia, where Craig was designing sets for a movie theme park.

At the end of 1989, the *Mayfield Messenger* highlighted the major stories of the year. A picture of me taken at the movie premiere was juxtaposed with a picture of the new chicken-feed mill built by Seaboard Farms across from my family's house.

19

In the spring of 1990, after years of living in the Northeast, I finally managed to move back to Kentucky, but I was still several hours' journey from Mayfield, and I did not go home for Thanksgiving that year. I was out of the habit. Janice lived in Florida. LaNelle was in Australia. LaNelle and I spoke on the telephone that morning, and I talked to Mama and Daddy on the telephone at about two in the afternoon, after they had finished dinner.

"That old squash made me sick," Daddy complained.

He never liked Mama's squash—her yellow crookneck squash mashed with bacon grease.

"Are you ready for the earthquake?" I asked.

He laughed. "I've got too much else on my mind to get scared by a crackpot," he said.

The earthquake hysteria had begun some weeks before, when a self-proclaimed climatologist predicted that the most devastating earthquake in U.S. history would hit the New Madrid fault, on the Mississippi River, not far from Mayfield. There had been a major earthquake along the fault in 1811, but few people lived in the region then. It was said that the force of that earthquake caused the Mississippi River to run backwards, and that it rattled dishes at the White House. The aftershocks lasted well into 1812. Since then, doomster prognosticators have been saying that the next earthquake will sink the whole region—from Memphis to St. Louis—into the Mississippi, and that the land with all the water reserves beneath it will turn into liquid clay.

Western Kentucky greeted the new prediction with fear and frolic. The stores were having earthquake sales. During the week prior to Thanksgiving, Daddy gleefully watched people on TV being interviewed in grocery stores as they stockpiled bottled water and toilet paper. Now, on the telephone, he told me about all these "crazy fools." He added, "If there ain't nothing to eat they won't need all that toilet paper."

Later that afternoon, Daddy's upset stomach suddenly grew worse. Then a huge headache slammed his brain and he collapsed.

"I'm dying," he told Mama. But he often said this for melodramatic effect when he had heartburn or an earache.

"Do you want me to call the ambulance?" Mama asked.

"No."

But then he lost consciousness, and she called the ambulance, half afraid he would be mad at her for doing so. She expected him to wake up and say, "Just take me behind the corncrib and shoot me." But surely this was only a spell, she thought. She called my brother, Don.

Don beat the ambulance to the house. Then the medics arrived and whisked Daddy off to a hospital in Paducah. Don and Mama followed in Don's car. They hardly recognized the familiar road.

Daddy was placed in intensive care. He had had a cerebral hemorrhage and was in a coma. There was nothing to do but wait. Mama called me and said, "Your daddy's had a real bad stroke." Roger and I arrived at the hospital at one o'clock in the morning, after a long drive in the rain, our car full of dogs, to find my mother numbed with disbelief, my father seemingly in a deep sleep.

Janice and her teenage son drove up from Florida, arriving by midmorning. LaNelle was summoned from Australia. In the darkness of uncertainty, she flew the length of the Pacific Ocean to Los Angeles, then to Nashville, where Don picked her up, as the rest of us still waited. She arrived at the intensive-care lounge in Paducah bearing macadamia nuts and books on Australian aboriginal culture and many snapshots. She brought kangaroo and koala souvenirs for the children. But her forced cheerfulness quickly faded. Australia didn't register on any of us.

I recall the intensity of intensive care. In the family lounge, all sensations were heightened—the ringing of the wall telephone, the slow sucking of strange machines, the pop-up appearances of the nurses who came to summon a family. Several families were camped out there, each stationed in a cluster of chairs and couches. Everyone jumped whenever the telephone rang. One family waited for word on a young woman whose lungs had been burned by a deadly mix of bathroom chemicals. The wife of a man with a brain tumor sat in a stupor. Mama settled among us in calm denial. We didn't know what went through her mind. She wouldn't talk. Ever thrifty, we fetched the remains of the Thanksgiving dinner and heated it in the cafeteria microwave. We huddled, cracking jokes like hickory nuts for survival. We lived in that lounge, napping and housekeeping in our little corner, clutching the mundane, elevating it to the surreal, charged by every sensation. We alternated between stoicism and despair. We imagined the reactions Daddy would have if he could see himself lying there in the hospital bed.

"If he woke up after laying flat on his back that long, don't you know he would be all stove up?"

"He'd bellyache for a month. I can hear him now."

It took about two minutes of family counsel to decide against heroic measures for prolonging life. We knew he would hate the idea of being hooked to machines. We discussed it briefly. And then in characteristic Mason fashion, we hung around in the hall for half an hour trying to decide what to do about supper. No one would take the initiative. Finally we sent for a pizza.

The days passed. Our friend Dottie brought us a station-wagon load of Chinese carryout food, with a tablecloth, cloth napkins, china plates, candles, chopsticks, and a bottle of wine with wine glasses. She arranged the dinner on the circular coffee table in the lounge. We lived in illusions, in shining glimpses of possibility. Daddy would miraculously wake up and we would all drive home.

Alternately, we told ourselves that slipping away in a coma was the best way to die. We thought he was lucky he didn't know his plight, lucky to exit this way, without suffering. Of course we wanted him to wake up, and we hammered at the neurologists. We demanded information, answers, assurances—which they could not give. We wanted him to live, to recover. But we knew he could not tolerate being an invalid. We didn't want him to spend the rest of his days in a wheelchair, helpless.

He had never trusted doctors. He wouldn't go to them except when he suffered severely. For years, he'd had a chronic earache, with a permanent ringing in his ears. When he had his ears tested once, he was pleased that the doctor could hear the ringing too. But his distrust of doctors made him skeptical of their methods—their horse liniment, their snake oil, their magic cures with cobalt and rotgut chemical potions. He knew people who had died from going to the doctor. He knew people who carried piss-bags plugged into their sides. Why would doctors do that to a person? He knew their character. He knew when they were putting one over on him. He saw how they acted superior, wielding their high-blown vocabulary to shame him. He hated hospitals so much he wouldn't even take his dog Oscar to the vet to be tested for heartworm, even though a neighbor's dog had died of heartworm. "Oscar don't want to go to the hospital," he said.

His cousin Mose had diabetes and wasn't supposed to eat much bread. "What that doctor don't know won't hurt him," Mose said. Daddy and Mose and all their kind continued to have eggs and fried toast and bacon or sausage for breakfast every day of their lives. Cholesterol was just another booger-man story they didn't have time for.

Daddy died on December 1, his mother's birthday. He didn't get to learn how the earthquake prediction turned out.

His death came much too soon, before crucial things had been said. Unanswered questions flew around like moths drifting toward a pilot light. We needed to understand his perversity, his stubbornness, his passivity. We needed clarification. He had been so silent. What had he made of us? We needed to show our love, heap upon him a backlog of long-intended expressions of sentiment. What do I do now? Mama wanted to know.

Instead of answers, we had food. Before the funeral, neighbors and kinfolks began bringing food to the house. They brought chicken buckets from Kentucky Fried Chicken, deli meat-and-cheese trays, loaves of white bread and pimiento-cheese spread, pies and cakes. A few made casseroles or cakes, but most brought prepared dishes from the supermarket. Store-bought costs more, so it has higher status.

The brick, faux-plantation-style funeral home in Mayfield is positioned between Wal-Mart and Kmart. It's an old funerary establishment, in one family for several generations. The place is dismal with its miserable purpose. We forced ourselves through its doors, dreading the private family preview of the enhanced body before the visitors arrived. We dreaded our own grief, the awkwardness of our sorrow. As we entered, our misery exploded through wads of Kleenex. The tears came like a poison we had to eject.

But the man lying there in the three-piece suit was not Wilburn Mason, only a garish look-alike, some store-window mannequin. Mama was unable to look at this grotesque version of her husband. Later, when the guests arrived, she could not stand beside the casket and greet people as was customary. She sat far down the front row of chairs, where the casket was out of her line of sight. The visitors came to her. "He looks real nice," they said. The rest of us mingled.

There was a lively evasiveness among the guests. People said, "It's nice to see you." Some avoided the subject of our loss. The Clear Springs kinfolks swam into focus, and then the old buddies Daddy hung out with at the filling station, and guys he had played with as a boy. They told us stories, things we didn't know, pranks Daddy pulled. The spirit grew lighter, more in keeping with Daddy's personality. But the flowers were incongruous, not his style. Many accompanying cards listed several names of people who had "made up" (paid for) some flowers together. Some of the offerings were plastic or silk, made to endure in the elements.

The next day, after the funeral—which was conducted at the funeral home chapel—we rode to Clear Springs in a Lincoln Town Car behind the hearse. A policeman led the procession, followed by the preacher, then the hearse, then the family. Just east of town, a red pickup truck broke into the line. The policeman stopped the procession and got out of his patrol car. He motioned for the truck to leave the line. When it failed to cooperate, he gestured more vehemently. Finally, in seeming chagrin, the truck veered out of the line and turned left into the parking lot of a motel. It blundered along, looking as though it couldn't figure out what had happened. And then the procession continued.

"Don't you wish Daddy could have seen that?" we said.

"He would have gotten a kick out of that."

We were seeing everything through his eyes. He loved anything that flouted convention.

All along the highway, the oncoming traffic saw us and slowed down. The drivers didn't whiz past, bent on their missions to the video store or the Piggly Wiggly; they pulled over and stopped on the shoulder of the road. All of them. It is the custom of the South. Some of the drivers were young people, including a few sorry-looking guys with unruly hair and rear-jacked cars. Farther down this two-lane state road, we came upon some construction work, and the oil-pavement trucks rolled out of our way. One of the workmen doffed his blaze-orange hard hat and held it to his chest.

Our little procession probably seemed eerily appropriate to all those motorists and workmen, for death was on everybody's mind. The earthquake was due that day. Schools were actually closed and grocery stocks were low.

Our Town Car was a sort of mortuary schooner. The trip to Clear Springs was a long, slow, peaceful ride through town and the countryside. I could see the landscape more clearly than I had since I was a child. We passed the old Arnett property, Granny's homeplace, and the family cemetery next to it. When we turned down the Clear Springs road, an old 1880 map of Clear Springs—a detailed guide to the past—came to mind. The map, which I had been studying recently, showed all the old houses and the names of the families who lived in them. It occurred to me that so little had changed since then; the nineteenth century was barely yesterday. The road was paved now, but it was still a country road, with the residences spread far apart. I noticed a ramshackle tobacco barn through the trees. Only a few brick houses were new. We floated past reminders of generations of Burnetts and Arnetts and Hickses, all relations of mine. The names on the mailboxes offered hints. I wanted to know the stories. Who were those people of my past? What had happened to them? What life would I have led if my family had never left Clear Springs? We passed the road where Mama had lived as a little girl with her grandmother, Mammy Hicks. We glided up Pulltight Hill, so called because mules had to pull tight when they trudged up its steep slope. McKendree Church was at the crest of the hill, and the cemetery was across the road. Both are still part of the old Mason homeplace; the Mason family supplied the land for the church. Literally, with scant preparation, I had been thrust back to my roots. Significance seemed embedded in the very ground. The cemetery was a miniature of the 1880 map of the community, I thought, gazing around at the stones that were engraved with familiar surnames.

Under a little blue tent, we sat on folding chairs beside the casket, which had an American flag spread over it. The preacher led a graveside service from a funeral manual—some words that didn't much register. I thought about the earthquake. It might erupt any second. The churches had been well attended the day before, a Sunday. A lot of people had added earthquake insurance riders, made new wills, held yard sales.

Daddy would have loved it if the ground had opened up on that raw December day and toppled him down in. He hated trappings so much, it would have been fitting if something had happened to undercut it all, to bring us all down to earth, into the earth, to show that all was folly.

I realized that we were sitting on Granddaddy's grave. Masons surrounded us. Herman and Bessie, Roe and Rosie, Robert and Ethel. We were on an artificial green carpet, like the astro-stuff Daddy had glued onto the front porch. The carpet had been spread over the ground; it extended down into the grave and out over the mound of dirt, as if we could not bear the sight of it. The casket was poised above the lined grave, which held a metal vault. The lid of the vault was waiting nearby. The flowers were banked on top of the carpet that covered the pile of dirt. Later the florists' stilts and plastic baskets would be arranged on the newly filled grave.

Because Daddy had been in the Navy, he received a military send-off from the mayor of Mayfield and another veteran, who wore V.F.W. hats and medal-studded vests. After the preacher finished, the mayor read a brief military service. Then he and his fellow vet folded the flag into a triangular package and presented it to Mama. She was cocooned in a long goose-down coat of mine from my snow-belt days. It was a bone-chilling day. Remote and preoccupied, she seemed like a chrysalis waiting until the time to emerge. We had been given our choice of "Taps" or a twenty-one-gun salute. We thought "Taps" would be easier on Daddy's ears. We glanced around for the bugler but didn't see anyone. Then in the background I glimpsed the mayor's V.F.W. companion holding something at arm's length, as if he had just found a bomb. It was a small tape recorder. He punched a button and a tinny rendition of "Taps" played.

I was outside myself. I was back in 1880, when the map delineated a simple agrarian economy. The Masons had been at the stable center of this community's history. What they passed down seemed to have arrived intact from the two brothers who first settled this ground in the 1820s. The Mason homeplace was only a little distance to my right, beyond McKendree Church. There, the Masons took my mother in after her grandmother died. I twisted around in my seat, gazing across the farmland to the southwest, to where Mama's grandmother, Mammy Hicks, had lived. I knew her house was still there, but I couldn't see it through the trees. My father's people and my mother's were commingled on this portion of land. Now I was here, slowed to a halt, forced to consider final things. The presence of the grave outlined the circle of life's journey. I realized that not everything had been accounted for. There was a large-scale forgetting all around me, through generations. But our history was mapped out here in Clear Springs, like the fencerows edging the fields that spread out in all directions. The history seemed to rise from the land, wrapping around me.

I knew little about our ancestors. "We came from England," Daddy had told me. "All the Masons here have big noses, and a lot of them have a hump. They got the hump when one of them married an Irish woman with a hump. Her whole family had humps—from being hod carriers, I reckon." He grinned.

Now, in my head, I could hear him talking, saying something typical, like, "I think I'll join the French Foreign Legion." I could hear him say "Hollyhocks!"—a comical word with an inherent scoff. He pronounced it "hollyhawks." He was sparing with words, but I realized now that usually when he spoke up, it was for the love of language.

I remembered a summer in 1975, when Roger and I explored the Borderlands—the coming together of northern England and southern Scotland. We rambled through sheep pastures, where miles of stone fences, which seemed centuries old, stretched out in all directions. Suddenly, the meaning and fact of my name struck me forcibly. Centuries of stonemasons had fashioned those walls. We came from people who built borders with stones. Over time, we had forgotten.

We left the cemetery in the Town Car. The driver backed out into the road on a blind hill, the top of Pulltight, directly across from McKendree Church. He blithely made a dogleg turn onto Panther Creek Road just as a speeding RC Cola truck, a huge eighteen-wheel rig, careened over the crest. The truck, braking, hurtled headlong behind us. We didn't notice. The others told us later that the truck braked and swerved, and blue smoke went flying up from the wheels. "You were nearly killed," they said.

"A handy place to get hit," we joked. "The cemetery's right here."

"And we've got the tape of 'Taps.' "

We gathered at the old Mason homeplace. I sat among the Clear Springs kinfolks, in the heart of Mason history, wondering, trying to feel back through generations, feeling a huge separation from this past, because my father was gone. I was trying to dig at his roots, hoping to find them alive, as one sometimes does when a potted plant seems to die. I saw my mother looking around at the kitchen, where her aunt Rosie had once reigned, and I thought about her deep involvement with the Mason family. This house was where my mother grew up, was courted, and had left to make her life for fifty-four years with the handsome man she once told me was "just larruping." I could not know the vastness of this separation, her bereavement.

For many weeks after the funeral I felt something that I had not known was intrinsic to grieving. It was a strange exhilaration. I couldn't hold my mind on the pain. Death was so painful that it knocked me out of myself into a celebration of life. Intensely aware of life's fragility, I drove along the Western Kentucky Parkway, drinking the landscape; every detail was fresh and remarkable. The lines of cedar trees growing like weeds out of rock crevices. The icicles hugging the faces of the limestone cutaways along the roadbed. The hazy winter pastures. The sprinklings of cattle—an all-white herd scattered on moon-color ground. Frost on dead grass. Leftover hay bales like giant shredded-wheat rolls. The winter landscape was a husk, a silhouette, a promise.

Everything I saw compelled my attention, yanked me out of my myself. It was a survival mechanism, this strange buoyancy. Some archaic words came to me to describe it, words I might have read in Granny's speller: a queer lightsomeness. I was lightsome, floating. I wondered if this was the way I was supposed to feel when I dedicated my life to Christ at the church altar when I was fifteen—charged with a new responsibility to celebrate life.

Life was a brittle frost-pattern on the window light—beautiful and fleeting. I was alive.

A farmer faces the fragility of life every day. It takes faith that his winter-dead fields will burst again with life. It takes faith to keep going, proof by habit. A farmer's belief in the sunrise and the changes of the seasons is the essence of his creed but also of his doubt.

Oscar and I walked to the pond. Oscar seemed eager for some action. He had looked around for Daddy, then settled for my company. Earlier in the week, seven ducks had appeared at the pond—six Muscovy ducks and a white one. I brought them some corn I had found in the stable. Daddy had collected some stray ears of corn the combine had missed. He had saved them to feed the squirrels. I rubbed the ears together and shelled the kernels onto the pond bank. Today there were ten ducks. I had heard that they had been moving around the neighborhood, fleeing coyotes.

Oscar and I made a complete circuit of the farm, roaming back half a mile through the fields. The soybeans and corn had been harvested, and no winter wheat had been planted this year, so the fields would remain stubbly and brown all winter. The ground was muddy. Oscar was busy, checking out all his favorite places. We crossed both creeks, which had slowed to trickles. Oscar splashed, I rock-hopped. The back field was ragged with cornstalks and briars and some kind of wavy plant that sliced my fingers when I tried to pick a few stalks for a bouquet. Daddy had kept paths mowed around the edges of the fields, against the tree lines. Already I could see what work needed to be done. Branches had fallen across the path in front of me. I picked them up and dragged them toward the creek. Oscar, on the lookout for rabbits, trotted ahead.

"Oscar likes to work," Daddy would say as they took off together into the fields or to the barn. Oscar loved it best when Daddy cranked up his three-wheeler (an outlawed all-terrain vehicle). Oscar knew the creek beds intimately, all the paths and coyote dens and rabbit holes. At the end of a walk he often disappeared into a briar patch, where he'd stay and work rabbits, eventually coming home with his face bloodied by briars. He was afraid of coyotes, and each time he got a scare he'd be careful about venturing out for a time, but then after a few days he'd get brave again. Oscar was also afraid of thunder; he could hear it well in advance, in time to run home and hide. Daddy seemed just as attuned as Oscar was to the wildlife and weather of the place. Every owl or coyote sighting was news. Each change in the wind, each storm and dry spell. More news circulated in the fields and along the creek beds than on the courthouse square.

As I walked around the fields, I contemplated what I knew, what I didn't know. My sister Janice and I had congratulated ourselves on how strong we had been. We hadn't expected to be. We had always thought we would go to pieces when we lost a close member of the family. But we hadn't. Looking at the farm, I thought that maybe everything Daddy was also resided in me and in the family and on this land. He gave me the seeds. I recalled sitting behind him on the corn planter, releasing the seeds and hearing "P.S. I Love You" play in my head.

Oscar and I returned from the fields. Oscar saw Daddy's car and dashed toward it with a joyful bark, then wandered desolately around the yard. Oscar seemed without lightsomeness. A dog's terms are clearer, more extreme. Joy or sorrow.

The car was a small, red Suzuki. Daddy favored unusual foreign cars. He had owned a Fiat and a Renault, and he had bought one of the first Volkswagens in the county. Just before I moved to Kentucky, I had traded my little Honda CRX for a station wagon. I got two thousand dollars trade-in from the dealer. Daddy was disappointed when he heard what I'd done.

"Why didn't you sell it to me? I was looking for a little car like that. I couldn't find one around here for less than three or four thousand."

"But I didn't know you wanted it," I said.

"Well, I didn't know you were selling it," he said.

This was so typical of us—misunderstandings and missed connections arising from silences.

Not long before that, he had gone to a car dealer in Paducah. He had found a used Honda he wanted in the lot. When he went into the office to buy it, a salesman talked at him for a while. Then the salesman said, "How do you intend to pay for it?"

Daddy bristled. He assumed the salesman didn't believe he could afford a car and would have to borrow. He was a farmer, in his jeans and feed cap.

"I was going to pay for it with *money*," he said, his hand clutching his wad of bills. He turned toward the door. "But I've changed my mind."

So instead, he bought the Suzuki, from a different dealer.

Now, in the glove compartment of the car, I found tapes of Jerry Lee Lewis, Chuck Berry, Bill Haley, and Muddy Waters. I remembered the foot-stomping old music we had listened to together from WLAC in Nashville.

Under the tapes, in a crevice, I found a small cardboard box. Inside was a ring set with what looked like diamonds. I showed it to LaNelle.

"I don't know diamonds from sequins," I said. "Is this real?"

"I don't know," LaNelle said. "Do you think he was going to give it to Mama for Christmas?"

We liked that thought. His way of romancing Mama was always off-key, a little tawdry. He brought her presents from flea markets—used appliances and antique oddities. Could he have bought this ring for her for a surprise? Would he have been that romantic?

We took the ring to Mama. "Look what we found," we said like little girls. We told her our theory.

She examined the ring. "No," she said. "That was a prize I won at the senior citizens, a grab-bag thing at a card game. It's not real. Wilburn was going to see what he could get for it at trade day."

Four

Clearing

20

Widows worry about grass. My mother anguishes over the upkeep of the farm. Nobody could keep it spruced up the way Daddy always had. He groomed the woods beside the road until it resembled a park. He gathered all the beer cans and fast-food packaging hurled from passing cars. He allowed no junk cars, concrete blocks, spare parts, chicken coops—nothing claptrap or trashy—to be visible from the road. He ran the Weed Eater along margins. He mowed the path along the creek to the pond. He mowed an expanse near the road, the site of his dairy barn that had burned. He circled meticulously through the small orchard of dwarf fruit trees.

That he isn't here to keep up the place according to his standards seems the most direct indicator of my mother's grief. When she hires people to mow, they don't take the time to clear the woods of leaves and fallen tree limbs. In the spring, she and Daddy always raked and burned the leaves and hauled limbs to the creek. Now she feels compelled to manage the spring cleanup alone.

"I have to keep this place up," she says.

"Don't," we say. "It doesn't have to be a park. Let it be a woods."

"But he was so proud of this place."

"But he's not here now. So it's not the same."

When she pauses, unsure how to respond, we add, "Nobody could take care of it the way he could. So he's irreplaceable. You wouldn't want to think somebody else could fill his shoes, would you?"

But she goes out and rakes until her body feels staved in. Breathing the leaf dust aggravates her bronchitis. A mist of chicken feed in the air settles on her bare arms; it is thick enough to scrape off. She telephones Seaboard Farms and instructs the management to install a finer filter.

What to do with the farm has become an ongoing dilemma, which prolongs itself into a basic state of being founded on inertia. Daddy had wanted Mama to live out her days on the farm, but now Mama's widow friends advise her not to. They have moved to town, and they say they're happier without farms to worry about. They were afraid to live alone in the country. Independent, they enjoy life in their simple little brick houses with minimal upkeep and rug-sized yards. All of them had been obsessed with grass. "A woman can't keep up a farm like that," they say. "You'll sell out and move to town. You'll wait two years and then you'll sell."

She thinks this is what she has to do. But her widow friends lead considerably more ladylike lives than she ever has. They play at crafts and decorate cakes and dust their knickknacks. Mama was always more ambitious; she wants to grow things and go fishing. Crafts are low on her list.

She waits. She keeps worrying about the grass, fretting about the pondweed. Surely she would be glad to leave Granny's house, we think, but she won't say what she really wants to do. We sense she is waiting for us to take the initiative, to advise her, to lead the way. She has always had bosses. She has never been on her own. She is not used to asserting her own wishes.

Two years go by, and still she has not followed her friends into town. She edges beyond the agonized "why?" of grief to a routine she accepts. We are more and more able to reminisce about Daddy; instead of dwelling on the recent past, I ask her about when they were young. I ask her to tell me about their wartime separation.

She shows me a postcard postmarked "Train 6, Omaha & Ogden Railroad." He wrote, "Hello sugar, I am still riding and seeing a lot of bad and pretty country. We will get to Calif. sometime tomorrow. Love Wilburn."

Mama turns the postcard over. The scene on the front is a classic butte in the Green River Valley of Wyoming. "After that I didn't hear from him for two weeks, and that was the hardest two weeks of my life. He was out on the water. I was nuts."

She repeats what she has often said, "He had his choice between the battleship and the destroyer and he took the destroyer. The other one sunk on the way back. It carried the bumb over. Some of the boys he trained with were on that ship. One was just a kid, under age. He was real fat."

All my life, I've heard the story of the choice between the battleship and the destroyer and how the battleship carried the "bumb." The next time I see my brother, Don, I ask him if Daddy ever discussed this with him.

"He told me he was offered the chance to volunteer for a secret mission. But he wouldn't do it. He was no fool." Don laughs. "Then I saw the movie *Jaws* and one of the characters told the story of the U.S.S. *Indianapolis*. The name sounded familiar. And I realized that was the ship Daddy had told me about. It was just like Daddy told it. The *Indianapolis* carried the bomb over, and it was torpedoed after it delivered the bomb. The story in the movie was very vivid." His eyes widen. "They told about how the sharks ate the sailors at the rate of seven to ten an hour."

A rigor runs through me.

"If Daddy had gone on that secret mission, you wouldn't be here," I say.

"LaNelle wouldn't be either," he says. "I've thought about that."

Sailor-gorging sharks might have wrecked this landlocked farm family. But Daddy came home and our lives resumed as if nothing had happened. I check Granny's 1946 diary again.

MARCH 11. *Clear, rather cool wind from the east. Wilburn got home last night, received his discharge from the Navy at Great Lakes, Ill., is home to stay. We gardened today. Bob went to the sales at the stockyard.*

MARCH 12. *Clear, and cold wind blowing from the south. We went back across the creek and burnt off broom sedge this afternoon.*

MARCH 13. *Partly cloudy, wind in south. We planted the garden. Mrs. Payne came to Christie's to sew this afternoon.*

MARCH 14. *Cloudy and rainy, wind in south. Cleaned out the wash-house and meat house. Bob went to town.*

MARCH 15. *Clear and almost still, little breeze from the south. We washed a big washing, all of Wilburn's clothes he brought home with him.*

Once he was safely home, her diary offers no evidence that the larger world exists, except for one entry from June 30. "We went down to Wilburn's to hear about the atomic bomb over the radio."

Our story could have ended out there in the Pacific, and our family farm would no doubt be long gone. But my father returned, the farm endured. It is ending now, decades later. I'm aware that something larger than myself, larger than our family, is ending here. A way of life with a long continuity, tracing back to the beginnings of this country, is coming to an end.

My mother has managed alone for a few years now. But the place is wearing on her. If the small family farm—the Jeffersonian ideal—had remained viable in America, my brother would probably be running our farm today and Mama would still be in her own house in the woods. Don does live nearby, but he works long hours for Coca-Cola and he has his own family. He and his young boys do some of the mowing around the place and tend to the pond. In this age, no one expects Don to spend the night at his mother's house so that she won't be alone. She herself would not allow that.

Mama speaks vaguely about putting the farm up for sale. Daddy often talked about "selling out," more to test the sound of the idea than to state a purpose.

"Do you want to move to town?" I ask Mama.

"Well, this place is too much for me to take care of," she says.

Beyond that, she won't give a straight answer. She won't say what she wants.

During visits home, I take her to see houses for sale, in neighborhoods of small houses, in parts of Mayfield she knows well.

"The rooms are so little," she says. "I'm used to big rooms. Look at that tooty dining room. I couldn't have one of my family dinners in that little hole."

The yards are pathetic, too small for pets. They don't have beautiful old trees.

"There wouldn't be enough room for a garden there," she comments of one place.

And of another, "That one's too close to the creek. It'll flood."

We drive all over town, as the movie location scouts did a few years before. What kind of place would make her happy? I know she will not be content in a puny brick box, in spite of what her widow buddies say. And she shouldn't live where there is much traffic, because of Oscar and her two cats, Chester and Susie. And she has to have lots of outdoor space. Country people have a phobia against houses built close together. None of the houses we see satisfy her.

She keeps vacillating. Finally she says, almost as if it were a secret,

"I kindly hate to see the farm go, to lose the Mason family name." She says this, knowing that no one in the family is ready to take up farming or to build a house in the shadow of the chicken tower. We realize, then, how important it is to her that the place stay in the family. A homeplace is where you were raised. This is our home. She wants us to care about it, and she doesn't want us to fight over it. She wants us to inherit it and carry it on somehow, as children did in the old days. The fierce hold a farm family has on its members is a measure of the value and meaning of a homeplace.

The little white house stands abandoned, too fragile for meaningful repair; and the house she lives in has sagging floors, peeling siding, termites. She is willing to make do, but we want better for her. We all live in nicer houses than she does, which makes us feel guilty. We're worried about her safety. It bothers us that she has to cross the busy road to reach the mailbox, and that she has to climb icy exterior stairs to the porch in the winter. We don't like her living alone on the edge of town with only the chicken tower and its spotlights for company at night. We want her to have some reward for her hard years, to have a house with conveniences that will ease her into old age. Cautiously, we are reversing our roles; we begin mothering her.

I suspect that what bothers her is the specter of the Big Fine House. A number of folks from Clear Springs saved their money and got themselves Big Fine Houses, mostly in town. Daddy believed such houses made people snooty. The house may be no more than an average-sized brick ranch with a utility room, a kitchen with built-in cabinets, a den, and an attached garage, but with its bath and a half, wall-to-wall carpets, and laminated kitchen counter it may seem grand. Most important is central heat—no more drafty old fireplaces and hazardous woodstoves.

In the fifties, the news that "she's got her a washer and dryer" was a sign of liberation. Until I left home, Mama used Granny's old wringer Maytag with the metal tubs; she and Granny built a fire outside under an iron wash kettle to heat the water. Sometime in the sixties, Mama got a washer and dryer—secondhand, some deal Daddy found somewhere.

Mama tells me now, "Back where I was raised, in the winter or in dry spells, we'd have to pack the water from the well up near McKendree Church. That was 'women's work.' The men could have dug a well down there, but they didn't care how hard the women had to work."

"Water was right under the ground," I say. "That's why the place was called Clear Springs."

"The men didn't see any need in making life easier for the women," Mama says bitterly. "I look back and see how women were treated and what we put up with, and I just wonder why we did it. I'm amazed."

"Then don't you think it's high time you had a little something for yourself?"

"Well, I'm too used to the old ways, I guess."

"Don't you think you deserve anything better?"

She won't answer.

Eventually we work out a deal. We'll help her buy a house so that she won't have to sell the farm. We've all promised to help maintain the farm somehow. She can still go fishing and have her garden there. She'll rent out the farmhouse and continue to lease the fields to a neighbor. The crucial point is that it will remain in the Mason name.

Again, Mama and I tour houses in town—some bigger houses than we saw before.

"I'm just an old country hunk," she says. "I won't be able to wear my old clothes at a house in town. I'll have to dress up for city folks."

A house with a swimming pool makes her laugh. "What do I need with a swimming pool?"

I say, "You could raise catfish in it."

Mama begins noticing that all the furniture in the nicer houses is like her antique furniture, except that much of it is imitation. Hers is real.

"Who would have thought that people in town would want that kind of old junk?" she says.

In all the houses we see country chic—reproductions of antique washstands and cane-bottom ladderback chairs and grandfather clocks. We see genuine antiques, too—pie safes, butter churns, refinished wardrobes that double as TV armoires. Mama has originals of almost everything she sees on display. It dawns on her that Granny's oak churn is now a prized collectible, and she regrets that she sold Granny's pedal-powered sewing machine. Suddenly Mama's own furniture seems legitimized, what people in town are decorating their houses with. It is no longer junk. In the end, it is the furniture in these nice houses that liberates her. She can begin to picture her things—and with them, herself—in one of these houses.

In the end we talk her into buying a better house than she would have chosen for herself. We feel guilty but pleased, triumphant but edgy. It is a three-bedroom brick house with an attached garage and a great room with a cathedral ceiling. We are aware that in some sense it is all wrong—too big, too fine. Making do has been Mama's profession. It is her habit, too deep to violate. And moving away from the farm—even a short distance, even if she still owns it—may be too much for her. I am aware of the contradictions of my own heart. Moving the elderly never works, I am informed. Their attachment to the familiar—their routines, their ways—makes the uprooting almost unbearable. But the decision is made.

On a spring day Mama and I explore the new house, planning the furniture arrangement. The yard is spacious enough for her pets, and it is protected from busy streets.

"There's a grapevine in the back," I report to Mama. "You can make jelly."

"Grapevines will take the place," she says matter-of-factly.

Liriope-bordered flower beds have been planted around the house with a landscaper's eye to successive blooms. A graceful Japanese maple is growing up against the wall behind the house. Mama examines it closely. "That will have to be cut back," she says. "Look how it's growing into the gutters. It'll work into the house."

Uprooted, she wants to uproot something else.

I go to the bank with Mama. She wears a grass-green sweatsuit and running shoes and no makeup. Forgetting her role in the transaction, she has intended to sit in the car while I pick up the papers.

"Come on, Mama," I say. "You're buying a house."

We sit with officials at a long shiny table in a private room at a state-of-the-art bank built to resemble a Southern plantation. In the preliminary idle chat, we discuss pets. The real-estate agent says he loves all animals except moles. He kills moles. All last summer he was after one particular mole that was tearing up the yards in his neighborhood. A neighbor who was especially annoyed by that mole's backyard antics used a nine-millimeter pistol but missed. Finally the agent got it. "I put it on his dinner plate for a surprise present!"

The banker says, "They used to use moleskin to make powder puffs."

Mama says, "My grandmother ruined a perfectly good knife a-skinning a mole to make a powder puff."

Later, I think how her comment seemed apropos. In her view, she is going to let a perfectly good farm go to ruin while she moves uptown into a ridiculous powder puff of a house.

The old house is in upheaval, torn apart by the preparations for moving, yet I'm dawdling, asking my mother questions about her past. Every object in the house seems to invite memory, but the pictures are the most compelling. I flip through the old albums. There's a shadowy snapshot of her grandmother, a formidable woman in an apron, her face hidden beneath her bonnet brim. I can imagine her skinning a mole without a second thought.

In one of the albums, there are some pictures of Robert Lee, Mama's father—snapshots I've seen many times but never deeply considered. Both of my grandfathers were named Robert Lee—Robert Lee Mason and Robert E. Lee. How much more quintessentially Southern could such a heritage be? I was named "Bobbie" for Granddaddy, Robert Lee Mason; it was traditional to name the first son— and that was supposed to be me—for the paternal grandfather. Granddaddy was the steady one, the one whose last name implies stonework—the rock fences of civilized, contained landscapes. My other grandfather was the wanderer. Robert Lee's face stares at me from a photograph. He is a handsome man, with thick hair and slick city clothes. There we are with him, in one of the pictures. Mama is holding Janice, who's an infant. I'm about four, gazing squint-eyed into the distance, as if I know already I am going to take off, just as Robert Lee did. He had deserted his family, and Mama didn't know him when she was growing up. But who was he? What did this negligent, insouciant man do to her soul—and ultimately to mine?

"Mama, what do you remember of your father?" I ask.

She's busy dusting the ceiling with a towel pinned onto the broom. I remember how she used to pin a diaper on the broom and swab the cobwebs away.

"He never loved me," she says, with a bitterness that could etch stone.

"How do you know?"

"I just do." She sets the broom down and fiddles with a pillow tassel.

"What about your mother?" I ask. "I don't remember ever seeing a picture of her."

"There's a big portrait of her in the attic at the other house," Mama says. "It got accidentally walled up behind some insulation, and I never could get it out."

"Oh, can we find it?"

"There won't be no use trying to get it out now," she says. "There won't be nothing left."

"How do you know?"

"We had another picture like it, and it crumbled to nothing years ago. I'm sure it's all crumbled to dust by now," she says, busying herself with a mob of worn dishrags.

I wish I could see that picture. Maybe the special conditions in the nest of insulation protected it. Maybe it survived. Maybe there would still be a ghostly impression of my grandmother Eunice's face—the grandmother I never knew.

A while later, Mama hands me a box of loose pictures. "I think there may be a picture of my mama in there. I don't know if you ever saw these."

It is a candy box. I remember how Daddy always assaulted a box of chocolates, punching down the centers to find the ones with nuts in them.

The large photograph on top is a school picture, in which parents are posing with their small children in front of a large two-room plank building with a dogtrot breezeway.

"That's Mammy Hicks holding my mother," Mama says, touching two small figures in the second row.

Mammy Hicks—my great-grandmother—appears thin and old, with fair hair pulled back tight. Her daughter Eunice is in her lap. She's a chubby little girl with long, dark curls. She is about six.

"That's your mother!"

"They said I had her black hair. She had a Burnett face, round and fat. They said she was the prettiest thing and she loved to laugh and she had little fat hands."

Mama shows me a thumbnail photo, the kind made in a booth at the dime store.

"That's my mother on the right and my Aunt Hattie on the left," she says, sitting down on the couch beside me.

I can barely make out two tiny, round faces with pompadoured hair. I need a magnifying glass—or perhaps a floodlight. I remember the searchlight at the county fair when I was growing up, how it would play across the sky like a giant windshield wiper. Looking for enlightenment here in these bits of the past is like playing that light across the night heavens. It blanks out the stars, but it seems to be looking for something significant to alight on. Of course, the searchlight at the fair was merely waving its big arm of light in order to be seen from afar. But I really am looking for anything that will illuminate the pathways from the past to my own psyche. I know how one set of grandparents helped form me, but the other set was always missing.

"Tell me more about your parents, Mama," I say. "What were they like? Could they sing or play the fiddle? What was your life like when you were growing up?"

"Oh, I can't remember." She laughs. "I declare, my mind's not two inches long." She jumps up and starts packing some pillows into a toilet-paper carton from the grocery.

Of course, all my life I've known the bare outline of her story. It was like a tree that had lost its leaves. Hanging from its bare branches was the lone orange that she received for Christmas one year. My mother always gave us more than we deserved, slathering love on us in compensation for her own deprived childhood. The night before Easter, she labored at her sewing machine long after supper, finishing our Easter outfits for church. Christmas was an extravagant production, with scads of presents—toys and books and clothes, usually including an outfit she had sewn for each of us. And she stuffed treats into our Christmas knee-socks hanging from the door facing—apples, Brazil nuts, chocolate creams, peppermint sticks. That Christmas orange was on her mind.

Drawing on the theory of chaos, I imagine how the Christmas orange comes down to me. In chaos theory, the smallest incident has far-reaching consequences. The ripple effect of the exhaust fan of an air conditioner in Paducah, say, may eventually affect a storm in Padua. I like to imagine how generations of the attitudes and behaviors of country people—a legacy of paucity and small shadings of pride and resistance and shame—intertwined and radiated down through time in increasingly complicated shapes. There is much more to my mother's story than the orange. I want to know the details. I want to color in the outline.

Later in the day, after I keep pestering her, Mama sinks down onto the couch again. "Where do you want me to start?" she asks.

21

At twenty-one, Eunice Hicks was afraid she was going to be an old maid. One of her sisters, Hattie, was already an old maid; nobody would marry her because she had fits. Another sister, Rosie, did not marry until she was thirty. Having children so late in life was risky; Eunice and her sisters knew of women who had died from bearing children too late.

Eunice was aware of the wild, red-headed youth up the Clear Springs Road, the rough, flirty boy who acted older than his years—Robert E. Lee. She liked the way he laughed and joked around. They had attended different schools, but she had seen him working in the fields, or hanging around the general store at Clear Springs. She had seen him driving down the road from the store to the river bottom in a mule-drawn wagon with his father. The sight of Robert Lee whipped her up inside like someone beating egg whites.

Eunice, who lived with her mother and raised tobacco and calves, had good things to start out married life with. She possessed a smart buggy and a healthy, fine-looking horse—a sign of status and prosperity. She owned a Hoosier pantry—a staple kitchen item of the time, a wooden unit of cupboards with a built-in flour dispenser funnel and a porcelain countertop. As a young woman of means, she was in a position to attract a respectable husband who owned some land. But instead, Eunice married the good-looking neighbor with the sexy swagger and not a penny to his name. The marriage was an immediate disaster, lasting less than a year. Robert Lee abandoned Eunice before their baby was born. He fled the county, driving off in Eunice's horse and buggy. Possibly they were legally his property, through marriage, but no one in Eunice's family saw it that way. He was a thief. And they never forgave him.

"You go straight to the courthouse," her mother told her when she straggled home in a neighbor's wagon, cradling her big belly. Divorce was uncommon in the 1920s, but Eunice, humiliated and angry, immediately filed the papers. Her mother and sisters all said she had married beneath her, and she realized it was true. Robert Lee hadn't even given her a real home, just a corner in his parents' house. He didn't own a farm. All he could do was hire out as a laborer. Everybody in the neighborhood let her know what a big mistake she had made. "You grabbed the first trifling tramp to come sashaying down the road," they said. "You're lucky your mama let you come back home after he run off."

Eunice gave birth to her baby and resumed life with her mother and her sister Hattie. Before long, Luther Moore, an older man with grown children, noticed her at a church supper. Luther had recently lost his wife. He was the opposite of Robert Lee—a respectable landowner. When her divorce was final, Eunice married him. With her baby, Christy, Eunice moved to Luther's pleasant cabin-style house, down the Panther Creek Road. Finally, she felt settled and provided for.

Christy's earliest memories are of living there with her mother and Luther Moore. She can recall the layout of the house, the long porch facing the road, the cistern at the back door. She remembers creeping into the bedroom and seeing her mother and Luther Moore in bed together. When she tried to crawl into bed with them, they pushed her away. Eunice said, "Now go to your room, go on," in a shushing tone, her hand shooing. And Christy retains another glimpse of the past: her stepfather went outside behind the shed, and Eunice told her child, "Don't go out there." Hushed warnings and secret loss were at the heart of Christy's closeness to her mother.

When Christy was four, Eunice grew big and Charley was born. Christy remembers the little baby and how afterwards her mother was wild with fever. Neighbors and kinfolks fluttered in and out as Eunice lay in bed suffering. She had convulsions. Christy was stowed in Luther's wagon on a pile of tow sacks and driven up Panther Creek Road to her grandmother's house. She didn't see her mother alive again. Later, everybody said, "Your mama oughtn't to have died. She wasn't tended to right." One neighbor told her years later, "I was there, and that doctor pummeled on her stomach. I saw him. He got up on the bed on his knees and worked his fists on her. That's what killed her."

Eunice's death unhinged the whole Hicks family and neighborhood. They couldn't stop talking about it, searching to cast blame. Rumors floated around, stories compounded out of fear and grief. A conspiracy theory evolved. A lame man in the neighborhood was reported missing—murder was suspected—and somehow he got worked into the speculations about Eunice's death. Maybe she was murdered because she knew something about the lame man's disappearance. Maybe Robert Lee was in on it. Eunice had been wronged once by Robert Lee, and there was talk that she had been betrayed again. People whispered and buzzed. It was a hot summer, good for porch gossip. Rumors were built on a purloined tarpaulin and a truck leaving out in the night. Someone heard the ghostly footsteps of the missing man—his hobbled leg thumping. Someone else saw a woman carrying a bushel of leaves to a cistern in the moonlight. All of these stray tidbits grew into a garbled suspicion of adultery and murder and a body dumped in that cistern. Who did what to whom isn't clear. There was likely little to any of this, just talk and superstition. But over the years, the suspicions spread like fungus creeping outward from the basic wrongs done to Eunice—abandonment, betrayal, death.

After Eunice died, her children were separated. The new baby, Charley, was raised by Luther Moore and his mother, and Christy stayed with her grandmother, Susan Hicks, known as "Mammy Hicks," the woman who would ruin her good knife skinning a mole. Mammy Hicks and her daughter Hattie, who still lived at home, looked for signs of Eunice in the little girl. They shortened her name, Bernice Christianna, to Chris. In her hair and her cheekbones, Chris favored Eunice, but now and then they glimpsed sinister traces of Robert Lee in her.

In her new home, Chris traipsed off to explore the fields and the outbuildings, until someone ran to catch her. The new place, with its vast fields and choked fencerows, seemed to swallow her up. Mammy Hicks owned sixty-two acres, with a good barn and a stable, an orchard, a smokehouse, and a henhouse. She even had a telephone, and she had once had an elegant two-story house, but it burned, destroying most of her fine furniture. A widow, she managed well with the help of her brother and her grown sons, who rebuilt the house and did the heavier farm work. The farm was a lonely place, though, for the only child, a spirited four-year-old.

She played alone, with the meager playthings that had been scrounged up for her. Her aunt Rosie gave her a little duck, and she treated it like a doll. She talked to it and carried it around.

"Chris wooled her duck to death," Mammy told her daughter Rosie later. "It liked to broke her heart when that little duck died."

"That'll learn her," Rosie said.

Chris played with the pig. Mammy always kept a pig named Pet—a new one each year. Pet was never penned up, and he would hang around the yard, waiting for scraps. Chris would scratch him on the belly and he'd fall over and raise his leg in ecstasy. But one hard-cold day in the late fall, the men would help Mammy string him up, slit his throat, bleed him, and butcher him. She smoked the hams and sides and shoulders in her smokehouse. She made sausage with her meat grinder and packed it into homemade sacks that were like sleeves.

Mammy Hicks was a practical-minded farm woman in a long dress and apron and a bonnet with a brim as deep as an awning, but she also aspired to refinement. She was literate when most women of her generation and place were not. She made sure her six children went to school, and she purchased a mail-order organ so they could be musical, like the Hurt family. Dr. Hurt boarded a piano teacher at his fine house for his six daughters. Mammy Hicks felt she was just as good as the Hurts, with their wraparound verandah and crystal chandeliers. So the affront to her dignity when no-good Robert Lee abandoned her daughter was immeasurable.

Mammy and Aunt Hatt decided that Chris was too little to send to school the first year. Even after she started to school, they wouldn't let her walk there by herself. And whenever there was something catching going around, they kept her at home. Chris's grandmother and aunt watched over her, but they were not affectionate with her. She longed for them to hug her or pet her, as her mother had done. Chris remembered wallowing in her mother's lap, daring to slide off until she was caught by the legs. Perhaps she reminded Mammy and Hattie too much of Eunice's shame? Did they see too much of Robert Lee in her? She had an independent spirit and was scampish. In a second-grade photograph, her head is cocked shyly, but there is an internal mischief bubbling, and a sly sense of privacy in her eyes.

As she grew older, Chris overheard the talk about her father, and she wondered about him. She wondered if he thought about her at all. He was worthless, a rascally snake-in-the-grass, everyone said. He was double-dealing and black-hearted and violent. He was rumored to have joined the Army. Once, Chris saw a group of uniformed soldiers trudging along the road. "They're just getting home from the war," Hattie said. "It takes a long time for them to make their way home." Chris heard people talking about the Blue and the Gray. The Civil War and the Great War ran together in her mind. She formed a picture of her father in a uniform, off in a war. She heard he had married again. She heard he was working on the river as a deckhand on a towboat. She knew he came to Clear Springs now and then. He hadn't disappeared entirely. His family was here, and he returned occasionally from the river, or some war, to visit them. But whenever Chris asked about him, Mammy Hicks would say "Hush!" and find a chore for her to do.

Half of her was doted on and the other half was a secret shame. Chris tottered between the two views of herself. She loved her aunt and her grandmother, and they loved the part of her that came from Eunice. Often lonely, Chris explored the creeks and fencerows. But sometimes they went fishing. Mammy Hicks's people, the Burnetts, would rather fish than eat cake. The Burnetts would be chopping out tobacco, and all of a sudden one of them would say, "I believe the fish might be biting." Their hoes would drop, and before they could think it through, they would find themselves lounging on the creek bank with fishing poles. Chris went fishing in Panther Creek with her grandmother and aunt and listened to them whoop and gossip. She liked the slippery feel of the fish. She learned to thread a hook with a squirming worm and drop it into the water. When storm clouds came, Mammy herded her and Hattie home like a mother duck. Mammy feared lightning the same as snakes. Lightning had burned her house down. Lightning was like snakes jumping in the heavens, she said, all lit up and jerky. "Snake fits," she said.

Mammy Hicks suffered from dropsy—heart trouble. Her ankles swelled. She was seized with spells of weakness and couldn't do her work. As her health deteriorated, one of her sons or daughters would come to stay with her most nights. Chris waited on the porch each evening, gazing longingly down the narrow dirt road, hoping someone would come to stay the night with her grandmother. Mammy was only in her sixties, but to Chris she seemed ancient, with her wrinkled, broken body and her puffy feet bursting from her shoes.

One afternoon, Mammy Hicks was sitting up in her four-poster bed eating watermelon when all at once she lurched and fell back on the pillow.

With a shriek, Hattie leaped to her mother's side. "Chris, reach in her mouth and get that piece of watermelon out," Hattie said. "Maybe she's choked on it. Go on, reach in there. Your hand's little."

Chris did as she was told. Her grandmother's head was limp, and Chris had to force her fingers past rotten teeth. The odor was like a putrefying dead animal. She pulled out the slippery piece of watermelon. But Mammy Hicks was dead.

It was the year of the stock-market crash, but the Depression had come early to the Clear Springs area. Throughout the twenties, the farmers of Clear Springs were in difficulty. They could grow enough food for their own use, but no one had much money to buy goods, even though there were two general stores. On Saturdays, to earn some cash, the farmers carried produce and chickens and eggs to Mayfield in their wagons. Although some families owned cars, the rural way of life had changed little since the settlement of Clear Springs a century before. Mammy Hicks's Montgomery Ward organ was as newfangled as anything around. Nobody owned a radio. Nobody had a bicycle.

My mother was ten years old. Hattie's sister Rosie decided that Chris could not be left alone with Hattie because of her fits. So Rosie brought both of them to live with her and her husband, Roe Mason, on their nearby farm. The Mason farm was well kept, with the borders scythed, the rail fences laid true. Chris had often visited the place, but now that she was coming there to live, she felt uprooted once again, and her life seemed insignificant. From a small ménage of women, Chris entered a huge household of cousins, hired hands, and boarders. Uncle Roe—Thomas Monroe Mason—had one son by his first wife and three children by Rosie, his second.

Chris and Hattie brought a wagonload of Mammy Hicks's possessions with them—her dishes, some furniture, her organ, her ice-cream churn. They also brought Eunice's fine things: her preserve stands and cakestands, her Hoosier pantry, and her bed with the high headboard and footboard—the bed she died in. At Aunt Rosie's house, Chris and Hattie slept in that bed in the dining room, near the kitchen fireplace.

The house was full of children, but none of Chris's own age to play with. She was outgoing, yet she was often lonely and bewildered. She hid in the attic and wrote little stories on a tablet. Or she explored the fields and the creeks. Along the fencerows, she found a kind of weed with a translucent lining in its seedpod that she could chew. It was like plastic. Years later, when plastic was developed, she claimed she had invented it. She discovered a banana tree growing in the woods. She picked a banana and ate it. She was sure it was a banana. She didn't often have bananas, but this truly tasted like one. She tried to follow hummingbirds. She played with cats. Cats went by colors—Blackie,

Whitey, Calico, Yeller. She dressed them in doll clothes. "She's always packing a cat around," Hattie explained to Rosie. Chris wore cotton dresses that Aunt Rosie made for her. Chris always wanted something tied around her waist. If she didn't have a belt, she used a string.

Mammy Hicks's organ occupied a place of honor in the parlor. It was a beautiful thing, with cutwork and fancy trim and colorful insets. It had a gorgeous stool, with a crimson velvet cushion and beaded embroidery. Chris loved to fool around on the organ, pounding the keys and pushing and pulling the stops. Although both Hattie and Rosie could play by ear—church tunes and folk songs—they wouldn't teach Chris to play. They were too busy.

Sometimes Aunt Rosie sent Chris a mile down the road to the store to get some sugar or salt or matches. Once, there was a penny left over and Chris spent it on chewing gum. Aunt Rosie whipped her with a hickory switch, but Hattie intervened.

"If she needs correcting, I'm the one to correct her," said Hattie, who jealously guarded her niece. "She's my baby."

"I'm not going to have her think she can just take what's not hers," Aunt Rosie said. "She got that from her daddy, I'll allow."

Hattie had the falling sickness. A lick on the head had triggered her seizures years before. The affliction made everyone a little afraid of her, as if it could leap out like a contagion. They assumed she was touched in the head. Little was understood about epilepsy—or "elipepsi," as some called it. They said she "had fits," like a dog in August. Her spells often came on at the time of her period, the women claimed. Sometimes when Hattie was hoeing tobacco she would suddenly keel over and begin jerking. She drooled, her tongue hung out, and her eyes rolled back. Chris was afraid for her aunt, and she tried to anticipate risky situations, since the seizures came on so suddenly. Hattie experienced both kinds—petit mal and grand mal. The petit mal seizures were only momentary lapses, and if Chris tried to intervene during them, Hattie lashed out at her furiously. Resisting Chris's warnings, she would deliberately sit on the edge of the high end of the porch, shelling beans and humming.

"Move away from there," Chris said. "You'll pitch off the edge if you have one of them fits."

"I'll give *you* a fit if you don't watch out," Hattie said.

Hattie loved to pick blackberries. One July morning, Aunt Rosie sent Chris along with Hattie into the blackberry thicket, as she often did, to help in case Hattie had a fit. On this occasion, Hattie did have one, and she fell headlong into the briar patch. Chris pulled and tugged on her, but Hattie was heavy. Chris ran back to the house for help, but when she returned with two of her cousins, Hattie was picking berries as if nothing had happened. That summer, she put up a hundred quarts of wild blackberries.

Hattie didn't like to be reminded of her illness. The family didn't want her to take chances, or do certain things—ride a horse, stay up late, eat kraut—that might bring on one of her spells. She probably was aware of the onset of a fit. Going into a grand mal seizure is said to be a strange, dreamy feeling; Hattie would feel as if she was about to throw up, or enter the gates of heaven—one or the other. It would be like escaping. It would be a sensation that something nebulous was passing over her. And then for what might have been for-ever . . . nothing. Afterwards, she would moan and cry, and as she became gradually aware of her surroundings again, it would be like climbing out of the cistern—dark and frightening. She would cry loudly during this phase. She would come to herself eventually, no doubt feeling as if she had entered through heaven's gates but had had to exit from the gates of hell.

The residents of Uncle Roe's big house tended to shoot each other down with hard looks and straightforward judgments, with incessant teasing and carrying on. They carried on to get attention or to get even. Carrying on could mean lamenting, complaining, harping, or teasing.

"She carried on and carried on about wanting that doll."

"Mama, make Chris quit aggervatin' me about that doll."

"If y'all don't shut up about that doll, I'm going to get me a switch."

Chris got nothing but an orange the first Christmas at Uncle Roe's, but the following Christmas she finally received a doll of her own. It was a large, beautiful doll with a porcelain head and hands and a soft, cuddly body. It wore pretty clothes and it could go to sleep. But one day the doll's eyes mysteriously fell into the back of its head. Chris shook the doll, and its eyes rattled. They wouldn't open again. She wrapped the doll up in rags so no one would see its face. She was afraid she would get a whipping. She hid the doll under a quilt, scared of what the others might say.

"You punched that doll's eyes out, didn't you?" Datha said when the secret was discovered. Datha was one of the cousins, eight years older than Chris.

"No, I didn't. They broke."

"I believe you punched that doll's eyes out. Mama, Chris punched her doll's eyes out."

Later, Datha's brother Mose said, "I heared you punched your doll's eyes out, Chris."

"No, I didn't. They fell out." Chris started to cry.

"She's gettin' a sull on," Mose said. "Like a old possum gettin' a sull on."

"She's always all sulled up about something or t'other," said Herman, Mose's half-brother.

"How would she like *her* eyes punched the way she punched her doll's eyes out?" said Uncle Roe, with a wheezy chuckle.

Chris cried and screamed. She wailed.

"Old squall-bag," said Herman.

"She punched her doll's eyes out, I believe," said Datha. "I never heard of a child punching her doll's eyes out. Have you, Mary?"

"I reckon not," Datha's sister, Mary, said. Mary was sweet, but she took her sister's side. "Why would you want to punch your doll's eyes out, Chris?"

"It's *my* doll! I'll punch her eyes out if I want to!" Chris was shrieking and stomping her feet. "But I didn't do it."

"She says she didn't do it, but she acts like she did," Mose said.

And so they carried on.

One Sunday afternoon they were playing ball. All the neighborhood children were there, lots of Burnetts and Hickses, some Tynes boys. Mose chased Chris through the field behind the house. He ran her halfway to the church, caught her, and quick as a jaybird pulled her dress up and pushed mustard down her pants. "I've been wanting to do that for the longest time," he said.

"She was as mad as a old wet hen," he reported gleefully to the others.

She was angry about that for years. Not long before Mose died, in his eighties, she asked him if he remembered the incident. She asked him, "*Why* did you do that to me?" He just laughed, as though remembering a moment of pure pleasure.

Chris was a fighter, with a quick temper. The boys liked to see her get mad, so they would keep on teasing her until she vibrated with fury. She was a spitfire, they said. When she fired off her temper, the family would say, "That's the Lee in her." Chris learned how to fight everybody except Uncle Roe, the boss. Nobody messed with Roe—he used a tobacco stick for serious whippings. He assigned tasks and then stood back watching while others worked. In the mornings, he would get up first and wake up everybody, then go back to bed till breakfast was ready.

Chris did not have to help in the kitchen. Instead, they sent her out-doors. She tended her own little garden. She fed the chickens. She ran cattle. When a cow strayed from the herd or broke through a fence, Roe sent Chris after her. Roe farmed about eighty acres—mostly corn, wheat, and hay, with two or three acres of tobacco. Like most of the farmers around, he did things the old way—the hard way. Tobacco was worked entirely by hand. It was the most difficult work on the farm—tedious and grueling. Before and after school in the spring, Chris toiled in the tobacco patch. At first she was too small to set tobacco—transplant the seedlings—but she could pull the seedlings from the seedbed and drop them in place in the row. Someone else came along behind and pressed them in the ground with a sharp-pointed peg. Seedlings had to be transplanted early in the day, while the dew still drenched the plants. She went to school shivering, wet and cold all over. Later in the season, topping and suckering tobacco—cutting the flowers and new shoots from the plants to make them pro-duce more leaves—were miserable chores. Chris wore a pair of men's overalls to protect her skin from the gummy, smelly plants as she hoed the weeds out of the tobacco. When she chopped a tobacco plant down by mistake, she would bury it; but Uncle Roe caught her once and gave her a whipping.

In the fall, she helped harvest corn. They gathered the dried corn by hand, tossing it into a mule-drawn wagon. The harsh husks slit her hands. After the crop was stored in the crib, Uncle Roe sent her to the weed-choked river bottom to cut down the dried cornstalks with a sharp hoe. After all the stalks were down, he burned the field.

Robert Lee came and went, sidling around the edges of the commu-nity, visiting his parents. Aunt Rosie and Aunt Hattie were determined that Chris should not go near him. He had stolen their sister's horse and buggy. He took advantage of poor Eunice and then left her. She wouldn't have died if she hadn't married him, they said. If he hadn't taken off, she'd be living still. But no telling what he would have done to Eunice if she'd lived. Poor Eunice—maybe she was better off dead. He would have carried her to Paducah and that would have led to no telling what kind of trouble. Chris grew to hate her father.

Then she saw him. She was at Crockett's store, across from school. She saw a man standing by the potbellied stove with some farmers. He had his back to her. She thought he looked familiar. Someone whispered to her, "That's your daddy." She stared at his red-brown hair. It was an ugly color, she thought. She described it later as "piss-burnt." He was tall and slender, yet muscular, and he had a worldly air—the way he stood by the stove jawboning with the men who lingered around the store. Hickory-smoked hams hung from the rafters, and a cat was curled up on the pickle barrel. Mr. Crockett was cutting slabs of cheese. It was a lazy wintertime scene, with dark coming on fast. Her father didn't look at her. But she could hear his loud laugh, his rough talk, forbidden talk. She realized she had seen him before. A few times after school she had noticed this man standing at the edge of the playground. Now she wondered if he had been there trying to get a glimpse of her.

"Don't let your daddy come close," the Masons had said.

"Run if you see him."

"Don't talk to any of them Lees."

"He done your mama wrong."

"He drove off in her buggy. He *stole* her horse and buggy."

"And he sold them. Her fine bay mare."

"She paid a hundred dollars for that buggy."

"That buggy and horse was worth over two hundred."

Chris hated her father. But she wished he would come forward at the store and speak to her, acknowledge her. She saw him gaze around the store. But he turned his back.

She knew that Robert Lee had married again and had two children, but it was not clear to her if he was still married, or where his wife was. He had brought the two young children, Thelma and Bill, to live with his parents. Thelma, the older one, entered school at Clear Springs. When Thelma learned that Chris was her half-sister, she pulled on Chris's arms, clinging to her. Thelma stuttered. Embarrassed, Chris fought Thelma off. She didn't want to be seen with any of the Lees. They were poor, and her father was no-account. But she didn't realize at first how Thelma was starved for love.

On the road by the school, a wagon sometimes passed. A young man with a lame leg drove the mules, and an older man sat in the back.

They hauled firewood out of river-bottom land they were clearing for one of the large landowners. The young man's hair was dark; the older man had red hair fading to gray. They were Lees. Chris avoided them. They were not family to her.

The good, productive fields were those low-lying lands along the river, a mile from the house. The Mason men worked down there. One summer Aunt Rosie sent Chris down there every day with dinner for the men. Chris rode a horse, bareback, with the buckets of food hanging across the horse's shoulders. She saw the wiggly snake trails in the dust on the path in front of her. While the horse drank from the river, she laid the dinner out on stumps—meat, vegetables, tomatoes, cornbread, green onions, a jug of tea. She left the fresh horse and rode back on a horse the men had been working. She felt deliciously free on those rides, as though the horse were her own and she could go anywhere. On the route, she had to ride past terrifying dogs. That summer a mad dog roved the vicinity. Dogs drooling in August, frothing and convulsing, were a common sight.

"My crack is scalded!" she told Datha and Mary when she dismounted.

Aunt Hattie was having seizures more frequently. She went on an excursion to Mississippi with a church group and wrote home a postcard in her exquisite handwriting, which wavered slightly. "Having an elephant time," she reported. Miraculously, she made the journey without complication. But one night in the bed she shared with Chris, she began having little fits, one after another. They were quiet but continuous, like sobbing. It was as though a lifetime of heartache were coloring her dreams. Hattie twitched, like a dog dreaming. Chris waited. She knew the fits usually subsided after a short while. The bed pulsated. Chris positioned Hattie's head so her tongue wouldn't slide back into her throat. She knew there was nothing to be done for Aunt Hatt's spells except to wait them out. But this time the throbbing wouldn't stop. The seizures continued, one after another, all night. Daylight came, and still the rolling continued, gradually growing wilder.

Aunt Rosie appeared. "How long's that been going on?" she asked Chris.

"All night, just about."

Aunt Rosie felt Hattie's face. Hattie's tongue lolled against the pillow like a fish, and foamy slobber soaked the bolster case. Rosie slipped back into the bedroom to tell her husband. "Hatt needs the doctor," she said sharply.

Chris got out of bed and placed pillows on the floor in case her aunt fell. She tried to push her toward the middle of the bed, but her weight was like a full feed-sack, solid and uncooperative. Hattie was beginning to jerk more forcefully.

Roe jumped in the T-model and went for the doctor, but he soon returned, cursing.

"He wouldn't even drive out here to see about her," Roe said, stomping through the kitchen. "He said either she'd come out of it or she wouldn't. There wasn't nothing he could do."

There was no treatment for a severe epileptic attack. When a person went into continuous seizures, the violent trauma would eventually wear out the body and the heart would stop.

By mid-morning Hatt's writhing had ceased. She was dead. She was thirty-nine years old.

Chris saw the others gather around, crying—Hattie's sisters and brothers and all the cousins. She had seen Mammy Hicks lying dead. Now Hattie. She could dimly recall her mother lying motionless and beautiful, her dark hair a shadow on the pillow, her small, fat hands crossed at the waist.

Hattie was laid out in a casket in the living room, and the neighbors streamed in, bringing food. By custom, the family kept a vigil throughout the night, for it was necessary to watch over the body until it was buried. Chris hid in the shadows, afraid. After the funeral, at McKendree Church, one of Chris's distant cousins—a little girl several years younger than fourteen-year-old Chris—said to her, "What are you going to do, Chris? Where will you go?" The child's question was uncomprehending, mere chatter. She was a spoiled only child with lots of dolls. But this question stayed in Chris's mind over time. The little cousin was looking up to her as a grown-up, someone with power. This child's innocent question contained the glimmer of a notion that Chris might have a choice.

"What *am* I going to do?" she had replied, with both sorrow and hope. For a moment it was as though she had a say in her future.

With the loss of Aunt Hattie, Chris may have finished constructing that secret place in her heart where she kept herself. She had pulled away from Hattie as she was slipping into oblivion, and ever after she held herself back from everyone but her own children. Having lost her mother, her grandmother, and her aunt—everyone who might have represented any source of maternal strength—she drove the last peg into that little chamber she fashioned to hide in, the special place within herself. She tried to be tough, and she was full of sass. But she expected everything she loved to be taken from her. She never expected to be anybody. She expected to work hard and to have little to show for it. She had seen enough of death to know what it was—final, irrevocable loss. She grew fatalistic about that. But Aunt Hattie's death also deepened her zest for life; it sparked her sense of survival, her determination to persevere. It nourished a growing capacity for joy, and it generated a whirling-dervish maternal energy. She had resilience, verve, and what she called daresomeness. These are what saved her.

22

It was Hattie's wish that if something happened to her, her niece Clausie should bring Chris up. Hattie had told Rosie, "Let Clausie have her; she's got money and no younguns." Clausie had married a well-off man and lived in Mayfield. She had a job, wore fine clothes, and drove a car.

"If she lives with Clausie, there won't be nobody there for her after school," Rosie said to Roe. So, without telling Clausie of Hattie's request, Rosie and Roe decided that Chris should remain in the large household at Clear Springs. They wanted to keep an eye on her. Chris, at fourteen, was a problem. Roe and Rosie were afraid she would repeat her mother's history—marry the wrong sort, or get in trouble. Her developing figure was attracting so much attention that all the neighborhood boys looked forward to coming over for ball games on Sunday afternoons in order to get into little teasing fights with her.

Roe Mason had greater problems than what to do with young Christy Lee. He was in danger of losing his farm, which was part of the original Mason homeplace—in the family for over a hundred years. He had never been in debt, but when the county dredged a ditch—the "drudge ditch," everybody called it—across the river-bottom land for drainage, all the farmers had to pay the expense. Roe did not have the cash for his portion and had to borrow the money from a relative, a judge at the courthouse. When Roe had trouble making the payments, the judge told him, "I wouldn't take your farm away, Roe. Just pay me the interest, and I'll see what I can do for you." The judge finagled a political office for Roe. For a two-year term he would become manager of the County House.

The County House was the poorhouse. At the time, paupers without families were cared for with county taxes. Leaving his own place empty, Roe moved his immediate family some ten miles away, to the other side of Mayfield, to a dismal house full of indigent strangers. That's how my mother came to live at the poorhouse. She had hardly ever been to Mayfield—a few times in the wagon when the men and boys went to trade on Saturdays—and she had rarely even had a Coca-Cola, but she was growing accustomed to the strangeness of moving away from home into some new situation.

It was a hellish hotel. The County House was a large wood-frame structure divided down the middle by a hall. Roe's family was crowded into two rooms. Chris slept with Datha and Mary in one bed, in the same room with Roe and Rosie, and Roe's son Mose occupied the other room with his new wife. Now Rosie was cooking for a larger group than ever, a dozen or more residents in addition to the family. The garden could not feed them all, so Roe bought food in bulk from a wholesaler at the edge of town. They had never had to buy common garden vegetables like cabbages and peas before. Aunt Rosie and the girls fixed three meals a day, cleaned the residents' rooms, and washed their clothes. One morning Chris was running a man's overalls through the wringer of the washing machine, and there was a turd in them—so large it hung up the wringer. The jaws of the wringer opened wide and locked, like someone gagging.

Chris carried meals to the sick, who were deposited in a separate little building. One room smelled so foul that Chris backed off in horror the first time she entered. The woman inside had cancer of the nose. Chris had never seen anyone so pitiful as this woman with the rotten hole in her face—a face with a permanent look of terror.

Another woman, who was very clean and fastidious, chattered about her son coming to see her. "He's coming tomorrow morning," she would say brightly each day.

Two men named Shorty lived there. One called himself a rambling man, from the song. He was always talking about hitting the road, but he never did. The other Shorty always talked about money. He was so enormous he could barely squeeze through doorways. When he eventually ate himself to death, his body required an oversized casket.

Chris knew one of the tenants as Aunt Mattie, a woman in her eighties. She was a distant Clear Springs relative who had never married. She toted an enameled pan with her everywhere she went. She carried her clothes in it, brushed her teeth in it, ate in it, even used it for a chamber pot. She was always walking somewhere. Back in Clear Springs, Chris had often seen her hiking briskly along, spurred by an inner purpose. Her sister had sent her to the County House because she couldn't keep track of her; Aunt Mattie kept wandering away from home. But Aunt Mattie ran away from the County House too, and Roe sent Chris to find her. Chris chased after her and found her half a mile away, near the highway. Chris plucked a willow switch and herded Aunt Mattie home. When the old woman slowed down, Chris switched her along. "She was give out when you got back with her," Aunt Rosie said to Chris the next day. "I had to carry her supper to her. Why, she's so old it's a wonder she didn't have a heart attack."

The woman who was expecting her son any day teased Chris and called her "Cricket" because she was so fast. "You're just a little cricket, a-flinging off that way," the woman said.

Her name was Hattie. Chris, admiring the woman's cheerfulness, confided in her about her own aunt Hattie. She gave her an old dress that needed patching. Hattie repaired the dress and wore it proudly. "I want to look nice for my boy," she said. "He's coming tomorrow."

Another man at the County House loved boiled cabbage, even though it always gave him painful gas attacks. One night Rosie served it at the boarding-house table, and she warned him to be sparing. "You'll get gas," she said. "You don't want another one of those attacks you get."

"But I love it," he said. "I love the way you fix it."

He took another helping. "Better watch that, Bud," one of the tenants said.

"I can't stop myself," he said. "I love cabbage better than anything."

At the table, the diners exchanged looks. He kept eating cabbage, taking helping after helping.

"Stop that, you'll make yourself sick," they said. But he wouldn't listen.

In the night, they could hear his groans. They could hear the rumbling fireworks of the gas. He got so sick he could not move from his bed. The next morning Roe sent for the county doctor, but the man soon died. Chris thought sadly of Aunt Hattie's ordeal, but she braced herself. Death was so ordinary, she observed. Children died from diphtheria and bloody flux. Anyone could die from locked bowels or lockjaw. Fevers and agues claimed people overnight; T.B. was pandemic. Women died in childbirth, and often the children died too. Chris was thankful to be alive, and she looked ahead.

The other Hattie's son never came to see her, and she died still hoping. No one claimed her body. Chris attended three or four burials in the two years she lived among these poor strangers. If their bodies weren't claimed, they were buried in wooden crates in an area at the edge of a field. The bodies were not embalmed. Seeing the unfortunate, the friendless, end their lives in poverty kept Chris from feeling sorry for herself. In nightmarish moments, she could imagine ending up homeless and unloved and perhaps crazy, but she fought that vision. Most of the time she felt a secret gladness, for she was better off than the people she waited on. She vowed that she wouldn't let herself end up like them. She was young. She was adventuresome.

An undercurrent of excitement churned through her. The place was so odd, with uncommon individuals whose life stories startled her. She was awed by anything new she encountered. She wore eagerness like a cloak. She walked a mile down the road to the eighth grade at Sunnyside, a two-room school. The students were country kids, like her, and she fell in easily with them. She giggled with the girls, played ball with the boys.

When fall came, she walked two miles in her too-tight, hand-me-down shoes to the city high school. But she found that the city kids were stuck-up, snotty. They mocked her worn shoes and her plain dresses, their eyes labeling her a country girl. They didn't invite her to parties or clubs. Sometimes she approached a bunch of girls, but when they saw her, their happy buzz halted. Yet she liked school and did well in her subjects. More than that, walking along the dirt farm road to town gave her a sense of independence. She liked venturing out, having her own life. She wasn't just Roe Mason's spindle-shanked ward. She was herself. She was headed somewhere.

Chris's cousins Datha and Mary found work in town and bought themselves some new clothes. The styles were changing—skirts and blouses and sweaters. Datha and Mary gave Chris their cast-off dresses. She wore them with long cotton stockings, which were always falling down, even though she tied them up with strings. Her lanky body was uncoordinated—tall and limber and top-heavy. She tagged along to play-parties with Datha and Mary, who were needing husbands. A play-party was a gathering where young people could dance when they didn't have a fiddler or a Victrola. They would sing "Liza Jane" and "Polly O" and swing each other around in circles to the music of their own voices. One night Chris went to a play-party at a neighbor's. Long after the party began, a young man with dark, oil-slicked hair slipped into the noisy house. He resembled an Indian, with high cheekbones and a long, pointed nose. His eyes were deep-set and brown. He stood around with his mouth hanging open. He wouldn't dance. He wouldn't talk. He was bashful and awkward, but he also seemed bemused, a little bit devilish. He was larruping, Chris thought—good-looking enough to eat. She knew who he was. She had seen him on his porch when she walked to school. He had been convalescing after scarlet fever, lounging on his front porch like a gentleman of leisure.

He was Uncle Roe's nephew, the only child of Roe's brother, Bob. Bob and Ethel Mason had often been out to visit Roe, but Wilburn had not come with them, so Chris had never met him before. Now, when she and Wilburn finally tiptoed into a clumsy conversation, he told her he had watched her walk along the road many times. She blushed. She loved to dance and she wished he would join the dancing with her. She couldn't keep still. He just stood there and grinned at her, as if he had a secret or was aiming to play a prank.

A few days later a boy at school told her that Wilburn Mason had said he was going to marry her. She was overcome with a tantalizing possibility that had never before entered her mind. For the first time, she began to have some real hopes for the future. When she walked past his house again, he was there, watching for her, and she waved.

"Where are you traveling to on them long legs of yours?" he asked, joining her.

As the days went by, he walked along with her. He lay in wait for her on Sunnyside Road as she walked home from school. He gave her rides in his jalopy. Soon they were going together. She felt as though she were holding her breath.

When Roe Mason's term at the County House ended after two years, he campaigned to be reelected. At the courthouse, a board convened to elect several officers. While waiting for the meeting to begin, Roe left to get a plate lunch across the street. While he was eating, his opponent bought off the votes and Roe lost the election. "Roe went to eat and it cost him the vote," the family teased him. "The dog would have caught the rabbit if he hadn't stopped to mess," they said.

Chris was disappointed. When Uncle Roe moved the family back to Clear Springs during the first week of 1936, she was in love. She didn't know how often she would get to see Wilburn, or if he would come to visit her. He had asked her to marry him, but she hadn't known what to tell him. She was embarrassed, afraid of what Roe and Rosie might say. Now she was afraid they wouldn't let him come to the house. They probably wouldn't let her marry him, she thought.

The winter farm work resumed. The family helped neighbors strip tobacco, working in stuffy barns permeated with the heavy odor of dark-fired tobacco, which had been cured over slow-burning hickory fires.

Chris drifted through daydreams. There were good reasons to marry, she thought, although she had not worked out a rational plan. She was not thinking at all. She was feeling and imagining life with Wilburn, who was twenty and out of school. Marrying would be a way out of her drudgery, she thought. She had trouble adjusting to the Clear Springs high school; the subjects were different from those at the city school, and the teachers were less qualified. She was out of step. Nobody encouraged her to stay in school. Datha and Mary and the boys had all graduated, but no one pushed Chris.

Uncle Roe didn't seem to approve of any of the young men who came around his daughters, Mary and Datha. He'd been a young hellion himself and knew what could happen. But he did not give Chris the trouble she expected. Wilburn was welcome because he was family. Chris and Wilburn weren't themselves blood kin, although they had mutual cousins; Datha and Mary and Mose were cousins to both of them. Roe and Rosie had treated Chris as someone beneath their station—she was a Lee—but now they were allowing a courtship not only within their station but in their own family.

On Sunday afternoons, Wilburn came to court Chris in the parlor. They sat on dark, fuzzy upholstery and giggled and punched at each other. He teased her incessantly. He told her that when he first saw her walking past his house, he thought she had the awfulest walk, so lanky and long-legged, striding along with that belt pinching in her figure. And then he told her she had the awfulest laugh, that high-pitched "hee-hee-hee-hee-hee." He grinned the whole time he was dishing out these jibes, which were his way of bestowing compliments, and she understood, seeing the mischief in his eyes.

He said, "Well, are you going to marry me or not?"

An unusual thing occurred then—an easing of the ban on the Lees. Aunt Rosie learned that Robert Lee's sister Mary was moving away to Detroit with her husband and little girl. Mary had inquired of Aunt

Rosie whether she could have Chris over to spend the night before she moved away. "I want to at least meet my niece before I go off," she said. Like many other tenant farmers in the area, Mary and her husband were leaving to find work up north. They lived in a small rented house up the hill toward Clear Springs.

"I reckon you can go," Aunt Rosie told Chris. "That way you can just walk down the hill to school the next morning instead of riding in the bus." The bus was a truck that went through the neighborhood picking up schoolkids. Chris was skipping school frequently by this point, and perhaps Rosie was concerned about that. But the real reason Rosie let her visit Mary surely lay elsewhere. She no longer needed to protect Chris. Chris was nearly grown, and Robert Lee's danger to her was passing.

Chris had never spoken with her aunt Mary, although she had seen her occasionally at the store. A handsome, angular woman with a good head of dark hair, Mary was outgoing and natural, and she was ambitious.

"I went back out to work in the cornfields too soon after I had my baby," she told Chris. "The blood was just a-running down my legs. But I kept on."

She was tired of the futile hand-to-mouth labor that faced them in Clear Springs. She and her husband, Tom, hoped to find work in the auto plants. Actually, people who had moved away from Clear Springs were now returning, whole families of them, because they had lost their jobs. They drifted back home to be fed by their kinfolks, who had land and food but not much else. Yet Mary was hopeful of finding something in Detroit.

The little rented house with its tacked-on kitchen and vine-covered porch posts reminded Chris of the house where she had lived with her mother and Luther Moore. Mary's little girl was asleep in a baby-bed. Chris wanted to hold her close. She noticed that the baby-bed was finely crafted, with wooden pegs and dovetail joints.

"What will you do with this littlun up there?" Chris asked.

"If we can both get work, we'd make enough money together, so maybe we can get somebody to take care of her," Mary said, lighting a cigarette.

Chris had not seen a woman smoke before.

"I got a surprise for you, Christy," Mary said after supper. Her eyes danced, and the smoke swirled around her like a filmy scarf.

Mary's husband, Tom, carried them for a ride in his car. Mary jiggled the fretting child in her lap as they traveled north through Clear Springs, past the school and the store and up the next hill. They turned left on a narrow dirt road, which was choked with weeds along the ditches. Chris felt she was going somewhere wild and forbidden. They drove a short way to the place where Mary's parents, the Lees, lived. They were Chris's grandparents. She had never spoken to them.

"My heart commenced to thumping," she told Mary later. "I wondered if my daddy was going to be there."

The Lees' house was a small unpainted cabin, much like the one Mary was living in, with a porch and a hickory split-shingle roof. In back, there were some outbuildings for corn and the mules and tools. A small blacksmith shop stood amid an orchard. The soil was weak and eroded, Chris realized, because the farm was situated up on the hill. The fields were odd-shaped and tree-studded, not spread out and regular. A patch of horseweed grew alongside the house.

She remembered seeing "Jimmo" Lee and his son Rudolph, Robert's lame brother, in the wagon going down the road. Jimmo was usually hunkered down on one leg in the center of the wagon, with the other leg stuck out straight in front of him. Rudolph drove a pair of mules, his helpless right leg dangling off the side of the wagon. She had never seen her grandmother before. Mary Luellen Lee was a large woman with stout legs and a jutting jaw and a coil of fine hair. Jimmo had faded red hair and a comical soup-strainer mustache that shielded his lips like a curtain.

Gushing with warmth, both of them took a lively interest in Chris. They joked with her. What impressed her most was their humility and their easygoing, jovial nature.

"Look at her," they said. "Now who does she favor?"

"Turn around there, youngun. Let's look at you good."

A number of people were visiting, but Chris did not know who they were. Robert Lee was not among them, but his younger children, Thelma and Bill, were there, along with some other scattered relations. Among this clan, Chris felt an eerie combination of the familiar and the foreign, as if she had gone to the courthouse square on a Saturday and found that everyone in the throng of strangers was related to her. Here, the Lees were all staring at her expectantly.

Rudolph, Mary's other brother, was about twenty-seven and unmarried. A leg brace protruded from his pants leg. He walked with a hickory stick worn smooth from use. Jimmo used a stick, too; his left leg seemed gimpy. Looking at the Lees, searching for resemblances,

Chris soon realized that she got her tall, slender build from them. She recognized their long fingers, as if they were all meant to play the piano.

Someone said, "Jimmo, tell about what Robert was a-doing on that last job. Where was he that time when he come back this winter?"

"He went down the river with a bargeload of tobaccy. He went *way* yander to *New*-braskie!" Jimmo's high-pitched voice rose even higher as he reached the climax of his remark. There was an explosion of mirth at the top of the scale, like the tone achieved by a country fiddler. Then he laughed.

The instant she heard Jimmo laugh, she recognized the sound. It was like the cadence of Uncle Roe's car engine after the ignition was switched off.

"Everybody always told me I had the Jimmo laugh," she said. "And sure enough, I do!"

They laughed together, distinctive "hee-hee-hee-hee-hee"s that started high and petered out. They tried it again. Jimmo's voice was musical, with an old-timey twist to his words. Someone had said he was Irish.

Chris found herself laughing naturally with these folks. They weren't like the industrious Hickses and the austere Masons. Why, she wondered, had she been deprived of such fun-loving people? They seemed to have a relaxed freedom that she found appealing. They were poor, but apparently they had plenty to eat, plenty of firewood, and they were handy. Jimmo had split the shingles for the roof, built the house, made the furniture, done the blacksmithing work in his own shop. She wondered if he had made that baby-bed she saw at Mary's.

Chris's glimpses of their place and their life were fleeting, but she was stirred. She wondered if her father could be as agreeable and full of fun. She wondered if he had ever had any feelings for her, after all. Perhaps she had been misled about him. She brushed the thought away. He was the grubworm curled against the peach seed, she thought. A thief.

In the kitchen, Grandma Lee clasped her granddaughter's hand and said quietly to Chris, "I remember the day you was born. I had a baby about two weeks after you was born. And it didn't live."

Later, it occurred to Chris that her grandmother had lost two babies the summer of 1919—her own child and her grandchild, whom she wasn't allowed to see.

That night at her aunt Mary's, Chris, cozy on a pallet on the floor by the fire, felt the unaccustomed pleasure of spending the night away from home. It was exhilarating to be away from the oblivious herd at Uncle Roe's. For a brief time, she allowed herself to imagine what might have been. She wondered what her life would have been like if instead of Aunt Rosie and Uncle Roe the Lees had taken her in. She couldn't help thinking it might have been so much easier. She might have had more love. But her father might have ruined it all.

"Will you write me if I write you?" Mary asked the next morning. "I want to write you."

Chris said yes. She looked forward to receiving letters of her own.

"I wish I could have knowed you before," Mary told her.

Mary cooked a sumptuous breakfast for her—biscuits and gravy and sausage and eggs—and fixed her a lunch to carry to school. Mary seemed happy—with her baby, with the excitement of going to Detroit. She hugged Chris.

"You just might want to go to Detroit yourself one of these days," Mary said. "I'll let you know how it is."

Chris wondered fleetingly what her life would be like if she went to Detroit. But mostly she wondered who she would be if she had been brought up with the Lees. Would she now be so enamored of Wilburn Mason? Or would he be someone unreachable, beyond her social sphere?

And I'm always wondering what my own life would have been like if I had been brought up in a situation like my mother's—without books and the radio and movies and patent-leather shoes, and countless other privileges, including parents. Mama didn't have a mother to sew for her, and to me this is an inadmissible thought. I'm haunted by the images of my mother's youth—the Christmas orange; the thrashing, pathetic aunt; the poorhouse horrors. But more than that, I'm riveted by the orphan state of mind, with the instilled sense of inferiority, the shame inflicted by the community. The tone of her childhood has cast a spell over her children, just as the landscape and folkways of Clear Springs still exert their influence, even on those who have strayed. Eunice's absence reaches me, too. And Robert Lee, my errant grandfather, is taking shape in my mind. I wonder about all those lanky Lees. I gaze at my own long piano fingers. Here I am, sitting with one leg tucked under me, and I wonder at the strange twist in my left leg that causes my foot to turn inward. This unexpected resemblance to long-dead ancestors is like discovering an old daguerreotype, a shadow image of a face that looks like mine.

....

Moving Mama is a job for archaeologists. It involves unearthing and sifting and cataloging. The history of her place is in the boxes and barrels in the junkhouse, the farm equipment and tools in the other outbuildings. All of it has to be evaluated, item by item, for its usefulness and monetary value. Mama speaks vaguely of having a sale. I know she would feel cheated if she got a penny less for an item than the price she saw in an antique shop. She would feel much worse if she sold the farm. Even if the farm brought a good price, she would still feel cheated—of its history, life, memory. It would be an insurmountable loss, to all of us.

She declares that she ought to get rid of extraneous items jammed in the outbuildings. But the indignity of submitting her belongings to the spectacle of an auction or a yard sale is overwhelmingly distasteful. I don't think she can bear it, and I don't think I can either.

"Your daddy saw a lot of farms go," she tells me. "And it always tore him apart to see the children at the auctions fighting over what their parents had worked so hard for."

"We won't fight over it," I promise.

Clearly she cannot part with anything. The sorting and saving could occupy the rest of our lives, I realize when I see her poring over a drawer of rags and scraps.

Impatient, and trying to be efficient, I say, "Take only the stuff you want. Put the rest in the stable, and we'll sell it later. We can't deal with all of it at once."

But in the turmoil of gathering to move, she doesn't know what she wants to keep, what to store away.

"Maybe these end tables are something you can replace," I venture to suggest. "They're not antique, and the veneer is wearing off."

"No," she says flatly. "I give too much for them to get rid of them. I'm keeping them."

Robert and Eunice hang over the forefront of my mind like a dust ruffle on a bed. For the time being, while we maneuver the move, I've stopped asking Mama to review her childhood for me. The past is not a place she wants to linger in. She can discard items of nostalgic value, but she will hang on to a tattered and begrimed old plastic shower curtain because "it still has some wear in it." My desire for simple order battles against the clutter of thrift. I'm one step ahead of chaos. Those jigsaw puzzles I worked as a child taught me to get every piece in place. If the pieces didn't fit, Mama says I got mad and tried to pound them in place with my fist.

Our house was always a mess. Mama was too busy to aim for a Good Housekeeping award. When someone drove up outside, we had to hurry to make the place presentable. We hurled berry buckets and toys and clothes into distant rooms. "Company's coming! Start gathering!" What a familiar sound, my mother's voice singing out from the past. Right now, my socks are drying on the chandelier.

Always be saving, Granddaddy said. It's an admirable habit, a lost art, a reverence for the resources of the planet. The habit of making do with what was on hand arose from the demands of pioneering and hardscrabble farming, long before the Depression. In one of my random sallies into genealogy, I recently ran across an estate inventory. After the death of Mama's great-great-grandfather James R. Hicks in 1892, among the meager odds and ends at his estate sale were one set of "crockerware," one looking glass, one bolster, and one lot of books. The books brought fifty cents. He had two beehives, with bees— commodities of great value, for sugar was scarce. He also had three lots of "tricks." What were tricks? What did it mean that Hicks had *three* lots of tricks? I discovered that tricks were doodads and miscellaneous objects saved for no other reason than that they couldn't be thrown away. Conceivably, they might come in handy (screws, buttons, pins), but tricks could also include odd, broken pieces of machinery, rusted-out cans, swatches of moth-eaten cloth. My mother has a world of tricks.

A few days before the move, I find Mama napping in her La-Z-Boy. She is exhausted from all the sorting and packing. "I'm half dead," she says, sitting up. "And I've got this Gravel Gertie throat."

Her hair is twirled with bobby pins under her U.K. Wildcats ball cap.

"I've had some disturbing news," she says. Her voice is hoarse from smoking.

She shows me a letter from her doctor. The letter says her tests show that one of her carotid arteries is sixty-percent blocked. When it gets to seventy, the doctor will recommend surgery, to prevent a stroke. The letter mentions dizziness and numbness, the symptoms of transient ischemic attacks—T.I.A.s—or little warning strokes. Mama says that since she got the letter that morning she's felt dizzy and numb.

"We have to talk with your doctor," I say, alarmed.

She lights a cigarette and rushes out the door, the sulfur smell of the match fading in a cloud of tobacco. She's not supposed to smoke, but she can't stop.

I anticipated feeling anger and impatience during the move. Now I am mute. The only important thing is not to lose her. She is my center. I'm only twenty-one years younger than she. She always says she was just a girl when she had me. I was so close to her that she often said she couldn't wean me. Now I can't face the ultimate weaning. I want her here. I want her to tell me now all the things I wouldn't let her teach me in the past. She is the source of my being. How can I *be*, without her?

I don't know what the stress of this move is doing to her. I stand back and watch my mother go through this cultural shock treatment, this uprooting, this clinging. And I don't know what I can do to ease the transition. Compared to the final journey into oblivion, moving to another house seems minor to me. But for her the subtext of this move is loss, a premonition of mortality.

When we talk on the telephone with her doctor, he is reassuring. He suggests that in about six months she ought to consider having elective surgery, just to be sure. He says he would have T.I.A. symptoms too if he got that letter. Anxiety, he says. He says third-year med students, when they study diseases, always develop the symptoms of anything they are studying.

"We don't have to worry about it now," I tell Mama. "Let's just take it easy."

She feels much better then. Her symptoms seem to vanish, and we plunge ahead, packing and sorting. Still, I keep an eye on her and wonder if moving is the right thing for her at this point. What if she doesn't live to enjoy her new house?

"That's stuff I'm getting rid of," she says of a few shopping bags in the center of the bedroom floor.

"Is that all?"

"You're just as bad as I am," she says, laughing. "You save ever little string and sack. You're just like Granny."

It's true, of course. But most of my possessions take the form of information, stuff I think I need to know. Books, magazines, pamphlets, catalogs, brochures, bulletins, journals, maps, letters, schedules, newspapers, clippings, file folders of outdated data. I stockpile words the way she hoards scraps of cloth and cracked pickle crocks.

Mama and LaNelle are talking on the telephone. LaNelle is in California, and I am on the extension phone.

"I think I'll have Granny's old clock restored and put it on the mantel of the new fireplace," Mama says. She noticed old clocks on mantels when we toured houses for sale.

"But you always hated Granny's clock," LaNelle reminds her. "The way it struck all night long, and the way she couldn't live without it."

"It's not hers now," Mama says. "It's mine."

"Now it's an antique," I explain to LaNelle. "It's in style."

"I wouldn't mind if you took that old clock and dumped it in the creek," LaNelle says. I sense her shudder across the miles.

When LaNelle and I talk privately about Mama's health, I ask, "Do you think this is too much for her?"

"I don't know. But being physically active will help her."

Mama and I continue our assault on the past. I nag her too much about smoking. I'm exhausted with resistance, with getting upset over the difficulties of the move. The work overwhelms us. Because I do not have a regular job with a boss and a time clock, I am available to help. At some point during the week, I express frustration at not getting any of my own work done.

"What work is that?" Mama asks.

"I write books."

"Oh." She has forgotten. She ponders. Then she says, "I hate for you to have to keep on writing, book after book. You need to rest and enjoy yourself. You'll burn yourself out."

Most of my childhood writings became landfill long ago. Daddy, who once advised me never to throw away anything I wrote, accidentally dumped a box of my scribblings into the creek, along with a jumble of glass and tin—trash to fight erosion.

We're awash in stuff. We lose track of what's worth keeping, and we can't find what we've saved.

"I spend the biggest part of my time hunting for something," Mama always said.

Anything we were looking for always seemed to be inaccessible, stored away somewhere at the bottom of a pile, or stuffed into one of the outbuildings, where it was exposed to the elements. For years, I kept a brassbound trunk in the corncrib. The trunk contained a stack of college newspapers, folders of my writings from my college years, all of Mama's letters to me when I was away at school, and souvenirs of my first trip to New York (swizzle sticks, Playbills). Now it is time to salvage this trunk, but when I open it, I discover that the wooden bottom has rotted through. I transfer the trunk's contents to some cardboard boxes. At the bottom of the trunk are my mother's letters. Some kind of insect has tunneled precise mazes through stacks of them, eating up her words like the most delectable nourishment. It is as though a jigsaw has been used to cut her letters into puzzles. I open one of them. Crumbs fall from the envelope. The letter unfolds like a chain of paper dolls. I read: "Yesterday ——— cows ——— since ——— all the way ——— never ——— hot peppers." My mother's precious words, the documentation of a decade, have been carved into a bizarre minimalist poetry. I am dismayed, angry at the way the most valuable things we squirrel away seem to be the most vulnerable. There is no way to save what is of real value. What endures is peripheral and empty.

In the corncrib I find Daddy's broken bootjack, which he had repaired with a piece of plywood. For years I'd tried to find him a new bootjack. Now I realize that even though his plywood repair job was crude, it had worked perfectly well for him. I also find Daddy's moth-nibbled Navy blanket, the one Janice and I used to sit on in front of the car at the drive-in theater. And then a while later I come across his seabag, out in the part of the junkhouse that he used as his gun shop. The seabag is white canvas, cinched at the top by a rope tied in a sailor's knot. The bag has probably not been opened in years. I hate to undo the knot. I will not know how to tie it up again. But I can't resist. I take the bag outside on the grass and open it carefully, for fear of black widows.

Inside, I find several shirts rolled up tightly and tied with twine. I pull out a pair of wool sailor pants with the initials W.A.M. on the inside pocket and my father's full name inside the leg. But most interesting is the fishing-tackle kit, given to sailors for an emergency—if the ship sinks and they're huddled in life rafts. It is made of an olive-green cloth like a carpenter's apron, with many pockets and strings to tie it up in a roll. Most of the tackle is missing, but there are some feather jigs and a wee harpoon and some fishing line. With the kit is a folded piece of thin paper—fishing instructions. The warnings about sharks give me a shiver. I imagine the frightened sailors on the cruiser U.S.S. *Indianapolis* frantically trying to read this little pamphlet, which looks as though it might dissolve in the sea. "Splashing with an oar or striking at it will usually drive a shark away. The tenderest spot in a shark is the end of his nose. His gills come next."

The fishing instructions range over a variety of survival options. You could eat seaweed, you could dry fish, you could skin birds and make a cloak. You could eat turtles, if you were careful. "After a turtle's head is cut off, the head may bite and the claws may scratch. Watch out." You could eat snakes, "even poisonous ones, if they have not bitten themselves."

I think of Daddy out in the Pacific, not knowing from moment to moment if he might have to begin fishing from a raft. He would have been belowdecks in the destroyer, a flimsy metal hulk known as a tin can; he would have been passing ammunition, unaware of what was happening above, the sounds of war like a million-amp rock concert. I wonder if he dreamed about those tender shark noses. I imagine him rehearsing his aim, practicing with that little harpoon.

Under the heading "Whales," the sole instruction is "Do not worry about whales."

Mama spends days emptying the outbuildings. She salvages a scythe and an ox yoke; the metal washtubs she and Granny used for years; the old iron wash kettle itself; a calf weaner; the milk cans I washed every day when I was growing up. She finds the stovepipe cover, the metal plate used to cover the hole in the ceiling when the coal stove was moved out of the house for the summer. It has Jesus' face painted on it.

She salvages a cast-off outdoor thermometer, a broken garden hose, cans of leftover glue and paint. She finds pieced quilt blocks bundled and tied with strips of selvedge. And tricks by the gross. In despair, I realize that all of this is making its way to her new home in town. She is afraid burglars might break into the outbuildings if she leaves anything here. I suggest putting out a welcome mat. I know that in trying to be lighthearted, I am unfairly dismissing the worth of her life. But the worth of her life is what I value most, and it bothers me that she's worrying about these bits of flotsam.

"I need to have a sale," she says.

She hires a man to haul off the trash. It all fits into one small trailer.

She's thrown out only items that are truly ruined and useless—the mouse-stained, the moth-eaten, the sodden and rusted and rotted. There is a bucket of thawed catfish and vegetables discarded from the bottom of the freezer, food dating back to 1985.

On moving day, Mama wears hot-pink pants and a pretty short-sleeved sweater embroidered with flowers. These aren't her everyday clothes. "I'll have to look like a rich bitch if I'm moving into a Big Fine House," she explains.

I realize how nervous she is, moving into a place where the houses are close together and where the neighbors might look down on her country clothes. Mama assumes that people in Big Fine Houses are in society, and she is afraid they will be unfriendly. She's in a tizzy, her cigarette smoke swirling behind her as she moves.

This house we are leaving is my birthplace, the site of my first memories. It is still a good, sturdy house, more solidly constructed than the little house next door where I was raised. I always regretted that when the bathroom was finally added, it blocked the breezeway I loved so much. It has been years since I sat in the porch swing or read a book under a maple in the front yard.

I think about Granny sitting in her rocking chair, twisting her hands in her apron and staring at the floor. Could she have imagined that her home would be abandoned by the family, rented out to strangers? Did she grasp the certainty that the hectic, high-tech world growing around her like pondweed—the foreshadowing of urban sprawl—was going to mean the death of the family farm?

Doesn't Mama want to get away from this oppressive place at last? This is the house Mama moved into the night of her marriage and endured thereafter. She should be glad to go. Yet this move is so radical. It is surely all wrong. I try to encourage Mama to be triumphant about her new house, but right now she is too tired to care. Her face is drawn, and she frequently touches her temple, as though a pain were shooting through.

"Is this whole thing a mistake?" I ask.

"I'll be all right," she says. "It'll just take time."

She hasn't had any more stroke symptoms. She is trying to limit the cigarettes, but she keeps forgetting.

. . .

I go to the pond with Oscar. This is my last visit to the farm while any of the family is living here. I feed the fish from a bucket of fish chow. A small black cat, a stray, crouches on the bank. I remember so many stray cats on this farm: a black cat crushed under Daddy's tire; another scrawny cat with starving kittens; Daddy's series of white cats. Not until I had owned nine white cats as an adult did I realize our shared partiality.

It is spring. The green lace of the trees is delicate and misty, like the first light of day. A sheen of purple lights the field—a ground cover of monkey flower and henbit, common weeds. Here I am again, facing this hard, eroding land, with the chicken tower behind me.

I go over the terms of our violent uprooting, trying to get clear: for Mama, the burden of operating a farm will be alleviated, and yet the farm will still be hers, close by. She has a good place to live in her old age, but she can still go fishing here, at her own pond. These small goals are accomplished with the aid of lawyers, tax accountants, and real-estate agents, in an operation as arcane as a tax audit. Nothing is simple anymore. To move Mama a couple of miles takes all the magic of the modern world: estate planners, title searchers, termite inspectors, veterinarians, insurance agents, cablevision providers, road maintenance crews, automobile mechanics, courthouse clerks, copying machines, fax machines, answering machines, billing systems, property surveyors, supermarkets, moving vans, pizza parlors, Chinese carryout emporia, florists, U.P.S., Federal Express, the Coca-Cola company, Wal-Mart, Kmart, the airline industry, and the federal government.

During the week that I help Mama move and get settled, I make many trips in my car—between the farm and the new house, and to the shopping center. On each short run, my tape of U2's *The Joshua Tree* blares out the exact raw notes of my emotions. The sound is a long drawn-out wail, a plea for freedom. For a few minutes, at full blast, I'm running down the road, free.

As I drive, I contemplate movement. My forebears left southern England, the borderlands of England and Scotland, and Ireland, and they headed for America. Whole families picked up and left, crossing the ocean, then traveling in wagon trains down the Shenandoah Valley on the Great Wagon Road. From North Carolina, they headed for the Cumberland Gap into the wilderness of Middle Tennessee. These were bold, arduous journeys, over a couple of generations. But when the Masons and the Arnetts got to Clear Springs, they planted their corn and stayed. A long settling began. A century later Robert Lee Mason and Ethel Arnett moved away, but not far, and they didn't loosen their Clear Springs ties. Daddy was rooted on this farm for seventy years, and Mama was here for fifty-nine.

With such a long settling after the initial spurt of adventure, even the smallest moves are wrenching. My grandparents moving here from Clear Springs. The Roe Mason family moving to the County House. My mother going to work at the factory in town. My grandmother being sent to Memphis and Hopkinsville to repair her mind. And now my mother moving to a house in town.

24

Late one spring afternoon, a couple of weeks later, I return to the farm to check on things. The two houses, emptied out, stand near the chicken tower like compliant whores. My grandparents' house looks shabby now that it is unoccupied, and the grass has shot up during recent rain. The irises and the wisteria have blown over. The renters have not arrived.

The other house has been empty for a long time. I go inside tentatively, imagining my young self still there, poring over my school lessons or sitting in the giant easy chair reading Nancy Drew books. The wallpaper is peeling. The old leak in the roof that periodically sprinkled my bed has caused the plasterboard ceiling to buckle. I remember many times sleeping with a pan, a washrag lining its bottom to deaden the sound of the dripping water. The floors, once shining hardwood, are smothered in moldy shag carpeting. The interior seems bedraggled and spent, as if the spirits that inhabited this space were glad to escape. Over my head, in the attic, remnants of a photograph of Eunice, my missing grandmother, may be trapped under generations of mouse beds. I have little hope of resurrecting her lost image, but I long to see such a picture. The story of my mother's childhood is fresh, since Mama and I have reviewed it, and I'm haunted by the two crucial family members who vanished so early—her parents. I always felt their absence from my mother's life, but I didn't feel their absence from my own. Now my mind is drawn to them—a mystery that I feel compelled to explore. The hole created in my mother's life yawns so wide and deep, I am washed with a grief decades old. But more than that now, I feel the hole in my own life. The loss of Eunice and Robert Lee is a void in our family history. If I could see a picture of Eunice, I might recognize something of myself; I would fall into place, a piece in the puzzle.

The attic is accessible through a hole in the ceiling of the little passageway between the main bedroom and the bathroom. The Sheetrock square that once plugged up the opening is missing, and the black hole gapes. An intense, musty odor of moisture and decay pours down from the attic like a heavy miasma. The hole is so small I realize why Mama used to send me up the ladder whenever she wanted to retrieve something she had stored up there. She would hold the stepladder steady for me to climb, but the ladder would sway, its hinge broken. I'd jerk the string on the attic lightbulb. There was no flooring up there, just a sheet of plywood laid across some of the joists. I would paw my way over the plywood, grab the box of Christmas decorations or whatever I had been sent for, and lower it carefully to Mama.

Now it is hard to think of standing on a wobbly ladder and wriggling through that tiny hole. Everything here always seemed to be dangerous to get to. For all our restraint—and our unwillingness to take chances or to move beyond the carefully configured boundaries of the farm—we were daredevils, living routinely with risk. My family operated on the edge. We lived with fire, electric storms, twisters. We drove on icy roads in cars with bald tires, low brake fluid, and cracked steering. We occupied a world without snowplows and seat belts and smoke alarms and lightning rods. (Daddy claimed lightning rods drew lightning.) We heated water in the bathtub with an immersible electric heater. Could you touch the water to find out if it was warm? We weren't sure. An electric space heater with a frayed cord sat beside the tub. LaNelle picked it up once from within the tub but for some reason did not get electrocuted. We ran barefooted over thorns, broken glass, and rusty cans. We nicked our legs on rusty barbed wire. The woodstoves had faulty flues, the porch steps had broken boards. Spiders grabbed our faces in the night; they inched under the sheets and prowled along our legs. We risked ticks, snapping turtles, diphtheria, measles, blood poisoning, "hydrophobie" (rabies).

The dangers at home must have paled in Granny's imagination, compared to the unspeakable evil in the outside world.

We never got food poisoning, even though dressed eggs and mayonnaise went on every picnic. We weren't concerned about botulism. Mama would scrape the brown part off the top of the food in the jar so as not to waste the rest.

And then there was the arsenic. Daddy bought a pound of arsenic for a taxidermy course he took by correspondence when he was a youth. He stuffed a mouse, a procedure requiring arsenic. I always heard about the arsenic stored in the junkhouse. He didn't know how to dispose of it, so he just stuck it away somewhere.

"I think it got sealed up in the attic of the smokehouse," Mama said recently when we were packing to move.

"Why are people always sealing up attics?" I wanted to know. The attic of Granny's house was shut up, too.

On the telephone, Janice said, "Don't you think he got rid of the arsenic? He wouldn't have wanted it around when we were growing up."

"Where would he get rid of it?" I asked. "In the creek?"

Don told me he had seen it. "Daddy kept it up above his gun shop. The cardboard box was dissolving."

"That's where my quilt frames are," Mama said. "They're worth something."

The arsenic weighed on my mind. Would it have lost its potency by now? Where could we dispose of it? What if it got into the pond? What if a tornado shot the little building into smithereens, dispersing the arsenic over the Jackson Purchase? I wondered if I was just being a worrywart, like Granny. Why didn't she worry about the arsenic instead of fornication on Fifth Avenue and whatever else she expected I would find in New York?

Of course, when I was growing up, country people were so fatalistic they didn't give a second thought to most of the daily dangers. The only one they would really address was vermin. It occurs to me now that people sealed off attics to prevent the spread of wildlife. In the winter, we could hear squirrels bowling overhead.

I stare at the hole above me, imagining the specter of Eunice Lee entombed there like some Edgar Allan Poe character. Eu-la-lee.

Nancy Drew would have no difficulty with this. For one thing, she would have her flashlight with her. And for another, somehow, a dependable ladder would be at hand. And in her adventure, the photograph, unscathed, would be neatly nesting in the insulation like an Easter egg. But here, in this scene, the frame of the hole above is collapsing, and water stains cover the rotting ceiling. No doubt my mother is right—there is nothing salvageable up there. The mice would have shredded Eunice's portrait into a pathetic confetti.

I leave the house and drive to town to run some errands. Later, I go to the drugstore to pick up the enlargement I've ordered of that tiny snapshot of Eunice and her sister that Mama gave me. Then I return to my mother in her shiny new house. The driveway and the brick path are clean. There is no mud, no weeds. I can sense how out of place she must feel in this pristine neighborhood.

She doesn't hear me come in. She is watching *Wheel of Fortune,* her favorite show. Her ginger cat, Chester, in her lap, gives me a haughty glance.

I examine the picture under a table lamp. The faded thumbnail snapshot has been blown up to five by seven inches. The results are astonishing. The faces are so clear, the dresses and hair full of rich detail. At last, I do have a genuine picture of my grandmother.

I show this blow-up to Mama—Eunice and her sister Hattie, smiling at us across time. After locating her glasses, Mama examines it skeptically.

"Why, that's not them," she says. "They didn't look like that."

"It has to be them!" I cry. "You said it was. And this is exactly how you described them."

Hammer that piece in place!

I definitely remember that she identified them. They fit her description: Eunice was short and fat and had a happy disposition, and Hattie was thin and troubled-looking. Mama studies the picture and still seems dubious, but she tentatively comes around.

I see two young women, perhaps in town on a Saturday afternoon getting their picture made at a booth in the five-and-dime store. They've made sure their hair is perfect; they've probably used a looking glass just before posing. Their hair is brushed to a rich shine and carefully wrapped around some huge rats (coils of hair or yarn) so that it sticks out at the sides like wings. Eunice, in a dark dress, has black hair. Hattie, in a white shirtwaist, is delicate and fair-haired. Eunice's full breasts are lifted within a high-necked dress that has streams of tucks over the yoke. I imagine Mammy Hicks making that dress, her old fingers working those fine stitches like tiny moles tunneling. Eunice has an impish face. She's biting her lower lip, and glee is in her eyes. She senses the irony and the fun of what they are up to—these country girls in town, shelling out a nickel to have their picture made. Their mother will scold them and take little interest.

Eunice seems outgoing and jovial. But Hattie appears frightened and shy. Mama favors Hattie more than she does her mother. And I resemble Hattie, too. I have her hairline, her lips, her nose, her eyes. But she seems slightly walleyed, as if she has to keep her eyes on two things at once, in case something might catch her.

Mama gets up, leaves the room, and returns in a moment with another snapshot she has found—three figures sitting in a field near a tree. I see flowers, probably daisies and buttercups. The photo is small, and the three people are indistinct, but I can tell they are dressed up, so I know it is probably a Sunday.

"That's my mama and daddy and Aunt Hattie," Mama says.

This is amazing. Mama has produced another rabbit from her hat— another long-lost puzzle piece magically materializing from the chaos of the move.

Robert Lee is sitting in the grass, wearing a jacket and a cap, a touring cap like people wore in the early days of the automobile. In the blur of his face I discern a hint of combined self-satisfaction and prankishness—the arrogance of youth. Eunice and Hattie are white swans. Robert looks as though he has gotten away with something. I wonder if this is his wedding day.

The photo holds such promise, young people on the verge. But their lives soon shattered. Robert Lee hovered on the edges of my life, just as he had on the edges of Mama's. I know that I saw him a few times in my early childhood. The memory of his red hair was once sharp and distinct, but by now it is only a faint blot. I stare at him and his sweetheart. I need to study Mama's old pictures of him again.

"Where's your album with those pictures of the Lees?" I ask Mama.

Her face is pasty. She's still tired from the move. Yesterday she said, "I'm tired as old Miss Tired."

"I'll look for it when I can," she says now. "I can't think where I put it."

Her new house has a place for everything. Janice and LaNelle, who are both artistic, have helped to decorate the place and arrange Mama's antiques. On the walls they have displayed some of the quilts that used to be stuffed in the top of a closet. Thanks to them, this house—which might have felt prissy and false, like something out of a magazine— feels like a home. It is comfortable and uncluttered, as if our lives have settled into place. But Mama still acts like a visitor.

I drive to the courthouse. The county records are in an annex filled with heavy, dusty books the size of valises. Both Robert and Eunice were born before births were officially recorded in Kentucky, so I can't find any indication of their origins. Instead, while poking around, I happen upon my own birth certificate. On it my mother's name is

Christy Mason, and her maiden name is given as Arnett. Arnett? Mama's maiden name was Lee. Arnett was Granny's maiden name—Mama's mother-in-law, the woman her life became so solidly bound to. I'm perplexed.

I remember the time Mama took her yellow-and-white cat, Abraham, to the vet after she had accidentally backed the car over his leg. When the receptionist asked for the cat's name, Mama became embarrassed—"Abraham" was one of Daddy's whimsical inspirations—and she blurted out "Yeller" instead. Is this what happened when she provided information for my birth certificate? Did she try to erase the shame of her blackguard father, Robert Lee? I'm not sure whether I should ask my mother about this. She has always said she despised him. Yet I know that within a couple of months of my birth she took me—her new baby—to Paducah to see him. For the first time, I wonder what was on her mind then. What emboldened her to show me off? Did she want to remind her father that he had abandoned her when she was a baby? To show him she had become a productive adult—without his help?

I'm not prepared for my next discovery. From their marriage license, I find that when they married in 1918, Eunice was twenty-one years old and Robert was *sixteen*. She was a grown woman, and he was only a boy. What does this mean? I try to imagine what kind of courtship they had. On the license, his occupation is given as farming. Robert's father, J. F. Lee, signed the license. And Robert signed it. Their handwriting is poor. After getting married, Robert certainly would not have finished school. I realize that Eunice died five years later, when Robert would have been only twenty-one. She died in childbirth, married to another man. What did Robert feel when he learned of her death? I'm shocked by the disparity in their ages. When she was sixteen, he was eleven. Now what am I to make of the mischief on her face in the dime-store portrait?

As I ponder this new information, my mind has done the easy arithmetic, the seven months between the marriage date and my mother's birth.

Later, while trying to locate the record of Eunice and Robert's divorce, I'm startled to find a document about the fabled horse-and-buggy incident. I hurry home with a copy to show Mama. The document is a "Petition in Equity," and in it Eunice Lee brings charges against Robert Lee. It is badly typed, full of errors. I read it to Mama, paraphrasing the legalese.

"Eunice claims that they lived together since their marriage, but then on May twenty-sixth—that was a month before you were born—he 'cruelly abandoned' her and she doesn't know where he went, but he took her horse. It was a bay horse about fifteen hands high with a white spot on its forehead, about eight years old. And he took 'one top buggy and harness.' She says that was all worth two hundred dollars. And she says he sold them to some guys, but she claims the price wasn't high enough and that he was in cahoots with them for the purpose of cheating her out of her property."

My mother is listening with a frown, as if a movie has begun—one she has already seen.

"Eunice filed this the very next day after he left her—and she's suing for alimony," I say. "She made up her mind real quick."

"It could have been building up to this for some time," Mama says. "He probably never treated her right."

"And listen to this, he took her money too. She says she had a bank account of her own money, about three hundred dollars, and that he took it all out and was planning to leave the state."

"That was a fortune!" Mama says. "She worked hard to earn that. They always said he robbed her."

This discovery confirms Robert Lee's knavish character. It's not news to Mama. I'm saddened, yet I'm pleased to find details that bring Eunice alive to my mind. She was proud, quick-tempered, saving. She owned a "top buggy." The description of the horse is vivid. The money in the bank reveals a thrifty, cautious nature. But she wound up in this plight. She is pregnant with my mother. And Robert has run off with all her resources, leaving her alone.

"It goes on," I say. "She says she is 'a very poor person unable to earn a support for herself and that he is a strong able-bodied man, capable of earning a living.' She's suing him 'for twenty dollars a month for the next ten years or the sum of twenty-four hundred dollars to support her in the station in life to which she is accustomed.' She's calling for his arrest. She says he 'so attempts to conceal himself that summons cannot be served upon him.' I guess that means he's in hiding, and she knows it." I read on. "And she's asking for a 'general attachment' against his property, and she's also suing those two guys who bought the horse and buggy from him. She's suing them for two hundred dollars."

"I bet she never got it."

"There's no record. I don't know."

"He never was a daddy to me," she says.

"Her handwriting was a lot like yours," I say, studying Eunice's signature. The capital letters are finely drawn, with a bit more flourish than my mother's writing, but the roundness of the letters looks familiar. "She had nice handwriting."

"Aunt Hatt had a beautiful hand," says Mama, as she examines her mother's signature. "But those fits caused it to deteriorate."

I show Mama a copy of her parents' marriage license and see her face fall when she realizes the date of her parents' wedding. "That can't be," she protests. "Oh, no."

I realize I shouldn't have shown her that. Quickly I go to another document I copied at the courthouse. This one is a sworn statement from the two men who bought the horse and buggy from Robert Lee. They deny all knowledge of the charges, they say they knew nothing of Robert's notions of defrauding Eunice, and they claim the horse wasn't worth more than forty-five dollars or the buggy worth more than fifteen.

"That's probably as far as it went," Mama says bitterly. "She probably didn't get nothing out of them or him, either one. He probably got across the state line."

Embarrassed for him and for myself, I offer excuses. "He was only a teenager," I say. "Maybe he was just a scared kid. He wasn't ready for a wife and child."

"He was grown," she says firmly. "Clausie said he was *mature* for his age."

I am trying to imagine a sixteen-year-old boy—not one of today's sullen teenagers hiding in his room with his sound system, but a self-reliant country boy—handy with tools, familiar with mules, accustomed to working alongside men. What would be on his mind, his horizons? He had no money or land. Eunice had a lot he might lust after—her full, attractive figure; her bay horse; that fine buggy; cash in the bank. He could have hung around her, impressing her with his way with a horse. Before long, he found himself in wedlock—committed to an extent he was unprepared for. When the prospect of a baby loomed too large, he abandoned his wife, escaping with her property. I run through the familiar story. But the question of blame shifts in my mind, like a kaleidoscope rotating. Eunice may have taken advantage of him—a boy. Who seduced whom? By heaping all the blame on Robert, the Hickses may have been trying to protect Eunice's own reputation. Still, it's not easy to forgive him, even at this late date. Back then, sixteen was a lot older than it is nowadays. But so was twenty-one.

Suddenly Mama stands up and throws out her arms triumphantly. She's beaming. "I just remembered—I was born premature! They said I was so little they were surprised I made it! They said I didn't cry for two months, and when I did—it liked to scared everybody to death! They said I didn't have any fingernails or eyelashers!" She lifts her hands in a thankful hallelujah, celebrating her legitimacy. For her, believing otherwise, I see, would be unbearable.

Later, we look through the album that has the photographs of the Lees. There are several pictures of Robert Lee, taken long after he abandoned Eunice and my mother. Instead of a child groom, he is now a grown-up. He's handsome in a flashy way, like an actor. He looks cocky, as though he has breezed in for the day from some glamorous place—Paducah, maybe—and wants to look sharp to impress the folks at home. His striped tie seems rather short, possibly because his large midriff is bulging above his belt buckle. He is about forty-two years old.

"He drank a lot," Mama says, pausing over another one of the pictures. "He made big money—road construction, I think. Back then you could make good money on a road crew. Mary was always saying he made a lot of money but he blowed it."

My mother and I and my baby sister, Janice, are in some of these pictures. Janice is a tiny baby, so it is 1944, probably August or September, doubtless on a Sunday afternoon, when families assembled for big dinners. The Lees, some sitting on wooden straight-chairs, are gathered under the trees in front of a small, plain, unpainted house with a porch. The roof is made of split-wood shingles, with a central chimney. Irises line a dirt driveway.

"There's the Plymouth, one of our oddball cars," Mama says, pointing to another picture. Several black cars and a truck with sideboards are parked under the trees. "I guess I drove it out there that day."

"Tell me about the time we drove to Paducah to see him when I was a baby," I urge her. She shuffles some of the loose pictures like playing cards.

Aunt Mary gave her Robert Lee's address and urged her to find him. Mama considered this for some time. Her curiosity had been held in check by her resentment, but now and then she had a notion that maybe he loved her, a little. Finally, she acted on impulse. Her cousin Shirley Hicks, from Clear Springs, drove out one Sunday afternoon in her new car and asked Mama to go riding. Mama put on her nice dress and combed her hair. She grabbed me and a blanket and some diapers, and we hit the road. I was two or three months old.

Paducah was a long, leisurely drive, and the weather was good. They played the radio. They honked at other Sunday afternoon joyriders. Mama liked being with Shirley, who had a spontaneous, warmhearted nature.

As they drew into the outskirts of the city, Mama grew nervous. What would she say to him? Maybe he wouldn't be at home. She had an idea he might be living in a slum, down by the riverfront. They stopped at a filling station and asked directions. The house was not far into town, near the train yard. They drove past the Illinois Central train-repair shops, where black locomotives resembling giant grasshoppers squatted menacingly. She expected they would get lost, but Shirley found the street without difficulty. When they located the house, they stopped in front of it and sat there for a while, until it got too hot to stay in the car. They went to the front door. Immediately, he answered her tentative knock.

"We found him at home, with that woman he was living with," Mama tells me. "She had a little girl with her." She assumed the child wasn't Robert Lee's, because Mary had not mentioned her.

My mother was rattled, meeting her father for the first time. But she had a way of being forward and blunt.

He was uneasy. He spoke hesitantly. They talked in non sequiturs.

"He just squirmed," she says. "I think he was put out that we come. He was nervous. He didn't know he was a grandpa—he was still a real young man."

Here she was, out of the blue, reminding him of his shameful past. And she sprang a baby on him, the grandchild he didn't know he had. I can imagine him standing there as if exposed—living in sin, wholly unprepared for his daughter's arrival. Perhaps he wondered what demands she might make on him. Maybe the woman he was living with didn't even know he had a grown daughter.

"The little girl was laying up on a bed in the next room with her shoes on, a-playing," Mama says. "I thought that was awful. I'd never seen any child on a bed with shoes on. That stuck in my mind."

They went outside presently and sat in the yard at the side of the house. It was a main street, and there was some traffic. After a while, he sent the little girl after ice cream. He tried to make sense of the baby in my mother's lap.

"He just looked at you and talked to you," Mama says. "But he wouldn't pick you up; he never held you. He didn't know what to say to you or how to make over a baby." My mother resented his lack of demonstrative affection, as if it made him inhuman.

"Go back," I say. I have a hundred questions. "I'm trying to see this scene."

As I pepper her with questions, I can tell she is thinking hard. "Yes, there was grass in the yard; it was mowed. It wasn't growed up. I can't remember seeing any trees. I don't remember if he had a car. It was a big house, one of those two-story houses built close together, kind of narrow—a gun-barrel house, it was called. It was an old-timey house with a porch. No, I don't know how long he had lived there. The place where he lived was on the first street past the train yard—behind a brickyard. It was all battered up, down in there. The house wasn't painted. It was wood—gray and weathered."

Each detail has been wrested from her with a question. She strains, probing the past, trying to visualize it. I know her memory must be vague, but some images loosen from the vapor and shine clear.

"What were they wearing?" I ask her.

"Not work clothes—they were cleaned up. They weren't dirty or ragged. Pretty good clothes. Sunday clothes, I guess."

"Do you remember what colors?"

She's exasperated with me. Why do I want to know such trifles?

"O.K.," she says, slapping the album down on the coffee table. "If that's the kind of thing you want to know. He had on tan pants and a light tan shirt. The woman was a lot shorter than him and had dark hair and had on a dark dress with white specks or flowers. The little girl had on frilly things. They wore ruffles and pinafores back then."

"Amazing!" I say. "Now I can see them. Like pictures."

"Oh, you're straining my little watery brain," she says with a moan. "All this talk. You make so much out of the least little thing." But she laughs then.

"Were you glad you went?" I ask.

She pauses. "There was something in me that told me I had to talk to him. I had to find him. And so I did. And I saw we had nothing in common. I knew he didn't want me. When I was growing up, they wouldn't let me have anything to do with him, but after I went out on my own, they couldn't stop me. It was just something I wanted to do, just see him and talk to him. Wilburn never said anything about us going down there to see him. I think I slipped off."

When she sighs, I hope it is a sigh of release, not pain.

Even though it had been a clumsy meeting, the ice was broken, and an acquaintance of sorts began. Soon after that trip to Paducah, Mary brought Robert Lee out to our farm for a Sunday afternoon. Mama helped Granny fix dinner for them. I imagine Robert awkwardly, tentatively, trying to respond to the opening his daughter created that day in Paducah.

"The menfolks stood around and talked," Mama tells me. "You know how men are—if they've got a big job they want to talk about it. They want to talk about money. He bragged about all the money he was making."

She didn't go out of her way to talk to him, and he hung back from her. I suspect he talked about money to impress her. He was showing her he had made his way out of poverty. For him, this would have been an enormous achievement—a boy with no prospects who had married too young, made mistakes, been driven away to pay for his mistakes, and then managed to do well despite it all. But I'm struck by his boorishness. He had robbed his wife—and by extension, his daughter. Any success he'd gained had come at their expense. The family's grievance always focused on his thievery. Yet here he was, the granddaddy of deadbeat dads, dwelling on the topic of money.

Mama doesn't remember talking to him that day, or ever talking with him to any extent, even though she was around him on a number of occasions during the next four years. "I didn't want much to do with him," she tells me now. "But the day I took you to Paducah—I knew I just *had* to meet him. He was so flabbergasted, he was speechless. But I decided I didn't need anything more from him. And I was satisfied with that."

From what I can find out, Robert Lee worked on the river when he was young, in the 1920s. He worked on a towboat as a laborer—anything from cook to deckhand. I imagine that after stealing Eunice's property he may have made his way across the river to Missouri or Arkansas. Working on the river, then, might have followed naturally. I picture him as a rowdy and randy young squirt, ready to engage the world. He strutted and bragged; he was sexually attractive; he knew the ways of the world, knowledge he gained on his visits to Vicksburg, Memphis, Cairo—all the river towns where he might have docked and gone on sprees. He wouldn't have retired to his room and read a book. From what I have heard, he was loud, rude, impetuous, adventurous, abusive to women. I imagine him exploding with obscenities, going into drunken rages. He would be in a whorehouse; he would be in bars, maybe in fights. He would always be looking for a chance—to test his skills, to pick up some change, to see what there was to see. He roamed and explored and caroused. A big hotheaded, hard-living son of a bitch. My grandfather.

After Eunice died, or maybe after she remarried, he would have made his way home to see his family. Visiting his parents at Clear Springs, Robert hung out at the store with his brother, worked with horses, did farm labor. He helped his father split shingles. He could work with his hands like an artist. The river was far away and foreign to this little community, so being a boatman probably seemed romantic. One of the neighbors gave Robert a nickname. He called Robert "Record," from the song "Steamboat Bill."

Steamboat Bill, steaming down the Mississippi
Is going to beat the record of the Robert E. Lee.

In the song, Steamboat Bill, pilot of the *Whippoorwill*, tries to outrace the redoubtable *Robert E. Lee*, the fastest steamboat on the Mississippi. But Steamboat Bill's boiler explodes from the fury of the race and now he's "a pilot on the ferry in the Promised Land."

I'm attracted to the idea of Robert Lee as a riverman. A rambler, a gambling man, a wanderer. No one else in my family that I know of ever strayed far from farm life, unless Daddy's Navy voyage counts. For generations, all the forebears I can name were farmers. But here was a principal figure in my immediate family cruising down the river. I try to picture Robert Lee on a towboat, steering barges of coal through the great confluence of the Mississippi and Ohio Rivers at Cairo, Illinois, the place where Huckleberry Finn's raft misses the turn toward freedom for the slave Jim. Robert Lee might have traveled all the way to Pittsburgh or St. Louis or New Orleans. I study the map. Could he have gone on the Missouri River to Omaha—"way yander to Newbraskie"?

My imagination is steaming down the river. I could hop onto Huckleberry Finn's raft, or Robert Lee's towboat—whatever's going.

Robert Lee died not many months after the Sunday afternoon in 1944 when we all had our picture taken together. My parents received a telegram asking them to meet the body at the depot. Our address had been found on a scrap of paper in his pocket. Daddy had given him the address some time before and Robert was still carrying it with him.

Mama is not sure where her father died, but she thinks it may have been in Mississippi, where he had gone on a job—maybe on a road crew. She said the workers were sheltered in tents, in cold, rainy weather. He didn't come out of his tent for two days, and when someone eventually checked on him, he was delirious with fever. He was carried to a hospital, but he soon died.

"He took double pneumony," Mama says. "I don't believe there was any penicillin then."

I wonder about all the pneumonia I had as a child—some of it without benefit of penicillin. How my mother must have worried over me, fearing I would die from the same disease that killed her father.

"The funeral was out at his mama and daddy's house," Mama says. "But before that, he was laid out for the public at a funeral home in Mayfield. Thelma, my half-sister, and me was the only ones there," Mama says. "Nobody knew about it, I guess. And that woman he lived with couldn't have come there because they weren't married. Thelma and me just set there. We didn't cry. He wasn't a daddy to either one of us. I didn't have any feelings. He made big money, but he never spent a penny on me. I got him a floral spray for seven-fifty. Back then you could get a big standing spray for seven-fifty. But it was still a lot of money."

25

On a sunny summer day much like the one in those 1944 photographs at the Lee homeplace, Mama and I are on a Sunday afternoon drive to Clear Springs. I'm still looking for Robert and Eunice. Mama wants to show me those old settings I've had on my mind, and I want to see my mother in the places of her youth. I remember her as a young mother—her bouncy black curls pulled back on top, her long, thin legs, her waist only barely beginning to thicken from childbearing. I remember her head thrown back in laughter.

On the drive, through some back roads, I'm mentally following the 1880 map of Clear Springs. Back then, the village of Clear Springs (pop. 1,422) had a post office and two doctors, a drugstore, a black-smith shop, a general store, and several houses. The map shows all these, as well as the farms all around, with the names of the owners. Twenty-two of my great- and great-great- and triple-great-grandparents are represented on that map. All the families I come from were settled in the community by then, except for the Lees, who would arrive by the turn of the century.

The farmland is much the same today, with tobacco and soybeans and hay and corn. But there are no stores now. The houses are modest; there's an occasional mobile home. Now and then we see a new brick house beside a dilapidated wood-frame house that has been allowed to weather and cure like an old ham. A very old tobacco barn appears gray and ghostly through a grove of oaks.

"That tobacco's out so late this year, I don't think it'll make," Mama observes as we pass a field with seedlings planted in a checkerboard pattern. She seems more interested in the crops of the moment than the reminders of the past. I can almost feel her quaver at some of the hard memories I've dredged up. Most of her generation of kinfolks out here in Clear Springs are dead, and we haven't kept up with the younger people.

We stop at Mammy Hicks's house, where Mama was born. Some years ago, it was remodeled into a barn; now it shelters farm equipment. The planks have weathered, and vines and weeds have grown around the place. Behind the house, Mama points out the old brick cistern, which collected rainwater from the roof. It is shaped like a milk jug, with its mouth and shoulders rising from the ground.

"I got a whipping once for playing around that cistern," she recalls.

We stand in the large doorway of the barn, and she gestures vaguely at the spaces inside. "Aunt Hatt's bed was over there in the corner. And here is where Mammy Hicks died; she was eating watermelon when her heart give out. Over there is where I slept. Mammy Hicks had lace curtains—they always said the Irish had to have lace curtains."

"They were Irish?" I ask.

"The old country. I guess they was Irish." Mama pronounces it "Arsh."

A wisp of ancestral memory floats across a couple of centuries to this spot. My mother was a child here.

Before that, Eunice had been a child here, the youngest of six children; their father died when she was a baby. Mammy Hicks looms in my mind as a no-nonsense woman who married a bit above her station. Her husband knew books. But his people had sided with the Union and might even have been bushwhackers. The fine organ that she was determined to have her daughters play was so much prized that when the house caught fire, Eunice and Hattie managed to rescue it from the second floor. I don't know how that was possible. Could they have heaved it out the window?

I try to imagine my mother growing up here, an independent little creature running around the fields, playing with the pig. She would have had a secure, steady family for several years, until Mammy Hicks choked on that piece of watermelon. In her home-cut bob, Chris is a sly orphan with her head cocked and bent down slightly, glancing furtively upward. In her furtiveness is a gleam of independence. I see my mother's life in outline, with the large, domineering Mason clan gathering around her, thwarting her wanderlust and collapsing her ambitions. Over the years, my mother, from a headstrong and spirited youngster, turned into a woman so bowed by circumstance and others' authority that she thought she didn't even deserve a house as nice as her grandmother's. Mama was at home with scraps and nubbins and hand-me-downs. The comfortable house she lives in now, I suspect, must make her feel that her life has been a most improbable journey.

As we drive farther into the country, I realize how isolated the Clear Springs community was in earlier times. Nowadays, of course, roads and wires connect it intimately to the larger world, but when my mother was a child, she rarely got to go as far as Mayfield. We pass a farm where, in 1880, Antnette Victoria "Bobbie" Mason had just married Mack Arnett. Antnette (a corruption of Antoinette, pronounced *Ant*-nit) would have eight children, and three would die as infants. She would die at age thirty-six, from blood poisoning, after giving birth to twins. I don't know how she got her nickname, "Bobbie," but I have a special feeling for her, this young Bobbie Mason who lived in that hard time when she would have been carrying water from the spring, scrubbing heavy britches on a washboard, drying peaches for winter, killing chickens, plucking geese. It was only a slight lurch in time that sent me down a different road, to life-saving penicillin and the radio and jet airplanes.

We pass McKendree Church; the cemetery where my father lies; the little house where wandering Aunt Mattie lived; names on mailboxes that are the same as the names on the old map. We see one of the country stores, abandoned now. We pass the spot where Dr. Hurt's magnificent house with its chandelier and music room burned years ago.

The gravel road leading to the Lees' house is just above Dr. Hurt's place. The Lees and the Masons lived barely two miles apart. What determination and care it required in that small community to keep Christy Lee from ever knowing her father! We turn and head uphill. On the corner, a distillery once flourished. Not far up the road, Mama locates the site of the Lees' homestead, and I pull off the gravel into a vacant, overgrown clearing. My mother's father was raised here.

"This is where it was," she says. "But the road's been built up, so the place is not up on a hill now."

The gravel, the color of paper grocery sacks, is muddy. Mama points out where the old house in the photographs had stood. The clearing gives the distinct impression of having been something else once, before nature began to reclaim it. In my mind, I arrange the house, the barn, a shed, the blacksmith shop, the orchard in this landscape. I try to see the straight-chairs in the yard under old shade trees that are no longer there. I can picture the porch, the spotted bobtailed dog, the hickory walking stick leaning against the tree. I remember

Mama in the pictures—she's casually gorgeous in high heels and a white piqué dress with eyelet ruffles.

We walk around, mentally imposing those old pictures onto the landscape. It occurs to me that there were no electric wires overhead in those scenes, even though Clear Springs had received rural electrification several years before. This place made a deep impression on me when I was a child, I realize now, for I have carried around a notion that my knowledge of country life extends back into the nineteenth century, back to the first settling of Clear Springs. That way of life is what I imagine here in the pioneer-cabin style of house—the handmade chairs, the roof with the hand-split hickory shingles, the pair of rickety old great-grandparents.

Mama says, "The first time I came over there, I remember how shocked I was that they didn't have any screen doors. The chickens and dogs could come right in the kitchen where we were eating. I wasn't used to that. The house wasn't very clean, but my grandparents were getting old and couldn't take care of themselves very well. Once, I was here and Grandma Lee went out in the yard and grabbed a chicken and killed it for dinner. I was so surprised at that. We always penned them up for a week and fattened them—that cleaned them out. I'd never seen anybody just kill one that was running loose."

In my imagination, Mama's grandparents are sitting side by side in straight-chairs in the yard. Grandma Lee's dark hair is parted in the center and pulled back in a knot. She has on shapeless brogans. Her dress is plain, a solid color. Grandpa's hair, lighter than hers, is graying. His fluffy mustache flows over his mouth. Wearing work clothes, he sits with one leg turned out at an angle.

Mama says she remembers when the place and her grandparents' belongings were auctioned off. "I got a wire eggbeater at the sale," she says. "Several people were bidding on it, but they saw I wanted it, and they stopped bidding so I could have something of my grandmother's."

There is a profusion of irises along the edge of the clearing. Grandma Lee's flowers have survived. Using a windshield scraper from the car as a tool, Mama and I dig up some of the tubers and stash them in a newspaper.

"These are the old-fashioned kind," Mama says. "The blooms will be little."

"Will they be all right for a couple of days, till I get home?"

"You can't kill iris."

"Evidently." These irises have been here for over fifty years. It pleases me that I can grow some of my great-grandmother's flowers and keep them going in her honor, but I think it pleases me even more that I recognize them from the old pictures.

"My daddy's funeral was here at the house," Mama says, as we straighten up from digging irises. "Granddaddy carried me out here. I don't remember if Granny come along with us. The funeral was in the house because my daddy's mother—Grandma Lee—was in bed sick. The roads were so muddy they couldn't get the hearse up the hill. They carried the casket up the muddy road and then packed it into the house."

Mama uses the verbs "carry" and "pack" frequently—she carries a cat to the vet and packs him into the office—but now I notice how these words emphasize her burdens. I remember what she said about the visit to the funeral home. Did no one sit up all night with the body? I wonder.

There was a chill in the late-spring air the day of the funeral. There were no flowers or food. Robert Lee's casket stood by his mother's bed, where she could look at him. His parents were brokenhearted, Mama says. "His death was such a shock to them. Grandma Lee prayed and prayed for him. She told me she had prayed his way into heaven and that he was O.K."

I remember seeing Grandma Lee, sick in bed, at this place. I was out in the yard, and she was in the front room, visible through the window. Her ancient, heavy bones, weighed down by her sagging skin, battled the bedclothes. She worried her head from side to side. She reached for me with gnarled, bird-claw hands. I remember the house and the small hillside of bare, hard dirt. And that was where I remember my grandfather Robert showing me something very important. He dug a cave in the side of the hill, a hole large enough to bury some hot coals from a fire, and he inserted a potato and closed up the hole. Some time later, he pulled the potato out with a stick. It was done and ready to eat. It was a sort of miracle, involving a little cave, on a dollhouse scale. The image of that potato cooked in the ground has stayed with me all these years, I think, because my grandfather came down to my level and revealed to me something filled with essential mystery—cave, fire, transformation.

Soon after Robert was buried, his sister Mary took their parents to live with her in Michigan. They were both in failing health and there was no one else to take care of them. "Mary rode with them in an ambulance because Grandma Lee was bedridden," Mama says. "The morning after they got to Mary's house, Grandma told Mary that Jimmo had wanted to have sex with her as soon as they got there. She said, 'As sick as I was, and he wanted that.' " Mama stifles a little laugh. "She didn't live long after that, and Mary brought her back home here to bury her."

"What if you had moved to Detroit instead of eloping with Daddy?"

She mulls over this. I can imagine it. The fun-loving, rebellious side of her would have had the upper hand then. In Detroit, Mama would have been cut loose from the Mason homeplace. She would have adopted a Northern brogue, gotten tough. Mary would have watched out for her.

"I might have gone up there," Mama says finally.

"What if the Lees had claimed you instead of Uncle Roe and Rosie?" I ask her. "What would your life have been like?"

She has a flat, simple answer. "I would have had more love from my grandparents, but not from my daddy. He didn't want me." Frowning, she stares into the distance. After a moment, she goes on. "Grandma Lee was real sweet. I believe she told me she had a baby at the same time I was born, but her baby died. Or did I just imagine that?"

In my snooping in the library, I have already traced that baby. It lived only a day. The name was recorded as "Vilent" Lee—probably Violet. I tell Mama now. Violet would have been her aunt.

Mama absorbs this quietly as we return to the car.

"It wasn't right that Uncle Roe and Aunt Rosie kept me away from those old people," Mama says suddenly. She is placing the newspaper-wrapped irises into the back of the car.

"I haven't had much of a life," she says after a pause.

I have stirred up too much, too many imponderables. I don't know what to say. We get in the car and turn out of the clearing. We head back down the Clear Springs road.

I'm coming to understand how memories are imposed on the past and also how they get lost. We reach a point where we do not know whether we remember an actual event or an imagined one; we cannot remember whether a significant event actually happened. In studying a photograph, which is documented proof of our presence at an event, we analyze the event as if we had been there, when for the purposes of memory we had not, for it has vanished from the mind. So I come near to inventing these old great-grandparents and this mysterious grandfather, while being as scrupulous to known fact as my brain will allow.

I don't know where Robert Lee worked or lived; I don't know what women he loved; I don't recall what his voice was like. A few people who vaguely remembered the Lees tried to tell me the Lees were good folks, that I shouldn't be ashamed of them for being poor. But Eunice's family and later my family held the shame of his poverty against Robert Lee. The Hickses and the Masons were upstanding people, thrifty and correct. They didn't let their chickens run around in the kitchen.

In one of the group photographs in Mama's album, my grandfather's hand rests gently on my shoulder. This is an important detail, I think.

As we drive down the road, images of him float through my mind: the boy in the meadow with Eunice and Hattie, the boy vamoosing with Eunice's horse and buggy and her money, fleeing to the river, running away from his crimes and responsibilities, rambling around. I'm haunted by the thought of him huddling feverishly in that tent, in the mud, coughing and dying.

What did he believe he was doing when he absconded with Eunice's fortune? Did that memory come to his mind as he lay dying, guilt rushing up like vomit? Did he think of that day in Paducah when my mother and I showed up, smashing our way into his Sunday afternoon? Perhaps in his fever he was tormented by the bay horse he stole, its fleeting hooves hammering in his brain.

Inexplicably, Robert Lee is buried in the Hicks graveyard, just off the main road in Clear Springs. The graveyard is enclosed with a wrought-iron fence. We drive through the gates and onto the grass. The place is well kept—neatly mowed and trimmed. Robert Lee and his family lie just east of Eunice and her family. I wonder if their proximity signals some kind of reconciliation in the community. Eunice has a tall, elegant stone, but others in her family closest to her grave aren't marked. Her sisters Hattie and Lillie are near her. Their sister Rosie is in McKendree Cemetery, with the Masons. Mammy Hicks is here. J. R. Hicks, who left the estate of books and beehives and tricks, is here too.

Mama points out what she thinks is Aunt Hattie's spot. "I always wanted to get Hatt a stone," she says, her voice low and mournful.

I take her hand as we walk several yards and stand before Robert's parents:

JAMES F. LEE	MARY LUE LEE
June 30, 1870	Mar. 31, 1881
Oct. 29, 1948	June 16, 1945

Grandpa Lee lived three years after Grandma Lee died. Both of them died in Detroit, far from the lives they had known.

"I think my daddy's right there," Mama says, pointing to a space to the right of Mary Lue Lee.

He has no headstone. But a small hunk of concrete, like the corner of a foundation, is there. It has gravel embedded in it. It lies in a bed of periwinkle and some scattered leaves. Robert is catty-cornered across from Eunice, he without a monument, she with a monolith, like a beacon—is she warning him away or beckoning him back? Her stone is old-fashioned and lovely. It says: COME YE BLESSED and GONE BUT NOT FORGOTTEN. Her name is misspelled "Unice." An image is carved above her name. It looks like a balcony between two portals, and a star is shining through a set of open gates. The gates of heaven are opening and a shining five-point star guides her in.

UNICE
Wife of L. O. MOORE
Mar. 29, 1897–Aug. 29, 1923

I see that her childbed fever occurred at the height of the summer heat. Nearby, her second husband, Luther Moore, is buried beside his first wife. One reads relationships and discussions here. Robert Lee ends on a note of eternal entrapment.

"After he died, Mary said that the woman he lived with told her he always loved my mama," Mama says. "She said he'd have nightmares and wake up calling out her name. She said he really loved my mother."

"I bet he did. He still had your name in his pocket when he died. I'm sure he loved you, too."

She laughs a little. "You make so much out of everything. But I reckon it's true. He must have felt awful when he heard she was dead."

I'm aware that we seem to be gossiping in his presence. This vacant spot hits both Mama and me hard, but we don't know what to say.

I'm aware that Robert Lee was a rounder, but I admire his bold sense of adventure and his desire to learn what he couldn't learn in the atmosphere of this community that held a curse over his head. I want to see his good side, and I want my mother to get out from under that old horse-and-buggy grudge.

I say, "I bet when he came back to Clear Springs he acted like he was really something on a stick. Remember how he combed his hair in those pictures? Not a *hair* out of place. But maybe he had a right to strut a little. He'd been somewhere and done things. He had gumption. I bet he didn't turn out as bad as some of them said."

Mama is listening, with her head down. After a while she says, "Well, just because he run off, I don't think they should have kept me from having anything to do with him." She touches her foot to the chunk of concrete that lies on his grave. It's like a piece of rubble tossed aside, casual and meaningless.

We're silent for a long while. Then Mama says, "I'll take back what I said before. If I hadn't had you children, I wouldn't have had much of a life. But I *did* have you. I just never had a chance at anything."

"That's because you didn't have parents to bring you up—but we did."

She adjusts her weight, as if she has been standing too long. "If my mama and daddy could just see me now," she says. "If they only knew how their youngun turned out."

"Well, I think you've turned out great!" I blurt.

I don't know what to say next. My lifelong habit of reticence holds my tongue. I don't know how to speak my gratitude for her sacrifices without sounding sentimental—which would be fine with her. But I try. I need to make her believe her worth, to know how proud I am of her for her strength and resilience.

"You've had an *extraordinary* life. Do you know how proud your children are of you? You're the best mama I could have had! And where would *we* have ended up without you?"

I pause, groping for more words.

"Just look at your parents," I say. "Look at what they missed. Robert Lee can't be all bad, or you wouldn't be as good as you are. I don't want you to hate him. If you hate him, then you hate yourself, and that means you hate part of me, too. But you know you don't hate your own children. Everything we are comes from you and Daddy. I think you and Daddy were always afraid we'd go off and not come back; you were afraid we'd get out in the world and then be ashamed of where we came from. But that's not true. We're grateful."

Mama has listened carefully. I've spewed all this, with an insistence that's nearly shrill, and now she's the one who seems speechless. Finally, she says, "You were the first one, and you were so little I was afraid you'd break." She looks me right in the eyes. "I was scared to handle you, so I raised you by the book. The book said feed you ever four hours. You were so hungry you cried yourself to sleep, and then when it was time to feed you, you wouldn't eat. I had to wake you up to feed you. You were never satisfied."

She smiles at my surprise.

"I didn't get enough titty? Well, that explains a lot!"

"You were always hungry," she says.

"So *that*'s why I had food dreams."

One reason to fashion a story is to lift a grudge. I can see my mother holding the weight of her life. It is too much to sum up or dispense with or bury. I know that it was up to my siblings and me to do what had been denied her, to take the chance she offered us. It saddens me that my mother had to raise me "by the book" because she didn't have a mother to teach her what to do. I'm aware that I am still that little child with the jigsaw puzzle, throwing a fit if the pieces don't go together. And Mama is humoring me. But now I feel we're closer to knowing what's in us, guiding us and bringing us together. What comes clearest is my own need to find the Robert Lee in myself. I'm the one who needs to lighten up, kick down the stone fences.

I'm walking away, toward the car, but when I look back I notice Mama is still at her father's grave. Again she prods the lump of pebble-studded concrete with her foot, then stoops to touch it, as if she were fussing with a floral arrangement. I meander through a row of Hickses and some Allcocks.

In a few minutes she joins me by the gate.

"He was awful young to die," she says.

"Just imagine—what if he had lived, and we could have gone down the river on a boat with him. Wonder what it would be like if he had lived and we could have gotten to know him?"

She smiles and shakes her head. "We'll never know."

"Let's go on a cruise down the Mississippi River," I say, taking her hand as we head for the car. "Let's hop on the *Delta Queen* and ride the river on down to Memphis."

"I'd have to take my fishing pole," she says. She starts laughing then.

I imagine Robert Lee on a towboat, towing me outward into the larger world, into the oceans, where the great migrations once rode the waves to the shore of the new continent. Some of these seekers threaded together and found their way to Clear Springs. Their history is elusive, the memory unreliable, as vague as the chemistry and flow of the ocean washing them to shore. I so much want everything to come clear. The old pieces dissolve like paper, but at last I feel I know where I am.

....

26

My mother and I are in her garden, and she is picking Kentucky Wonder beans. It is shortly after dawn. We have driven to the farm from her new house, which she has now occupied for over a year. She works bending from the waist in the timeless stoop-labor position. She parts the vines and plucks three beans simultaneously, threading the pods between her fingers.

I like to see her in her garden. I know she misses living here at the farm. But her bones are brittle, and I am glad she does not have to climb rickety wooden steps. I wish she felt strong enough to go fishing in her pond. Several months after moving to her new house, she suffered a light stroke, so minor that for a couple of days we thought it was only her nerves. With that warning, she agreed to have the corrective surgery her doctor had recommended to unblock her carotid artery. After recovering from the operation, she was livelier and more clear-headed, with more bounce. Now she seems restored, with no lasting damage from the stroke. She has tried to quit smoking several times.

Near the garden, the house where I was raised sits forlornly in the woods; weeds and grass and bushes are slowly strangling it. A hole has appeared in the roof, as if a concrete block has been dropped by a passing airplane. It reminds me of the hole punched in the new roof of the movie-set garage to make it look old. I'm on my way to the creek to pick blackberries, but I can't resist circling around our old house one last time. In my gumshoes, I almost step on a nail sticking up from a shingle that is dissolving in the mud. I have spiked my feet on rusty nails on this farm before. I notice a nearby sinkhole carpeted with leaves—that was the septic tank. If I stepped there, I might disappear.

A bulldozer is going to crush the house, flatten it, and push it a few hundred yards through the woods to a depression in the ground, an old pond site. The bulldozer will bury the house there. We don't know when the bulldozer will arrive. Maybe tomorrow, maybe next week, or not until the fall. It depends. Mama has been avoiding the issue. I know she must feel sad at seeing the house go to ruin. She doesn't mention it often, but she admits that the house is a dangerous wreck and an invitation to vandals.

I share her melancholy. But I'm also feeling energized: the morass of loss I've been in is finally dissipating, like a fog clearing so a plane can take off. I feel wide awake and lightsome; I've come full circle—that is, far enough to know where I've been. Every summer now, I have an irresistible urge to pick berries.

The fields are laid out behind the woods like quilt blocks, with the shaggy fencerows stitching them together. The landscape is an array of greens, pale and dark and misty and gold-tinged. Soybeans grow all the way to the far creek, and popcorn has been planted in the fields across that creek. This land around me has a hold on my heart, yet I wouldn't want to live here, on a farm that has an industrial sewer pipe running beneath its fields like the bowels of a monster that has settled from outer space. I'm content to live—within driving distance—on my own piece of ground with my husband and pets.

It feels strange to be walking on this place without Oscar. He is in retirement, too feeble now to scamper in these fields.

Granny's old house is rented out. Through the trees, I see two little girls bouncing on a trampoline in the yard. In a flash, I am six years old, jumping on the bed in our new house. I remember the sheer joy of jumping, trying to hit the ceiling, with the faint possibility that I might just fly on up to the sky.

The chicken tower is whirring, spinning its guts to produce food for fowl, and the vomit smell of it is laced through the air.

In sophisticated gatherings, I'm sometimes given to conversation stoppers. I might mention the time I sang with a gospel quartet, or how my family didn't have an indoor bathroom until I was eight years old, or how I had to sleep with a pan to catch the water from the leak in the ceiling. I might let slip that my Granny made her hair curlers out of pipe cleaners covered with scraps of leather. Usually, nobody present can identify with these memories. There's an awkward pause and then someone striving for a sympathetic connection will mention summer camp in the Adirondacks, or they'll say they always liked fresh, home-baked bread. So, perversely, I volunteer that we fried our toast. I have grown to cultivate my idiosyncratic revelations, now that I'm no longer humiliated by them; sometimes springing them is fun, though rather unfair of me. I time the mystified pause, then the quiet scramble back to familiar conversational territory. What is apparent, though, is that these revelations rarely get through to people. They don't know how to categorize what I've said, so they continue to assume that my background was basically like theirs, with regular garbage pickup and ballet lessons. Or if what I say registers at all, they may reduce it to some pathetic image of poverty based on the movies. Which of course is not the story at all. The story is of distinctions and interweavings and shadings.

I have met people who left their country origins behind, seemingly with ease and good riddance, in favor of the delights of urban fellow-ship and opportunity. I have dared repeatedly to plunge in over my head, but with my country reserve, I can't casually summon the knowledge I've gathered and jump into intellectual conversations; I can't serve on a committee or run for office or feel easy at a cocktail party. The rural temperament still has a hold on me that I won't let go.

But this is fine with me. I don't want to enter academic discourse, don't want to run for office. I'm beginning to understand what my father must have felt when he returned after the Navy. He had sur-vived the war. He decided what was important. And he knew who he was. He renewed his vows to the land, even though there was little prospect of prosperity.

I imagine his sense of resignation came down to him through his-tory: from the pioneers, who learned to cultivate stinginess and stern-ness on such matters as seed corn and labor; and from the Civil War, which filled an entire culture with a profound sense of loss. After lurching through Pacific waters, my father was stilled, as a cow is held in a stanchion while being milked. Coming home, he found peace in honoring the violent necessities of the soil and the seasons, and in bowing to the authority of his father. Undeniably, his nerve failed him—in part, his resignation was a defeat. But I think he also loved his place in the scheme of things. In part, he chose his life.

Emerging from a bank of berry bushes, I gaze around at Daddy's fields, the margins grown ragged now. Tire tracks from giant farm machines have reshaped the mouth of the creek where the pond empties. I'm surrounded by my father's horizons. This piece of ground fought him, and he fought back. He fought the gullies and the Johnsongrass and the blackberry briars.

I read so much into my parents. I read the character and history of America in them as if they were a book. I read them in the ground, in the patch of grass where their barn used to be, in the sentinel yuccas by the driveway, in the lightning-scarred oak trees at the edge of the woods. I link them to the early journeys over the ocean, the revolving generations, the plow turning the furrow. While riding the rows on his tractor, Daddy mulled over the way the world works, just as I've done while sitting at the controls at my desk. I reach to know his mind, as I grab for a post, an anchor. But I always knew where my center was—here, on this land. This is my parents' greatest gift—this rootedness, this grounding. It is what has let me roam. I've been like a hawk on a gyre, flying off, ranging as far as I can—yet always spiraling back, securely tethered to home. Unlike Daddy, I won't come back to roost here. I want to stretch my wings farther.

The chicken tower's reflection shines in the still pond like a magnificent tableau from a science-fiction fantasy. It is still huffing away, like Godzilla. Lately, Mexican immigrants have moved into the area to take the low-wage jobs offered by the chicken-processing plant on the other side of town. They have traveled this far to find a better life for their families, to make money to send home. What solace and promise do they find in the sight of these green fields, so wide and welcoming, and the narrow boundaries of suspicion that sometimes greet them in the aisles of the new Wal-Mart Supercenter?

For a long time, I've been preoccupied with why some folks stay and some stray. I read about a scientific study of cats in the wild. It had been assumed that cats who established a territory, or home base, were the successful ones, while those who remained roamers were the losers. The study uncovered evidence that the transients, not the residents, might be the more resourceful cats, accepting greater risks and more varied opportunities for prey and mates. It was almost as though they were exercising imagination. It's an old question—the call of the hearth or the call of the wild? Should I stay or should I go? Who is better off, those who traipse around or those who spend decades in the same spot, growing roots?

The way I see it, a clever cat prowls but calls home occasionally. The answer is the mingling of sunlight and shadow; it's ambiguity, not either-or. The best journeys spiral up and around—the journey of Odysseus on the wine-dark sea or Bloom in the winding streets of Dublin. In the Zen journey, when you return, you know for the first time where you came from. We're always yearning and wandering, whether we actually leave or not. In America, we all come from somewhere else, and we carry along some dream myth of home, a notion that something—our point of origin, our roots, the home country—is out there. It's a place where we belong, where we know who we are. Maybe it's in the past—we dream of our own clear springs—or maybe it's somewhere ahead. In its inception, the idea of America was heaven on earth. Now that dream is fractured and we're looking for the pieces. Maybe we'll never find what we're looking for, but we have to look.

After all my comings and goings, now I see that I *am* my mother—and all of my forebears. I am plainspoken like Granny. Sometimes I realize I am talking to myself the way Granddaddy used to do—as if there were two of me. Sometimes I have a thought that I know Daddy must have had. Sometimes I think I have an original idea, but I know that some great-great-grandmother hunched over a quilt frame quite likely had that same thought. I feel Robert Lee in me, surging downriver. I am so much my mother that I can feel myself inside her head, feel her in me. From this berry bush I can see Mama in the garden, working the soil just the way she learned from Mammy Hicks and Aunt Rosie. I feel the ache in Mama's bones, the promise of young Eunice, Aunt Rosie's need to mastermind, and Daddy's shy detachment, his sly asides.

I think of something I want to tell Mama. Recently, I saw a hummingbird fly into my living-room window, its long beak stabbing the glass. Stunned, it fell to the ground and lay on its side, still breathing. It was a female. Her feathers were green and gold—iridescent, like a peacock's. The minuscule feathers overlapped like fish scales. The bird lay there, her exquisitely designed clothing on show. When she began to stir, I set her upright in a hanging flowerpot. Eventually she gathered the strength to buzz away like an oversized bumblebee.

A country person's social isolation can be stunting, but then again he may have a chance at clearer glimpses of the ultimate—like the hummingbird that slammed into my window. A city dweller has more faith in human possibility and can dream up a skyscraper, but a rural person knows life's limits. It occurs to me that the sorrow of this knowledge is the basis of the large-scale forgetting of our past, the loss of memory that has perplexed me so much. In agriculture, the individual is lost in repetition; the world recycles. Memory seizes only what is out of the ordinary.

My berry box is almost full. I head back across the field toward Mama.

Mama always knows where the moon is, and when to plant seed potatoes, and what potion to paint on a sick child's chest. She knows how to read the sky. My father knew when to expect birds to arrive or cows to calve; he knew how to fix almost anything without spending a cent. He could tell time in his head. He claimed he could approach any dog without fear.

I can't sew up a chicken's injured craw. I can't drive a tractor or cook worth beans. I can't put in a zipper. I tat words and save hummingbirds and come home to pick berries. Then I get eager to leap outwards again. Maybe someday I'll move to Vermont. I'm planning to take up piano, and I'm going trekking in Ireland, and then maybe I'll study lepidoptery. Or why not math? It turns out that the ultimate mysteries may be there. There's more than was dreamt of in Miss Florence's philosophy. I'll give chaos theory a whirl. Wonders are crashing into me, birds striking my window. I can't catch my breath. A summer dawn hits me nowadays like a stun-gun.

Maybe I'll just sit still and grow quiet and contemplate what is close to home. It would be a good time to let the colored-glass bits and floating feathers and song snatches in my head settle, so that some clear light can shine through. I recall Mama writing me that Granny, bedfast and obstinate, was driving her up the wall. What will I do if Mama requires such care? All I know is that I imagine I will do what needs to be done, even though I think I can't.

At the garden, I see that Mama has filled her buckets with beans, and now she is scraping some weeds that are popping through the dirt around her okra. She can't abide the weeds coming through. She doesn't let them get over a tenth of an inch high—barely visible. She scrapes the crust of the soil and turns it to aerate it.

"How many berries did you get?" she asks, straightening up. I show her my box. "Well, that'll do for a pie," she says, as she scrutinizes my berries. She moves into the tomato row. "I'm not going to hoe anymore," she says. "The wind's in the north, and I'd better not."

"Why?"

"Whenever Granny tried to hoe when the wind was in the north, the plants would die."

"I can't feel any wind." I set down the berries. Mama can sense the direction of the wind when it is so subtle that not a leaf is stirring, even when she is indoors.

Mama says, "I've seen the wind blow in all four directions in one day. It does that when it's trying to get back to the north."

I remember to tell Mama about the hummingbird.

Her face brightens. She says, "I never saw a hummingbird land in a tree till just a few years ago. It wasn't no bigger than my thumb."

Then I think of something else I know will interest her. I tell her about the cat who goes walking with Roger and me and our dogs. "Every time we go for a walk, our orange cat comes along with us. He thinks he's a dog. We try to sneak off, but he comes trotting along. He gets slowed down if we go for a long walk, and he has to be carried. If we leave him somewhere along the way, he just sits and waits at that one spot till we come back and get him—the way a kitten does."

Mama laughs while I'm talking. Her silver curls flow from beneath her baseball cap. She says, "I never knew a cat that would go for a walk. Which one of your cats is that?"

"Fergus."

"Fergus?"

"The name's from Ireland—the name of an ancient hero. Anyway, I thought it was the kind of name Daddy would have liked."

She grins. "Yeah, he would have got a kick out of that. Fergus." She leans on her hoe. "I tell you, he could come up with the oddballest names for his animals. Buford. Happy Jack. Hubert. Alphonse. Elvira. Irving."

A fluff of memory floats in like a paper airplane. "Why did you call us 'Pusservin' when we were little?" I ask. "I always thought you meant 'Preserving.' Were you saying 'Puss *Irving*'? Or what?"

"Law, I don't know. Pusservin—it was just a name I called you younguns." She leans over to gouge out a sprig of pigweed—pig presley—that has encroached upon her field-pea vines. I feel the strain in her back and share her small victory when the weed comes up roots and all.

Five

The
Pond

27

October 4, 1996

A couple of months after I went blackberry picking,
something unexpected happened. My mother told
me about it on the telephone. As usual, I asked
so many questions that she said, "Oh, you're
straining my little watery brain."

It had been an unusually hot summer, and my mother had gotten out of the habit of stirring about, although she still drove to her garden at the farm each morning. When she lived at the farm, she had kept active all summer, but at the new house, she felt inhibited from going outside. There were so many houses around, with people to see her and make her feel self-conscious. She was stiffening up with arthritis, and her muscles were still weak from her stroke a year ago. The doctor told her she had severe osteoporosis, but he didn't seem to think that was unusual for someone her age—seventy-seven. Her daughters nagged at her about exercise. They went on and went on about muscle tone and skeletal support. It made her tired to listen to them.

Now that it was autumn, the weather was a little cooler, and she longed to go fishing. Her daughters had given her a new rod-and-reel for her birthday over a year ago, but she had hardly made use of it. She knew the fish were growing big. When Wilburn restocked the pond, just before he died, he had included two five-pound catfish.

One sunny day in early October, after her dinner at noon, she impulsively went fishing. Leaving the dirty dishes on the table and the pots and pans on the counter, she stowed her tackle box and her rod-and-reel in the car and drove to the farm. She parked the car in the shade by the stable, near her garden, and headed across the soybean field toward the pond. She knew the fish would be biting. She was quicker in her step than she had been lately, but she picked her way carefully through the stubbly field. The soybeans had been recently harvested, but she did not know if the men who leased the land had gathered the popcorn they had planted in the back fields. It had been several years since she had been across the creeks to the back acreage.

She was walking through the field behind Granny's house. Only one car was in the driveway, and she did not see any of the renters. The trampoline in the yard reminded her of a misshapen hospital cot. The black dog chained to the wash-house regarded her skeptically, pawed at the ground, and sat down lazily. With his chain, he had worn away her grapevine and turned the grass into a crescent of dirt. The old place had so much time and heart invested in it, too much to comprehend. Now it seemed derelict and unloved.

She was out of breath when she reached the pond, but she recovered quickly in the warm air. The leaves on the trees along the creek were beginning to turn yellow and brown. The pond was full and still. The pondweed had diminished somewhat this year because Don had released two grass-eating carp into the water. They were supposed to eat their weight in pondweed daily. She had told Don to make sure they were the same sex. She didn't want the pond overrun with carp, which could be a worse calamity than pondweed.

She felt good, eager to fish. She baited her hook with a piece of a chicken gizzard she had bought the week before. It was ripe, a piece of stink bait to lure a catfish. After wiping her hands on the grass, she cast out and reeled in slowly. It was pleasant to stand on the bank and watch the arc of her line fly out. She was standing at the deep bend of the pond, near the old lane. The water was exceptionally high, nearly reaching the rim of the pond. The wind was blowing from the east, and her floater drifted to the left. She reeled it toward her.

Lately she had been reviewing her life, reflecting on the hardships she had endured. She bridled at the way the women always had to serve the men. The men always sat down in the evening, but the women kept going. Why had the women agreed to that arrangement? How had they stood it? What if she had had an opportunity for something different? Wilburn, amazed by her paintings, once said, "Why, if you'd had a chance, there's no telling what you could have accomplished." She didn't know. The thought weighed her down, taunting her with something lost she could never retrieve, like a stillborn child.

After a while, she got a bite. Her cork plunged down and then took off. A fish was carrying the bait across the pond, against the wind, rippling the water, flying across. She reeled in and felt the fish pull steady. It was a big one, but she didn't allow her hopes to rise yet. It seemed heavy, though. She worked it back and forth, feeling the deep pleasure of hooking a fish. It grew lively then. It was a fighter. As it resisted, she gradually realized its strength. She was afraid her line wasn't strong enough to bring it in. She would have to play it delicately.

She had never felt such a huge fish pulling at her. With growing anticipation, she worked the fish for an hour or more. But time seemed to drift like a cloud. She thought of LaNelle's Lark at the bottom of the pond. Wilburn had sunk the dilapidated car at the high end of the pond to reinforce the levee. Its hulk would be like a cow's skeleton, she thought. She did not allow the fish to take her line near that area.

She thought she knew exactly which fish she had hooked. She had had her eye on it for years. It was the prize fish of the whole pond. She had seen this great fish now and then, a monster that would occasionally surface and roll. It would wallow around like a whale. Since the first time she'd seen it, she had been out to get the "old big one." Her quest had become legendary in the family. "Mama's going to get that old big fish," they'd say. But she hadn't imagined this would be the day. It was as though the fish had been waiting for her, growing formidably, until this day. It had caught *her* by surprise.

Slowly, the fish lost its strength. She could see its mouth as she drew it nearer, as it relaxed and let her float it in. The fish was gigantic, more immense than any fish she had ever caught. From the feel of it and now the glimpse of it in the murky water, she thought it might weigh thirty pounds. If only she could see Wilburn's face when she brought this fish in.

She had never landed a fish larger than eleven pounds. She had caught a ten-pound catfish at a pay-pond once, and she had hooked the eleven-pounder in this pond. She knew that landing this one would be a challenge. She would have to drag it out, instead of raising it and flipping it out of the water.

Finally, the fish was at the bank, its mouth shut on the line like a clamp-top canning jar, its whiskers working like knitting needles. It was enormous. She was astonished. It touched the bank, but without the smooth glide of the water to support it the fish was dead weight. She couldn't pull it all the way up the bank. She couldn't lift it with her rod, nor could she drag it through the weeds of the bank. She was more worn out than the fish was, she thought. She held the line taut, so that the fish couldn't slip back in the water, and she tugged, but it didn't give. The mud was sucking it, holding it fast. Its head was out of the water, and with those whiskers and its wide wraparound mouth, it seemed to be smiling at her. She stepped carefully through scrubby dried weeds and clumps of grass, making her way down the shallow bank toward the fish. Knots of pondweed bordered the water. Gingerly, she placed her left foot on a patch of dried vegetation and reached toward the fish.

The patch appeared solid. For a fraction of a second, the surprise of its give was like the strangeness of the taste of Coca-Cola when the tongue had expected iced tea. The ground gave way under her foot and she slid straight into the pond. It wasn't a hard fall, for her weight slid right into the water, almost gracefully. On the way, she grabbed at a willow bush but missed it. She still had hold of the line, even though her rod-and-reel slipped into the water. She clutched at dried weeds as she slid, and the brittle leaves crumpled in her hands. Then the fish was slipping back into the water, dragging the rod. She snatched the rod and felt the fish still weighting the end of the line. Quickly, she heaved the rod to the bank. She caught hold of the fish and held it tight, her fingernails studding its skin.

She was gasping at the chill of the water. She could not touch bottom. She was clutching the edge of the bank, and the water was up to her neck.

She hadn't imagined the pond was so deep next to the bank. The fish in her hands, she hugged the bank, propping herself against it with her elbows. She tried to get a toehold against the side of the pond, but as she shifted her weight, the solid matter fell away and her foot seemed to float free. She kept a tight hold on the fish, pointing its head away from her so it would not grab her fingers. Sometimes a channel catfish would grip bait and not let go, even after the fish was dead. It could bite a person's finger off.

She still couldn't touch the bottom, but she balanced herself against the side of the pond and held the fish's head out of the water. The water helped buoy the weight of the fish. The fish gaped, and the baited hook floated for a moment. The hook was not even sunk into its flesh. Then the fish clamped onto the hook again.

The fish was a fine one, she thought. It would make good eating. She was pleased, even amazed that she had caught it. It had lost much of its strength. She would have to wait for it to die. When the mouth stayed open, it would be dead, even if it still seemed to be breathing.

She managed to scoot it up onto the bank, inching it in front of her. She laid it in the ooze, placing it by the gills. Its gills were still working, its mouth loosened now. She held it down hard against the mud. The fish gaped, and she lessened her pressure. She floundered in the water, repositioning herself against the muck. She realized the water no longer seemed chilly.

The water was high, submerging the lower branches of the willow bushes. The willows were only a few feet away, but she did not want to get near those bushes. She was sure there were snakes around the roots of the willows. The snaky tendrils of the pondweed brushed her legs. She kicked and stirred the water while holding on to a tuft of grass.

To make her way to the shallow end, she would have to maneuver around the willows. But she would have to launch too far out into the pond to do that. She wasn't sure she could swim, yet her clothes did not feel heavy. She was wearing her old tan stretch-knit pants and a thin blouse and a cotton shirt and tennis shoes.

She noticed it was shady in the direction of the shallow end, so she decided to stay where she was, where she could feel the sunshine. She expected that someone would see her presently and come to help her out. With difficulty, she twisted her body toward the road, where cars were passing. She let out a holler. More cars passed. She hollered again. The cars were driven by the blind and the deaf. Their windows were rolled up tight.

"Hey!" She let out a yodeling sound, and then a pig call. "Soo-eeee!" She tried all the calls she knew, calls she used when she had to reach the men working in the fields, sounds that could carry across creeks and hollers. "Sook, cow!" she called, as if summoning a herd of milk cows.

There was no one at the house now, but she thought the renters would be there soon. The car she had seen was gone. Her car gleamed fire-red at the stable. In the smooth surface of the pond before her, stretching toward the soybean field and then the road, she saw the up-side-down reflection of the chicken-feed mill. The sky was bright autumn blue, and the reflection of the tower was like a picturesque postcard, still and important-looking.

Balancing against the bank in the water up to her neck, she gazed across the field toward the houses and the road. In that panorama, her whole life lay before her—a rug at the foot of the feed-mill tower. She saw her own small house in the clump of trees. The bulldozer still had not come to demolish it. She was sure the house could be fixed up, if she could only tend to it. Leaving it vacant had caused it to deteriorate. The loss of her house probably hurt her more than anything about the farm. But she couldn't keep everything up. It was too much for her. She'd had the stable repainted—a clear red—but it needed more work. Her thoughts weighed her down with the heaviness of the farm's history. Her memories mixed together in a mosaic of hard bits, like chicken grit. She saw the calves, the horses, the corncrib, the gardens, the henhouses, and other buildings no longer there. She saw the onions and potatoes she stored in one of the stalls. She saw mules and tractors and bonfires of leaves. What she saw before her eyes now was the consequence and basis of her labor. Years of toil were finished now; sometimes she wondered what it had all been for.

She seized a clump of grass but could not nudge her weight onto the bank. It was like trying to chin herself on a high bar. She did not have the energy. Then the grass pulled loose. The fish gaped again, and she managed to push it farther up the bank. She avoided its mouth.

Time passed. For a while, she lay horizontal in the water, clutching grass; then she rested vertically against the sludge of the bank. When occasionally her grip loosened, she had to dog-paddle to keep afloat.

She was panting. She held herself steady until she gathered her strength, then she tried again to pull herself up. She could not. The water seemed quite warm now. She thrashed, to scare off snakes. If she could grab a willow branch, she was sure she could pull herself out, but the thought of snakes underwater around the willow roots made her tremble. Snapping turtles were there too, she felt sure.

The shade covering the shallow end had grown deeper and longer now. She needed to stay here in the sun.

A pack of coyotes could eat a person. Wilburn had said that was not true, but she believed it was. Last year, one of the neighbor women carried dinner to the farmhands at work in one of her back fields. She parked her car on a lane beside the field, and as she started toward the gate with the dinner she saw some coyotes running at her, a whole caboodle of them. She raced back to the car and slammed the door just in time. The coyotes clambered all over the car, sniffing.

Sometimes the siren of a passing ambulance started the coyotes howling. All along the creek, a long ribbon of eerie sound followed the siren. If the coyotes found her in the pond, she could not escape. They might smell the fish, she thought. That would draw them like bait. Her dread hardened into a knot. She thought she ought to pray. She hadn't been to church much lately. She had trouble hearing, now that they had a microphone. Its squealing hurt her ears.

Cars passed. She thought she saw her son's van under the trees. She thought he might be sawing wood. She hollered to the air. After a while, she could tell that what she had thought was the van was only some scrap metal glinting in the sun.

The soybeans had been harvested only a week before, and the combine had missed multitudes of beans. She could see clumps of them dotting the field. There was so much waste. It bothered her. The land itself was washing into the creek. She pictured herself in the pond, washing over the levee in a hard rain and then sweeping on down through the creek.

If Wilburn came along and saw her here, he would grin at her and say, "What are you fooling around in the pond for? Got time on your hands?" She wondered what it would be like to while away the hours in a country club swimming pool. She had never had time to idle like that. She did not know how people could piddle their lives away and not go crazy. She had stopped going on the senior-citizen bus tours because they wasted so much time at shopping malls. She told them she'd rather eat a worm.

She recalled falling into water before—it was familiar. She was a little thing, fishing in Panther Creek with her grandmother and aunt. Suddenly she slid off a log, down the bank, and into the water. Mammy Hicks and Aunt Hattie laughed at her. "You got wet, didn't you?" Hattie said, bobbing her pole. A whole life passed between those two splashings.

Her hands were raw. She thought she could see snakes swirling and swimming along the bank some yards away. She had never seen a cottonmouth at this pond, but a snake was a snake, poisonous or not. She shuddered and tightened her grasp on the grass. She kicked her feet behind her. Her shoes were sodden.

A pain jerked through her leg—a charley horse. She waited for it to subside. She did not know how much time had passed, but the sun was low. She was starting to feel cooler. Her legs were numb. She realized she could be having another stroke. For the first time, it occurred to her that she might really be stranded here and no one would know. No one knew she had come fishing.

She scrambled clumsily at the bank. Now she knew she had to get out. No one was going to come for her. She knew she should have tried earlier, when she had more strength, but she had believed someone would spot her and come to help her. She worked more industriously now, not in panic but with single-minded purpose. She paused to take some deep breaths. Then she began to pull, gripping the mud, holding herself against it. She was panting hard. Little by little, she pulled herself up the mud bank. She crawled out of the water an inch at a time, stopping to rest after each small gain. She did not know if she felt desperation. She was so heavy. Her teeth were chattering from the cold, and she was too weak to rise. Finally she was on the bank, lying on her belly, but her legs remained in the water. She twisted around, trying to raise herself up. She saw a car turn into the driveway. She hollered as loud as she could. Her teeth rattled. After a moment, the car backed up and drove away.

The western sun was still beating down. She lay still and let it dry her. As her clothes dried, she felt warmer. But her legs remained in the water, her shoes like laden satchels. She pulled and pulled and crawled until her legs emerged from the water. She felt the sun drawing the water from her clammy legs. But as the sun sank, she felt cooler. She crawled with the sun—moving with it, grabbing grass.

When she finally uprighted herself, the sun was going down. She stood still, letting her strength gather. Then she placed one foot in front of her, then the other.

She had to get the fish. Stooping, she pulled it onto the grass, but she could not lift it, and she knew she could not pack it to the car. It was dead, though its gills still worked like a bellows, slowly expanding and collapsing. It had let go of the hook. Leaving the fish, she struck out across the soybean field toward the car. No one was at the house. She reached the car. Luckily, the key had not washed out of her pocket while she was in the pond. In the dim light, she couldn't see how to get it in the ignition. For an interminable time, she fumbled with the key. Then it turned.

Instead of following the path around the edge of the field, she steered the car straight across the beanfield. She stopped before the rise to the pond and got out. As she climbed toward the pond, her feet became tangled in some greenbrier vines and she fell backwards into a clump of high grass. Her head was lower than her feet. She managed to twist herself around so that she was headed up the bank, but she was too weak to stand.

She lay there in the grass for some time, probably half an hour. She dozed, then jarred awake, remembering the fish. Slowly, she eased up the bank and eventually stood. When she reached the fish, it appeared as a silhouette, the day had grown so dark. She dragged the fish to the car and heaved it up through the door, then scooted it onto the floorboard behind the driver's seat. She paused to catch her breath.

The sun was down now. In the car, she made her way out of the field to the road. Cars were whizzing by. She was not sure her lights were working. They seemed to burn only dimly. She hugged the edge of the narrow road, which had no shoulders, just deep ditches. Cars with blazing headlights roared past. She slowed down. By the time she got into town, the streetlights were on. She could not see where to turn into her street. A car behind her honked. Flustered, she made her turn.

When she got home, the kitchen clock said 7:25. She had been at the pond for seven hours. She opened the back door, and Chester the cat darted in, then skidded to a stop and stared at her, his eyes bugged out. She laughed.

"Chester, you don't know me! Do I smell like the pond?"

Chester retreated under the kitchen table, where he kept a wary lookout.

"Come here, baby," she said softly. "Come on." He backed away from her.

She got into the shower, where she let hot water beat on her. Memories of the afternoon's ordeal mingled in her mind like dreams, the sensations running together and contorting out of shape. She thought that later she would be angry with herself for not pulling herself out of the pond sooner—she could have ventured into those willow bushes—but now she felt nothing but relief.

After she was clean and warm, she went to the kitchen. Chester reappeared. He rubbed against her legs.

"Chester," she crooned. "You didn't know me." She laughed at him again.

She fed Chester and warmed up some leftovers for her supper. She hadn't been hungry all those hours, and she was too tired to eat now, but she ate anyway. She ate quickly. Then she went out to the garage and dragged the fish out of the car.

She wrestled it into the kitchen. She couldn't find her hatchet. But she thought she was too weak to hack its head off now. Using the step stool, she managed, in stages, to get the fish up onto the counter. She located her camera. The flash didn't work, but she took a picture of the fish anyway, knowing it probably wouldn't turn out. She didn't know where her kitchen scales were—lost in the move somewhere.

She was too tired to look for them. She found her tape measure in a tool drawer.

The fish was thirty-eight and a half inches long. It was the largest fish she had ever caught.

"Look at that fish, Chester," she said.

With her butcher knife, she gutted the fish into a bucket. The fish was full—intestines and pondweed and debris and unidentifiable black masses squished out.

She could feel herself grinning. She had not let go of the fish when she was working it, and she had gotten back home with the old big one. She imagined telling Wilburn about the fish. He would be sitting in front of the TV, and she would call him from the kitchen. "Just wait till you see what I reeled in at the pond," she would say. "Come in here and see. Hurry!" He would know immediately what she had caught. She had a habit of giving away a secret prematurely. Her grinning face—and her laughing voice—gave her away. When she had a surprise for the children, she couldn't wait to tell them. She wanted to see their faces, the delight over something she had bought them for Christmas or some surprise she had planned. "Wake up, get out of bed. Guess what! Hurry!"

Acknowledgments

Portions of this book first appeared in somewhat different form in *The New Yorker*. I am grateful to my editor and friend there, Roger Angell.

Some material about the Cuba Cubs is drawn from my story "State Champions," first published in *Harper's*. Some small bits about my childhood reading and writing appeared in my book *The Girl Sleuth*, first published by the Feminist Press, 1975.

The story of Peyton Washam, the hapless pioneer, is from *Kentucky: A History of the State* by J. H. Battle, W. H. Perrin, and G. C. Kniffin, 1885.

The 1880 map of Clear Springs is from *An Atlas of Graves County, Kentucky*, published by D. J. Lake & Co., Philadelphia, 1880.

Harriette Simpson Arnow's imaginative re-creations of life on the Middle Tennessee frontier—*Seedtime on the Cumberland* and *Flowering of the Cumberland*—inspired and informed my journey into the past. Through those books, I was able to imagine the trail of most of my ancestors, especially the Masons, who traveled down the Cumberland River to Western Kentucky in the 1820s.

Most of my genealogical research was done at the Kentucky Historical Society and the Graves County Library. I'm especially grateful to Don Simmons for his privately published transcriptions of miles of microfilm of local records and abstracts from Mayfield newspapers. These helped me form a clearer picture of Clear Springs and its inhabitants in earlier days.

As always, I am indebted to Lon Carter Barton, Graves County's historian, and Thomas D. Clark, Kentucky's historian laureate, for their profoundly insightful guidance into the past.

My thanks to Erika Brady, folklorist at Western Kentucky State

University, Bowling Green, Kentucky, for her research help, especially for locating the words to the song "Steamboat Bill."

For reminiscences of Robert Hazel, I am grateful to Wendell Berry, Kyra Hackley, James Baker Hall, John Kuehl, Ed McClanahan, Gurney Norman, and David Polk.

For critical readings of the work in progress, I am grateful to Mary Ann Taylor-Hall, James Baker Hall, Cori Jones, Lauren Lepow, Kate Medina, and Binky Urban. Special thanks to Lila Havens.

The names of a few individuals who play minor roles in this narrative have been changed to assure privacy.

I appreciate the permission from my friends Frank Cantor, James Baker Hall, and Guy Mendes to reproduce photographs they took.

I salute my many Clear Springs cousins, whose heritage I am proud to share. And I am indebted to everyone in my family for their indulgence—especially to my mother, who has always been my chief inspiration.

My husband's encouragement and confidence in this project were essential.

BOBBIE ANN MASON is the author of the novels *In Country* and *Feather Crowns. Feather Crowns* was nominated for the National Book Critics Circle Award and won the Southern Book Award. Her short-story collection *Shiloh and Other Stories* won the PEN/ Hemingway Award for First Fiction and was nominated for other major prizes. Her fiction has appeared in *The New Yorker* and elsewhere.

Five generations of her family, going back to the 1820s, are rooted in the farming community of Clear Springs. She lives in Kentucky now with her husband and dogs and cats.

About the Type

This book is set in Fournier, a typeface named for Pierre Simon Fournier, the youngest son of a French printing family. Pierre Fournier made several important contributions to the field of type design, pioneered the concept of the type family, and is said to have cut 60,000 punches for 147 alphabets of his own design. The Fournier typeface was released in 1925.